A
BACUP MISCELLANY

Prose and Verse by Local Writers
past and present

Compiled by
Harry Craven and Ronald Y. Digby

* * *

Edited by
Kenneth F. Bowden

* * *

Illustrations Edited by
John B. Taylor

Borough of Bacup Amenities Committee

1972

ACKNOWLEDGEMENTS

Many thanks are due to all the authors whose work is included in this book, and who would, had space permitted, have appeared in a "Who's Who". Thanks are also due to the Rossendale Free Press for permission to use anything out of their pages, to the Accrington Observer and Times, the Evening Star, Burnley, and the Lancashire Evening Telegraph, Blackburn; to Joan Pomfret, F.R.S.A., for granting the use of material out of her book "Nowt So Queer", and also to the publishers, G. Gerrard of Brierfield; to Cassell & Co. Ltd., for allowing us to include an extract from "Nothing So Strange", the autobiography of the late Lord Francis Williams who spent his boyhood days at Britannia; to John J. Haworth for access to and use of Moses Heap's Diary.

Permission to use copyright photographs has been readily granted by the Rossendale Free Press, the Evening Star, Burnley, A.H. Leach & Co. Ltd., and Messrs. Hutchinson & Co. Ltd. for the photograph of David Billington.

For the cover of the book, the map is reproduced from the Ordnance Survey map with the sanction of the Controller of H.M. Stationery Office, Crown copyright reserved. Thanks are also due to the Borough of Bacup for permitting the use of their coat of arms, and to the Lancashire Evening Telegraph for the photograph of Bacup centre.

If the compilers or editor have unwittingly infringed any copyright, their sincere apologies are tendered to any copyright owners who might notice such infringement.

The compilers thank the Borough of Bacup Amenities Committee for publishing this book, and the Borough Librarian, Mr. K. F. Bowden, for sponsoring this publication and for taking on the task of being Editor, and Mr. John B. Taylor for editing and captioning most of the photographs.

The editor wishes to thank all the individuals who have loaned photographs and material for this first Bacup Miscellany, and not least to the staff of Bacup Public Library whose teamwork has enabled the Borough Librarian to devote a major portion of his time to the preparation of this book for press.

HARRY CRAVEN

1907 – 1971

(see page 121 and following section)

FOREWORD

Ninety years ago, Bacup was granted a Charter conferring upon the town the status of Borough, and it is likely that in the near future that status will be surrendered in favour of an amalgamated Borough of Rossendale. Those ninety years have seen tremendous changes in the fortunes and appearance of our town. But one thing has not changed – the character of its people.

If this little book has anything to say it is about the character of the PEOPLE of Bacup – their warmth, their friendliness, their humour, their directness. This is why the Amenities Committee of the Borough Council have agreed to its publication.

Much of the dialect of yesteryear has disappeared from common usage. So have the clogs, the cloth caps and (most of) the cobbles. And yet these are the tools which seem to bring to life most vividly the true characteristics of the Bacupian. There have been few craftsmen more adept in the use of these tools than Harry Craven ("Ross-en-Dale") to whom this book is dedicated. Harry could find humour or nostalgia in the most inanimate of objects. Such was the skill which has placed him in a long succession of great Bacup "characters".

We are indebted to Ronald Y. Digby for conceiving the idea of this book and compiling most of the material, together with Kenneth F. Bowden who has edited it.

The history of Bacup extends much farther back than its incorporation as a Borough. I feel sure it will continue to have a character of its own, which writers like Harry Craven will preserve, long after it has ceased to be an independent Borough.

Alderman GEORGE E. MILLS,
(Chairman, Amenities Committee, Bacup Borough Council).

CONTENTS

POETRY

IN AND AROUND

"ROSS ENDALE" – *poems by Harry Craven*

BEFORE LIVING MEMORY

WITHIN LIVING MEMORY

Lord Francis Williams was a farmer's son, but he didn't follow in his father's footsteps. He took up journalism, first provincially, then in Fleet Street, and he was so successful that at the age of thirty-two he was the Editor of the Daily Herald. He was Controller of the Press and Censorship at the Ministry of Information under Churchill as Prime Minister; his career took him to the San Francisco Conference, to 10 Downing Street as personal press advisor to Clement Attlee, and to the B.B.C. as a Governor and famous television personality. In 1962 he went to the House of Lords as a life peer.

Lord Francis wrote a number of books, including three novels, and in 1970 his autobiography, "Nothing So Strange" was published by Cassell & Company Ltd., by whose kind permission the following extract from it, which describes his boyhood days at Britannia, is included in this Miscellany.

MY BOYHOOD DAYS AT BRITANNIA

(an extract from "Nothing So Strange", the autobiography of the late Lord Francis Williams).

"The new farm was on the Lancashire-Yorkshire moors between Bacup and Todmorden, one of the bleakest stretches of country you could come across. There were a few meadows on the lower slopes of the farm, but most of it was moorland with tufts of coarse grass suitable only for grazing sheep. My mother looked after the house on her own and my father did all the farm work except at harvest time when the Irish came.

"The farmhouse was an ugly stone building on the hillside above the village of Britannia which was the site of the highest railway station in England. Yet I remember it as a place of great happiness.

"The farm was called Hogshead Farm and according to a local story, of which my mother soon learned, had once been a head-quarters for smugglers who brought brandy across the moors and stored it there until it could be disposed of in Manchester not many miles away. There was a vaulted cellar in the farmhouse which gave some credence to this and since smugglers always have treasure to hide my mother felt sure that they must have left some bags of gold about the place somewhere. My father took up two stone flags in the kitchen which seemed to her to be loose and then conducted a major excavation in the vaulted cellar which my mother decided was part of a tunnel which had been walled off.

“This proved to be the case, but when my father managed to break through the wall, it was not to disclose cases of gold coins or even hogsheads of brandy, but merely a rough tunnel used for digging coal out of the hillside. There were several such tunnels going into the moorside, some of them with rusted narrow-gauge railway tracks along which ponies had drawn coal tubs. Some of these tunnels went a long way under the moor and were ventilated by air shafts bored down from the moor surface. The low roofs of the tunnels were supported by pit props but with age and disuse many of these had rotted away and the tunnels were very dangerous. So were many of the air shafts which were of considerable size and were surrounded by inadequate fences of stakes and wire to deter sheep from falling into them which, however, they did with lamentable frequency.

“When first we lived at Hogshead Farm we went to the village school at Britannia. Britannia was not more than two rows of stone houses opening direct on to a street of stone sets with their frontdoor steps holystoned to a shining whiteness and the Britannia Mill with its tall chimney at one end.

“Those were the days of half-timers and in school the elder boys and girls who had started working half time at the mill when they were twelve would put their heads down on their desks in the afternoon and go fast asleep. They had to be at the mill at five o’clock each morning and were wakened just after four by a knocker-up who went round tapping bedroom windows with a long pole. They needed *sleep* more than lessons and the two teachers *understood* this and did not often disturb them or let us do so. Except for my sister and myself and a family called Watson who lived in a large decrepit house halfway along the road from Britannia to Hogshead Farm, all the children at the school wore clogs and most of the boys were clothed in rough suits of corduroy of a peculiarly evil-smelling kind. It was before science had discovered how to take the smell out. When the room became hot -- there was only one schoolroom with two classes, one at each side of the room -- the stench became almost unbearable, especially if it had been raining and the corduroy was damp. This had a good effect on my character. It made me careful to avoid getting into fights. I could not stomach rolling about the floor locked in combat with anyone who smelt like that.

“The village depended entirely on the cotton mill and the men and women and children all worked in it. This did not affect their independence of character, no doubt because under the system then ruling in the cotton industry each family looked after a loom or set of looms and were paid on results. They were in a sense sub-contractors and, like my father, felt they were their own bosses. They conducted long, bawdy and derisory conversations across the floor of the weaving-shed by lip reading and called the manager and the over-seers, who were among the chief butts for their wit, by their Christian names. The first week in August the mill closed for Wakes Week and practically everyone in Britannia except us went in a char-a-banc to Blackpool, taking their year's savings with them. All they left behind was a shilling or two in a tea caddy on the mantel-piece to tide over until pay day came round again after they got back. It was a point of honour to return with nothing in one's pockets.

"At Britannia I could roam about the moors at will, walking and scrambling for miles until I was tired, when I would fling myself down on the short grass and give myself over to dreams as the peewits called in the sky above me. Usually I had an old collie dog as my companion and she would lie down close beside me and let me rest my head on her if I wanted to as though she were a pillow. Sometimes one or two boys from the village school would come with me and we would try to catch the horned sheep that roamed about the moor and see how long we could stay on their backs. If it was one of the big old rams we caught it would make straight for one of the high dry-stone walls and leap onto the top, leaving its rider sprawling among the stones.

"On Saturday mornings we would sometimes walk across the moors to Bacup to a cinema hall known to everyone as the flea-pit, where we had the wonderful experience of seeing early Charlie Chaplin films, and Buster Keaton and the Keystone Cops and other such now legendary figures of the cinema's age of innocence. They came to us on a flickering screen with a piano strumming at the side without any preparatory warning, so that like Cortez on his peak in Darien we were struck silent with the wonder of it all, or would have been had we not been compelled to uncontrollable laughter. And there was one wonderful day when my father took us to see Buffalo Bill -- the real genuine Colonel William Cody -- and his circus in a field outside Bacup -- that circus which as the posters weeks ahead had told us had been seen and admired by all the crowned heads of Europe, which did not surprise us, for what was a crowned head compared to Buffalo Bill and all the real cowboys and Red Indians he brought with him?

"There was also a tremendous day when everyone lined the streets of Britannia to cheer the first tram from Rochdale to Bacup, decorated with flags and with the driver clanging his bell and the Mayors of Bacup and Rochdale riding on the platform wearing their chains. We felt as though now at last we were in the centre of things, linked to the world and all its wonders.

"Such peaks as these were rare, of course. For the most part pleasures were more modest, like helping with the hay at harvest time. Two or three of my friends from Britannia school would come to help and at the end of the week, when my father paid the Irish labourers who came over in a team and who slept in one of the farm buildings, he would give each of us 3d for our week's wages. When we had it we would swagger down to Britannia and go to the fish-and-chip shop where we would each order a penny mixture -- a bowl of peas with chips on the top -- on which we would sprinkle salt and pepper and vinegar with a professional hand. We would buy a bottle of pop to drink -- there was a glass marble in the neck which you had to press down before you could get the pop to come gurgling down your throat -- and would sit on the bench at the side of the shop and eat our penny mixtures and drink our pop and listen to the grown-up conversation, and would not, as my grandmother used to say, have had the King for cousin.

"In winter the moors were covered with snow and we would toboggan down the hill above the farm. When the milking was done and supper cooking in the oven my mother and father would join us and we would race each other down the long slope, my mother and I on one toboggan, my sister and my father on the other to make it fair, or so my mother would say, with a man to guide each one with heels ready to jam in the snow to swerve or stop. The moon would come up and all the world would be bright and glittering. Afterwards we would go in to supper and after supper my mother would cook chestnuts on the bars of the kitchen grate and we would read aloud to each other.

"We were still living in Britannia when the war came -- although I was in Oswestry with my grandmother on the day it started. It did not affect us, or most of the people in Britannia very directly. My father was too old to join the Army and was told that it was his duty to stay and produce food. The Britannia mill was busy on contracts for army clothing, so that most people were better off than usual. I was in the Scouts and on Scout nights we would be posted to guard a nearby reservoir -- although against what was never quite clear.

"My sister and I were by now at a secondary school at Rawtenstall -- a small textile town famous for its brass and silver bands which had won many contests in more peaceful days -- and I can remember how we all gathered together in the main hall shortly after I went there to cheer the captain of the school and four other sixth formers who were leaving to go straight into the army. Within a few weeks three of them were dead, the first names on the school's roll of honour.

"We did not, however, live out the war in Britannia, but moved soon after it began to Middleton, near Manchester, where my father had found a slightly larger and more cultivatable farm."

(Note: The School mentioned above was the Bacup and Rawtenstall Secondary School which has now changed its name to Bacup and Rawtenstall Grammar School.)

* * * * * * * *

"The character of the people of Bacup is as marked as are the natural features of the Valley, pronounced, individual, blunt, sometimes even to rudeness. When once known, they are never forgotten, and are recognised all the world over. Their dialect is peculiarly their own. They possess a two-edged wit and homour. It is said they love like angels and hate like devils. True as steel in their friendships, they are thrifty, but not mean, hard working and enterprising; quick to take advantage of any new thought and ready to pursue it to a successful conclusion."

(J. H. Brearley).

THE BACUP NATURAL HISTORY SOCIETY
(established 1878)

It is from the pen of the Society's first Secretary, James Holmes, that we can cull a brief synopsis of its early history. At the outset the Meetings were held in a large upstairs room at Hempsteads, then occupied by a Mr. Nicholson, who was a local tailor, and took an active interest in local flora and fauna. Later, the Meetings were held in the tea-rooms of the Co-operative Society.

The very first lecture by Mr. Henry Kerr was held on March 1st, 1878, under the title "A Visit to the Sea-birds on Walney Island". During this period, the Society was known as "The Bacup and Rossendale Field Naturalist Club", being extremely well attended, and proving to be a source of educational advancement for the numerous people interested in Natural History.

One early member who was prominent at that time was Mr. E. O. Lord, who was an expert Microscopist and who contributed valuable work and stimulated much interest in minute forms of life.

About 1879, another prominent member, Dr. Worrall, offered a cottage adjacent to his own home, and here it was -- where the Maden Public Baths now stand -- that the Society acquired its first "permanent" home, when it was decided to amend its name to The Bacup Natural History Society.

Following the furnishing of the new premises, Dr. Worrall and others loaned microscopes, and the place became a constant resort for the members every evening. Mr. Robert Smith, a local shoemaker, taught Geology, together with splendid co-workers like mine-manager Mr George Scott, who discovered many rare coal-measure fossils, the rarest of which is now housed at the British Museum in London as *Cyclops Scotti.*

The Society also had with them a young student, Mr. Herbert Bolton, who afterward became known as an authority on "The Geology of Rossendale", the book he wrote that is now widely recognised as a standard work on the subject. (He eventually became Curator of the British Museum.) Classes of various subjects of natural science were formed including Botany, Entomology, Ornithology, Anatomy, Anthropology, and Taxidermy, being fairly representative of the Society's early activities.

Later, a newsroom was started, taking in technical and scientific journals to further extend the members' abilities.

In addition, a Mr. A. Foulds constructed a large aquarium and stocked it with perch, roach, minnows, and other species. During this period, before present-day pollution, *trout could be seen in the Irwell at Broadclough.*

On the 10th of May, 1889, the Society removed from Rochdale Road to St. James Square, on part of the site now occupied by Woolworth's and the Electricity Showrooms. Here for approximately 37 years, the "Nat" contributed much to the cultural life of the town.

Following the Society's compulsory removal from St. James Square, new premises were found at Zion Buildings, which proved to be sufficiently commodious to display to advantage one of the finest mineral collections in the north of England. These premises were officially opened by Dr. J. Wilfred Jackson, D.Sc., F.G.S., senior Assistant Keeper of Manchester Museum, on November 6th, 1937.

Our present-day headquarters are situated in Yorkshire Street, in the old Hare & Hounds public house, which we acquired in 1948, and in accordance with past tradition the Society has always maintained an unbroken sequence of Lectures during the winter months. These have been well attended by the general public, with rambles and visits to places of interest in the summer seasons.

The Society can look back with justifiable pride to its various achievements over the long years, acknowledging the many faithful services of its working-presidents who rendered "yeoman service". The list of Presidents reads:

Thomas Aitken (of "The Holmes")	1878 to 1889
George Shepherd (Alderman, of "Shepherd's Tent")	1889 to 1897
Rev. J. S. Doxey (Vicar of Christ Church)	1897 to 1909
James Horrocks (Councillor)	1909 to 1939
James Hargreaves	1939 to 1948
Edmund S. Pilling	1948 to 1972

The last named President, who was elected in June 1948, was a keen naturalist who devoted a lifetime to the pursuit of his studies, and was particularly well known for his popular lantern lecture "Old Bacup".

In order that the Society's cultural activities could continue and prosper, a series of annual "Lancashire Neets" were instituted just after the First World War. These evenings began as a night of Lancashire dialect verse and song, and later became plays which took the form of Northcountry comedies, and a long succession of 'Players" became so expert that the performances fell little short of professional standards. Amongst their productions was a three-act Lancashire comedy "A Bit o' Peace and Quiet", written by the then Borough Librarian of Bacup, John A. Vickers, and performed in March 1954.

During the past few years this popular type of entertainment has been allowed to lapse, which is nothing if not a sad reflection on the apathy of the people of our time. (However, a Lancashire Neet staged in memory of Mr. Harry Craven, who was closely connected with the "Nat", on January 29th, 1972, drew a full house of over 350 people at the Mechanics' Hall. On this occasion, Lancashire dialect items were given by members of the Edwin Waugh Society and the Lancashire Authors' Association, with Messrs. Clifford Heyworth (Bill o' Bows) and Ronald Y. Digby as comperes.)

In conjunction with the Society there is a flourishing Camera Club which has been in existence for more than sixty years. It runs competitions and promotes its own series of lectures each winter.

The scope of the "Nat" is much wider than the title suggests, and it has always been interested in Lancashire history and traditions. Many prominent Lancashire dialect writers have lectured there. Particular mention should be made of the late Sam Fitton of Shaw, whose works were collected and published by Ammon Wrigley under the title "Gradely Lancashire". After Sam gave his lecture, he presented two of his paintings to the Society. One upon the clubroom walls "A Naturalist's Nightmare" shows his rich sense of humour. Many years ago, Mr. Sim Schofield gave a lecture on Samuel Laycock's writings. Laycock will always be remembered for his two masterpieces, "Bowton's Yard", and "Bonnie Brid". The "Bonnie Brid" anticipated in the poem was a boy, but turned out to be a daughter, and Mr. Sim Schofield married her eventually. The well-known Accrington geologist, Mr. John Ranson, actually gave 50 lectures to the Society, a wonderful record.

Brief mention should be made of the Society's museum. There is a wealth of material. Reproduced on another page is the chart indicating the placings of the collection of flint arrowheads, scrapers, and implements of the later Stone Age assembled by Mr. J. R. Chew and Mr. J. T. Pickup, both of whom were members of the Society. But besides these and other fossils may be seen a fascinating collection of domestic bygones -- kitchen utensils many years old. There is an apparatus used for the now almost obsolete game of KNURR AND SPELL.

An omnibus time-table shows the times of horse-drawn buses from Bacup to Rochdale and Bacup to Haslingden. This service, dating from July 1, 1879, was run by the Bacup Omnibus, Conveyance & Livery Stables Co. Limited. The Company's office was at Pippin Bank, and the Manager was William Roberts. There were four omnibuses each day to Rochdale, with an early and late omnibus to Facit only. The journey took 1 hour 5 minutes, and the stops were at Britannia, Shawforth, Facit, Whitworth and Ending.

The Company also ran four omnibuses every day to Haslingden. This journey took 1 hour 15 minutes, with stops at Stacksteads, Newchurch, Cloughfold and Rawtenstall.

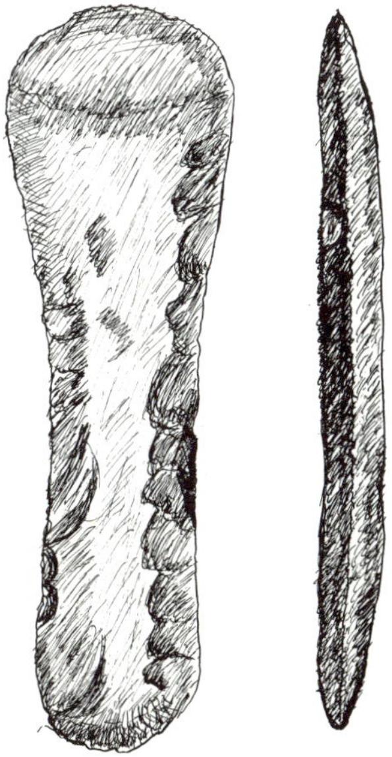

(Half original size)

COLLECTION OF FLINTS PRESENTED BY

MR. J. T. PICKUP, BACUP,

TO THE NATURAL HISTORY MUSEUM

1. Spearhead. (Middle Hill, Shawforth, 21 January 1915)
2, 2A, 2B. Pigmies - - various local places
3. Scraper (Middle Hill, Shawforth)
4. Spearhead. (Tooter Hill, 24 October 1914)
5. Leaf arrowhead. (Tooter Hill, 28 October 1917)
6. Scraper. (Shore Moor, Littleborough)
7. Scraper (Knowl Hill, Ashworth Moor)
8. Arrowhead. (Hades Hill, Shawforth, 6 February 1915)
9. Arrowhead. (Hameldon, Crawshawbooth, 3 July 1915)
10. Borer. (Shore Moor, Littleborough)
11. Arrowhead. (Whittle Pike, Edenfield, 21 May 1918)
12. Arrowhead (Cheesden, Ashworth Moor)
13. Arrowhead (leaf shape) (Gorpley, October 1919)
14. Arrowhead. (Middle Hill, Shawforth, 22 February 1919)
15. Arrowhead. (Trough Edge, Shawforth, 4 September 1917)
16. Arrowhead. (Hameldon, Crawshawbooth, 20 June 1914)
17. Arrowhead. (Hades Hill, Shawforth, March 1914)
18. Knife. (Hameldon)
19. Saw. (Shore Moor)
20. Leaf Arrowhead. (Flower Scar, Bacup, 23 January 1918)
21. Spear or Lance head. (Shore Moor, 8 July 1916)
22. Borer. (Shore Moor)
23. Broken Lance Head. (Shore Moor)
24. Borer. (Intack, Rooley Moor)
25. Arrowhead. (Shore Moor, 13 January 1918)
26. Combination Scraper. (Knowl Hill)

(Note: After becoming blind, Mr. Pickup could still give expert knowledge about flints by examining them with his fingers.)

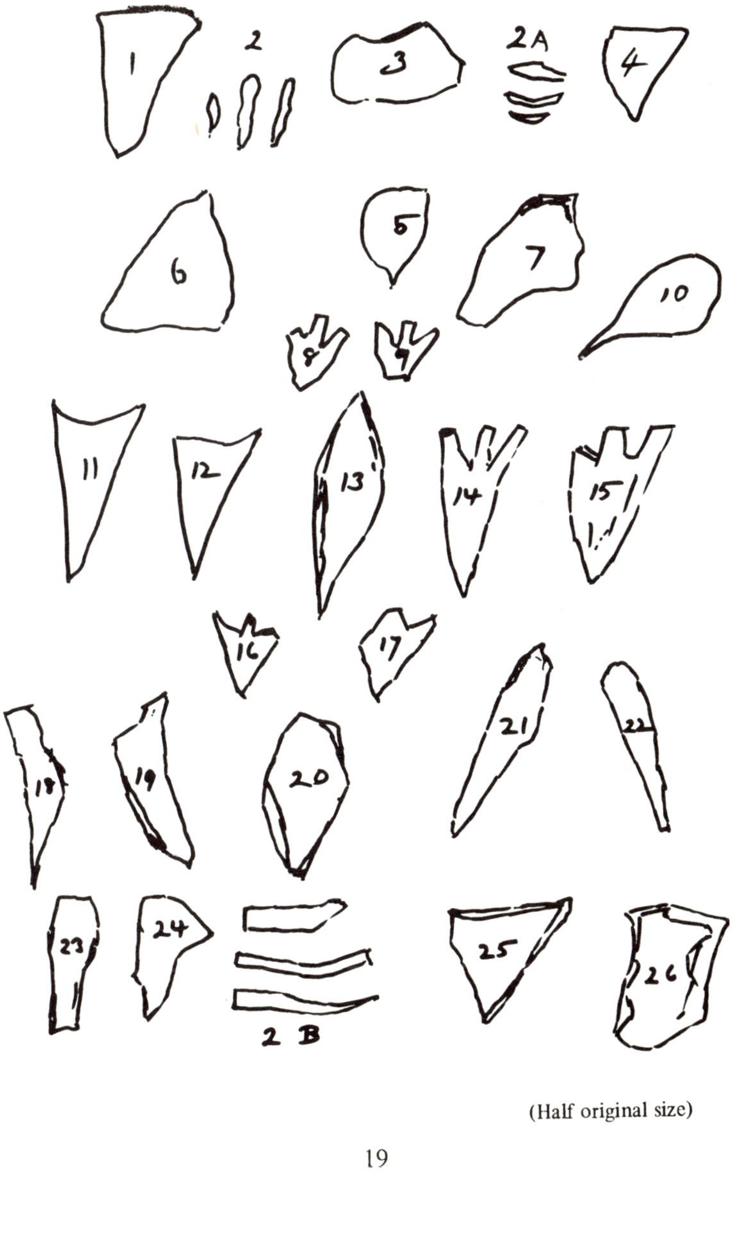

(Half original size)

BIRDS OF ROSSENDALE

The birds of Rossendale are by the very nature of the place birds of the hills. The birds of the lowlands liking the cover and warmth of lush vegetation give up the struggle and fade out about Irwell Vale and Ewood Bridge. Here may be found the blackcap and whitethroat, the yellow-hammer and linnet. Above this even the floor of the Irwell valley quickly reaches 500 feet above sea level and facing west is open to the strong winds from the Atlantic. This exposure to wind and weather brings about the bleak conditions which limit the extent of many species. One exception is the valley of the Limy at Crawshawbooth which, running from north to south and sheltered by the steep side of the Cribden range has richer woodland with better cover. Here may be found the tree creeper, lesser spotted woodpecker, spotted flycatcher and redstart. In and around small woods and suburban gardens are to be seen the usual common birds, blackbird, songthrush, mistle thrush, greenfinch, chaffinch, robin and wren, blue and great tit and the ubiquitous magpie. The coniferous plantations round the reservoirs at Clough Bottom and Haslingden Grane form a habitat for the tiny goldcrest and the coal tit.

Having thus briefly dismissed the birds of the lower lands and the woods, a consideration of the birds of the hills must make up the greater part of an account of the birds of Rossendale. A newcomer to Rossendale might find the hills cold and almost empty of birds during the winter months, with spring coming late and snow lying sometimes in April and May. Yet in some ways spring may be said to come early for the hill birds return to their breeding grounds by the end of January. First come the skylarks in the third and fourth weeks of January, followed by the lapwings in mid-February, snipe a little later and curlews in March. Flocks of golden plover begin to build up on favoured feeding grounds especially the improved hill pastures round The Hile, roosting at night on the higher peat mosses of Smallshaw Heights. Most of these golden plover belong to the northern race and will move on to their breeding grounds in northern Europe during the last week in April. By this time the males are resplendent in full breeding plumage with jet black face, throat and belly separated by a clear white margin from the beautiful gold speckled upper parts. Those of the southern race are already paired and have established territories on the higher peat covered hills -- Cowpe Moss, Hailstorm Hill and Knowl Moor.

Thus by March the hills are transformed. The cock birds of hills and open spaces establish their right to territory by wonderful aerial displays combined with vocal efforts which correspond to the singing from perched song posts of woodland and garden birds such as blackbird, thrush and robin. It is these displays which bring a special magic to the hills particularly at dusk on a March evening. Then the air itself seems almost alive with sound and motion. The lapwings hurl themselves about in crazy flight, sometimes upside down, sometimes almost dashing themselves to pieces on the ground, and all the time shouting out their song of defiance to any possible intruding male. This song, for such it is, as much as the song of nightingale or blackbird, must be one of the most familiar spring sounds on the hill pastures. It goes pees-weep-weep-weep and through it may be heard the swish of air against the wing feathers.

The snipe's aerial display is somewhat different in character. It flies round in a wide circle occasionally diving a short way towards the ground. During the dive may be heard the familiar "drumming" or bleating noise, not a vocal sound but caused by the flow of air vibrating the extended outer tail feathers. The curlew also delivers its beautiful bubbling call while on the wing, perhaps the most emotive sound in spring among the hills of Britain.

The highest moors, level areas 1300 to 1500 feet above sea level, have thick peat overlying boulder clay, with many small pools, boggy patches, and cotton grass. This is the habitat favoured by the golden plover and a small wader the dunlin. The dunlin is perhaps the rarest of the waders to nest on the Rossendale fells. There may be four nesting pairs on the largest hill mass which includes Cowpe Moss, Hailstorm Hill and Knowl Moor, with one or two pairs on the Musbury, Haslingden and Oswaldtwistle Moors. The birds return in April to the hills and the males establish their territories and attract a mate with a wonderful trilling song delivered on the wing. The nest is extremely difficult to find, being a slight hollow usually partly covered by grasses. The hen bird sits very close and the best chance of finding the nest is when she flutters from the eggs almost underfoot. Both birds are very tame in the nesting area and will stand or walk around only a few yards away while one is searching for the nest.

Two other waders need to be mentioned. The redshank nests in small numbers often only a single pair on the hills between the valleys of the Whitewell and the Limy. This is a handsome bird looking very black and white in flight and having bright red legs and beak. The common sandpiper is a summer migrant arriving usually in May. It nests mainly round the sides of the reservoirs.

The red grouse is a bird which is closely associated with the northern moors. It has declined somewhat during the last twenty years. I have seen nests on Smallshaw Heights and Holcombe Moor, and more recently have come across the odd covey of young birds in the Rooley Moor and Knowl Moor areas but these usually appear to be isolated instances of breeding. There are no large areas of heather in Rossendale and this is the main food of the red grouse. It may be that the amount of heather has been reduced by overburning. Certainly the plant food on which grouse feed in Rossendale is the crowberry which forms mats of growth on the south facing slopes from Hailstorm Hill to the Naden Brook Valley and this is where I most frequently see grouse.

Of the small birds of the hills the skylark and meadow pipit are the most numerous. The skylark is in fact the commonest nesting species on the Rossendale hills. I have for some years taken part in the Common Bird Census for the British Trust for Ornithology. This has been done on a 200 acre plot in the vicinity of The Hile. The figures for breeding pairs on this plot have been 50 to 60 skylarks, 15 to 20 meadow pipits, 15 lapwings, 6 snipe, 5 to 10 twites, 4 reed buntings, 4 blackbirds, 1 curlew, 1 stock dove, 1 wheatear, 1 magpie. The skylark and meadow pipit both have song flights by which the males indicate their possession of territory. That of the skylark is well known. The meadow pipit's display is a much shorter one, the bird rising only twenty or thirty feet, then planing down on outstretched wings.

The reed bunting is an interesting addition to the birds of the hills. Up to ten years ago it nested as far up the valley as the sewage works at Ewood Bridge which was similar to its usual habitat round rushy ponds and marshy areas on the lowlands. It appears to be a successful species which is increasing and expanding its range to the wet rushy patches much higher up the hills and I have even seen it in winter above the 1000 foot level. The cock is a handsome bird with a black head and white collar but his song consists of just a few short jangling notes.

The twite or mountain linnet is rather a special bird of Rossendale since its habitat requirements limit it for the most part to hill country with rough grassland and heather and it breeds only very locally along the flanks of the Pennines. It nests in small colonial groups of from two pairs to five or six pairs which return regularly to certain favoured areas. The first flocks return in February or March but it is usually late April or May before nesting is begun and I have found nests still containing young ones in August. This late nesting would appear to coincide with the ripening of the seeds of many of the hill grasses, needed for an abundant food supply for the young. The twite eats the seeds of many weeds. I have watched it feeding on ragwort, thistle and knot grass. Oddly enough a favourite feeding area when the birds arrive back in Rossendale is on the bare patches in the goal-mouth and centre circle of football fields, where presumably the studs of many boots have churned up the surface and exposed the seeds of knot grass, dock and plantain which can often be seen growing on such patches later in the year.

Hills and moors imply the presence of hill streams, and numerous fine little valleys descend into the Irwell and its tributaries. Many of these are deeply incised and the steep sides provide the main wooded areas of Rossendale. The streams themselves provide a habitat for two species specially adapted for feeding by the water. The dipper can actually walk under water and feed on the aquatic insect life which abounds among the stony beds of streams and the bottoms of ponds and lodges. It was formerly restricted to the smaller unpolluted streams but with the clearing of the Whitewell, Cowpe Brook and even stretches of the Irwell, it is now commonly seen even in the centre of Waterfoot and Rawtenstall. Rather like a small dumpy blackbird with a white breast its constant bobbing movements are well adapted to the lively pattern of foam-flecked water among which it feeds.

The other bird of the streams is the grey wagtail whose name belies its beautiful appearance in which the grey of the back and head is combined and contrasted with a gorgeous saffron yellow on the under part of the tail. Like the dipper and in fact like many water-side birds it has a constant and active movement which helps it to blend with the rapid movement of the waters.

The birds of prey are quite well represented in Rossendale. The kestrel is often to be seen hovering over rough grass even among built up areas, its chief prey being the short tailed field vole. It nests in derelict farm houses, on ledges in quarries and at least one pair in a hole in the side of a mill chimney in Rawtenstall. The merlin, a tiny falcon of the moors, has nested sporadically in the Knowl Moor --

Whittle Pike area. The commonest owl is the tawny owl whose hooting is a familiar sound especially in the autumn when the males are establishing their territories. The barn owl is much rarer with perhaps one pair in the whole area. The little owl, originally introduced into Britain from southern Europe, has made itself at home in Rossendale, nesting in the old quarries and derelict farm buildings. I have photographed the young of this species in the Hile-Brex area. Both the little owl and the short eared owl may be seen hunting during daylight hours. The short eared owl mainly appears as a passage migrant in the autumn but there are increasing signs that it is moving in as a breeding species especially where new coniferous plantations provide a suitable habitat.

By the very nature of evolutionary processes, slow changes are constantly taking place in numbers and distribution of living things. Even within the limited area of Rossendale over a relatively short period of twenty years, some changes have become evident. The increase in the numbers of the reed bunting, and its expansion into the hills from the lower lands, has already been mentioned. Another significant change has been in the habits of some species of gulls, Twenty years ago the herring gull was rarely seen in Rossendale, a fact also mentioned by C.K. Parker in his "Birds of Rossendale". The lesser black-backed gull was known mainly as a passage migrant on its way through moving south to the Mediterranean in autumn. The lesser black-back was the first of the gulls to move inland and change its habits from being mainly a coastal species. It began to nest in considerable numbers on the northern Pennines and discovered a lucrative source of food on the rubbish tips of the industrial towns of the Pennine flanks. This food supply appears to have caused a change in migratory habits and gradually more and more lesser black-backs began to winter in England rather than migrating to the Mediterranean. In the early 1950's 100 or more lesser black-backs could be seen feeding on Stacksteads tip during the winter. In 1951 a single herring gull appeared with them. Three or four years later there were equal numbers of herring and lesser black-backs at the tip and today the herring gulls are in the majority. Great flocks of gulls numbering many thousands roost on the reservoirs including Haslingden Grane and often at first light flocks may be seen moving up the Irwell Valley towards the rubbish tips, with a return movement the opposite way during late afternoon. The latest species to join the inland movement is the great black-back which has appeared in small numbers among the herring and lesser black-backed gulls. The black-headed gull has of course been an inland nester for much longer. There was a small colony of these birds in the hills south-west of Musbury Tor in 1948 and I understand that numbers were much greater during the war years.

The carrion crow is another species which has moved into Rossendale during the last twenty years and breeding pairs are to be found in most localities often in the remoter parts at the heads of valleys, for instance at Clow Bridge and Lench.

Wildfowl are to be seen on the local reservoirs, in greatest numbers during the autumn and winter. Flocks of mallard numbering 50 to 100 are present on Ashworth Moor reservoir, usually with a few teal among the flock. The goldeneye is the commonest winter visitor among the ducks and again is most commonly present at Ashworth Moor reservoir between October and March. Numbers are usually about 10 or 15 but occasionally flocks of 20 or 30 may be seen. The males are very handsome in their black and white plumage, especially in the spring when they are moving back to their breeding grounds in northern Europe. Other species of duck which occur from time to time include scoter, scaup, tufted duck, pochard and wigeon. Flocks of pink-footed geese often pass along the Irwell valley during the winter. The valley seems to provide an east-west routeway between the Ribble and Humber estuaries which are important wintering areas for this species of goose. Shelduck also pass through in late summer and autumn when birds from the Lancashire coast are on a moult migration to the coast of Germany.

An interesting winter visitor is the snow bunting which comes from the Tundra regions of northern Europe and from the slopes of the higher mountains -- in the Scottish Highlands for instance where it nests at altitudes of over 3000 feet. In some years small flocks winter on the Rossendale fells feeding on the seeds of the hill grasses. The cock birds show a great deal of white including two large patches on the wings which become very noticeable in flight.

It is almost impossible to mention every species of bird which may be seen in Rossendale -- there are the passage migrants and winter visitors for instance fieldfares and redwings. The latter may be heard passing overhead on almost any mild night in October and November when the thin high pitched flight call "tseep" can hardly be missed if one's ears are receptive to sounds other than that of the motor car. What also of the spring migrants -- the house martin that builds its mud cup nest under the eaves of buildings in Rawtenstall and Waterfoot, the swift which colonises the crevices under the eaves of the larger old mill buildings, the swallow, yellow wagtail and willow warbler. There are the rare winter and passage migrants the waxwing and the crossbill, an occasional arctic tern, red throated diver, greenshank or green sandpiper.

Yet as I pointed out earlier, it is the hill birds which give ornithology in Rossendale its special character, its special beauty and wildness. To quote a line from a letter written to me from southern England, "I wish we had such birds around here". So may I end with a plea that we should cherish and protect the unique wild life of the hills of northern England.

ROSSENDALE ANECDOTES

When the evacuees arrived at Waterfoot during the war, there were two black boys with them, and one of the reception committee, something of a humorist, did his best, in his own way, to make them feel at home. He took them into the Arcade chip shop and in his own words, "Gave 'em a good feed o' black peighs".

When the landlord called for his rent at a tumbledown old cottage in a Rossendale hamlet, he was taken aback when the old lady who lived there asked for "electric leet to be put in". "Electric leet?", he exclaimed, - - "at two an' ninepence a week th'art lucky to ged dayleet".

"Is this mon a trained singer?" a man asked the steward at Waterfoot 'Con' on a concert night. "Oh yes", said the steward, "He was trained at Milan". "Milan?" said the man -- "tha means Mill End".

PREHISTORIC MAN IN ROSSENDALE

"Flinting" was a popular pastime in the late 19th and early 20th centuries.

In 1878, Captain Aitken of Bacup led the search for evidence that prehistoric man roamed our local hills by his discoveries of arrow-heads and other artifacts found in this area. During 1879 he was joined in this work by Robert Law and James Horsefall. Between them they visited thirty-four sites, wandering as far as the Saddle-worth area finding some 3,824 flints and of these 83 were positively identified as "worked flints". A list of their finds for the years 1879-1882 appeared in the Journal of the Yorkshire Geological & Poly-technic Society published in 1882.

Ammon Wrigley, antiquarian and historically-minded poet of Saddleworth, began to study the Neolithic Period at the turn of the century and eventually he became an authority on this subject. Most of his collection of flints was donated to Oldham Museum.

No evidence of Palaeolithic (Old Stone Age) man has been discovered in this part of the Pennines due to glacial conditions prevailing at that time. For thousands of years he travelled Europe making and using his all-purpose hand-axe, a tool which later developed into flint blades. These were used for a variety of purposes. It can be said that through this long evolutionary period the ancestors of modern man had by 40,000 B.C. made their appearance as homo-sapiens (Upper Palaeolithic).

Thousands of years were to pass before the first settlers to visit our area came into the country via France and Belgium. They are known from the finding of their very small flints with secondary working called microliths, many of them less than half an inch in length lying scattered on what must have been in 10,000 B.C. their temporary camping sites. These tiny flints would probably be used for setting in wooden shafts for arrows, or glued with resinous substances to a wooden, bone or antler shaft to make a saw-like implement or as arranged in illustration (g) to make a deadly weapon for the hunt. These Mesolithic (Middle Stone Age) people relied on hunting, fishing and the gathering of wild fruits and seeds for a living and were nomadic in character moving to and from forest-free areas of scrub, sandy territory or rocky outcrops. Their rough hearths and working floors are found preserved below the peat.

Other immigrant people more capable of dealing with the forest conditions of that time later fused with our Pennine Tardenoesian race to influence one another in acquiring skills. As time went on they became a more insular race, as it was also at this time that England became separated from the continent, and the climate became wetter, changing the vegetation cover, the pines giving way to oak and alder on the heavy clay soils.

The small geometrical flints associated with Mesolithic occupation can be found in our district by looking at areas of sandy exposure where the surface of the peat has weathered away either through erosion or fire. Scatterings of these flints have been picked up at Trough Edge, Bull, Knowl and Tooter Hills. It is quite certain that more of these microliths await the searcher on other of our local hills.

While these hunter-fishing people were living their nomadic life on our hills, over in the Middle East folk were living a much more settled pastoral life and it is this civilisation which reached these shores around 3000 B.C. causing such an impact that it has been called the Neolithic Revolution (New Stone Age).

These new immigrant farmers from France, Belgium, Holland and Germany brought with them new technical skills such as weaving and pottery. They grew corn mostly wheat, kept fair-sized herds of cattle and pigs; they had domesticated the dog and practised mixed farming, laying the foundation of present day agriculture. Using their polished stone axes they made a great impact on the forest trees and scrub with their "slash and burn" tactics. A very fine example of a flint adze found on Tooter Hill is in the local museum, and reproduced elsewhere in this Miscellany. In the museum one can also see several Neolithic examples of flint arrowheads in the J. R. Chew collection.

Other than a farming economy was their interest in religion and their belief in a Mother Goddess and the life hereafter, for these Neolithic people built the first "henge" monuments and chambered tombs. In the north of England the latter are represented by long barrows and cairns. Interested in obtaining better quality materials, they set up a mining industry at Grimes Graves in Norfolk, and traded the flint nodules thus obtained throughout the country. This trade in flints along with the trade in polished axes, which were now being made from fine-grained rocks as well as flint, would possibly be carried out by itinerant families who were specialists in mining. It is interesting to record that rough-cuts of axes made at

Great Langdale have been found in Hampshire and the Firth of Forth.

Our Early Bronze Age is recognised as beginning with the arrival of successive waves of warrior peoples from the continent in 1900 B.C. These invaders are called Beaker Folk from a highly distinctive type of pottery they used. Quickly subduing and occupying much of this country they absorbed the Neolithic people and culture into their own way of life. They brought with them simple metal equipment from Europe and soon organised trade with the Irish and Scottish smiths, from whom they purchased flat copper axes, awls and tanged and rivetted daggers. Flint continued to be used though, and very finely chipped daggers and knives were made from this material. Their religious zeal was responsible for creating the two magnificent monuments of Avebury and Stonehenge.

Although there is nothing to see of their domestic abodes we have evidence that early Bronze Age man visited our local moorlands. Being archer warriors, they used flint to tip their arrows, and beautifully made tanged and barbed arrow-heads have been found in several localities within our area. Amongst several examples in Bacup Natural History Museum is a finely worked tanged and barbed arrow-head from Thieveley Pike

Stone circles, standing stones, avenues of stones and burial mounds are the main monuments of the Bronze Age, and it is from the latter that evidence of their way of life is being assembled from the artifacts found by excavating these burial sites.

In 1960, Mr. Farnworth and Mr. Tyson of the Bury Archaeologists decided after consideration of the derivation of the name Whitelow Hillock in the Irwell Valley to visit the site and discovered a cairn structure which was subsequently investigated.

Fully documented, this site, which was patiently excavated over a period of years by the quadrant method, revealed a primary and twelve secondary burials.

Situated at a height of 814 feet (National Grid 805163), Whitelow Hillock is one mile south-east of Ramsbottom and three miles north of Bury. The ruins of Grants' Tower overlook the site to the south. The Hillock mound itself has a diameter of ninety feet with a small central cairn. It is ovoid in shape with a north/south axis and is made of sand and gravel. An outer rim of stone defines the barrow's circumference.

The primary burial in the cairn structure, for which the barrow was originally intended, was contained in a pit twelve inches deep and fifteen inches in diameter which had been dug into the hard yellow gravel below the leached horizon. A two inch layer of soot and charcoal covered the bottom of the pit followed by a deposit of cremated bones. Among the bones was a calcined flint blade one and a half inches in length and also a bronze awl which had been deliberately broken before deposition. The pit was then filled with soot and charcoal and closed with a sandstone slab eighteen inches square and four inches deep. On this stone cover the orange coloured gravel had been replaced and finally capped by the cairn of stones.

The secondary burials were contained in collared urns (see sketch k) which were found inverted in small earthen or stone cists, scattered throughout the barrow.

Grave goods included flint knives, leaf-shaped arrowheads and sherds of an incense cup 3 inches by 3½ inches were found in the filling of one of the pits suggesting that it perhaps accompanied an unurned cremation.

A clay stud, shaped like a pulley one inch in diameter, was found with one of the urn burials and experts have suggested various uses for this article, dress fastener or charm pendant. A bronze awl received the attention of expert Mr. Thomas of Birmingham, who suggested that the date for this artifact is probably the 16th or 15th century B.C.

There are cairn burials in the area under review which have become badly weathered and exploited for stone. Shawforth, Cheesden, Middle Hill, Thieveley Pike, Deerplay, Stiperden and Shore Moors, Knowl and Hades Hills are all places where artifacts have been found or interesting relic monuments still exist.

It is worth noting that an old road runs by the Whitelow barrow and during excavation a 9th-century Northumbrian and a 3rd-century Roman coin found near to the surface suggest a very early date for this old road between Bacup and Bury.

Many sites of archaeological interest must still await the investigator and, as the ever encroaching peat or vegetation spreads over the surrounding moorlands, finding these sites and associated artifacts will become even more difficult. One could follow the example of the Bury archaeologists and deduce sites from present day geogrpahical names, an exercise which in the case of Whitelow Hillock proved of exceptional significance to a better understanding of the original settlement of our area; and work of this nature breathes life into the ancient flints, axes and other artifacts housed in our museums.

Summary of evidence for the existence of pre-historic man in Rossendale:

Paleolithic Man	No evidence
Mesolithic Man	Scatterings of small geometrical flints at Trough Edge, Bull, Knowl and Tooter Hills.
Neolithic Man	A flint adze found on Tooter Hill; flint arrowheads in the J. R. Chew collection in the Bacup "Nat" Museum.
Bronze Age Man	A cairn at Whitelow Hillock has been excavated. Artifacts have been found at other cairn burials and relic monuments still exist.

I would like to place on record the help I received from Mr. Pilling, the curator of Bacup Natural History Society's Museum and from the Bury Archaeological Society in compiling this article.

For further reading:

Clark, Grahame: Prehistoric England (out of print)
Bennett, W.: History of Burnley, part 1 (Burnley Corporation)
Celoria, Francis: Archaeology (Hamlyn)
Dyer, James: Discovering archaeology in England & Wales (Shire)
Hawkes, Jacquetta & Christopher: Prehistoric Britain (Chatto)
Ordnance Survey: Field archaeology (H.M.S.O.)

Illustrations

a. Microliths (Mesolithic) showing secondary working

b. Neolithic flint axe

c. and d. Neolithic arrowheads

e. Beaker arrowhead

f. and h. Bronze Age arrowheads

g. Suggested method of using microliths (East Africa) Sketch

k. Collared Urn – Bronze Age (Sketch)

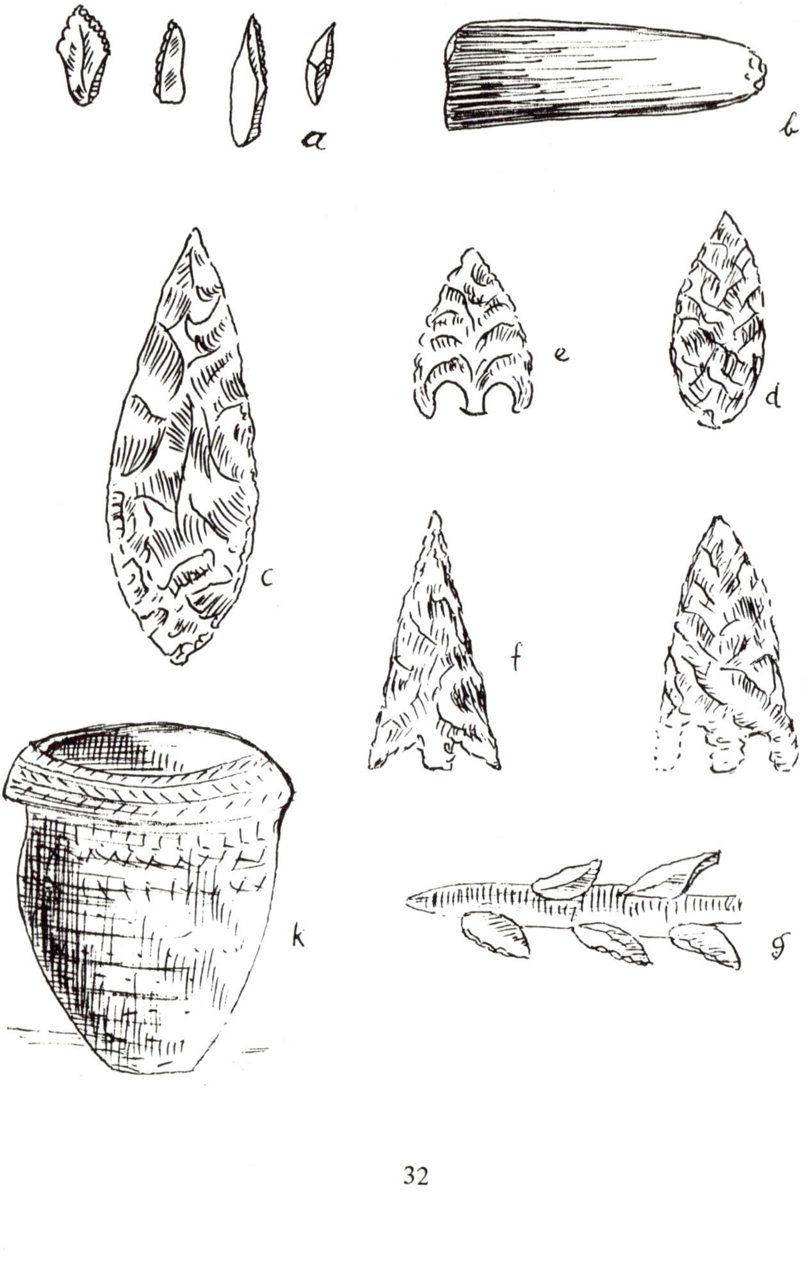
a
b
c
e
d
f
h
k
g

BACUP: ITS CHARACTERISTICS AND HISTORY

As most of you are aware, Bacup is situated at the head of the Rossendale Valley, shut in by hills on all sides. It is part of the Forest of Rossendale, which was included in the Forest of Blackburnshire, along with the Forest of Pendle, Trawden and Accrington, at the time of the Norman Conquest. Its retention of the dialect, quaint characters and customs, is largely due to its inaccessibility and isolation.

There are many theories as to the derivation of the name Bacup. In the records its spelling has changed fourteen times, in eight of which there is an "o" in the last syllable -- cope. My opinion is the one that has come down through the ages, that a place receives its name from its own peculiar character. Men received their names from the place of their abode or occupation. I have rambled over our hills at all seasons, and have always been struck by their appearance. In summer, when the twitch grass, as we call it, is in bloom, their colour is a rich red brown; in winter a darker brown. What more natural than Red Brown (for which the saxon word is bay) and Cope Hill? The name is spelt this way on eight occasions. Thus Bay Cope and Red Hill. Viewed from the hills, the valleys below when they were heavily wooded, the trees and bracken in leaf, the colour would be the same red brown; hence we get the name Rossendale from its appearance, the Russet Dale.

The characteristics of a Bacupian are his double-edged wit, bluntness, suspicion of strangers (whom he calls foreigners). He is enterprising and persistent in effort to master anything he undertakes, and clannish even to stupidity.

The earliest authentic history we have dates back to the year 1200, although we have many evidences of the ancient Briton, the Saxon and the Dane before that time. About the year 1200, during the reign of King John, Roger De Lacy, one of the Lords of the Honor of Clitheroe, granted to the monks at Whalley Abbey that portion of Rossendale known as Brandwood. As a result of this gift Brandwood, by being cleared and cultivated, was the first part of the forest rendered suitable for the habitation of man. The success of the monks led the Lord of the Manor to portion out and establish compastures or vaccaries, over which he placed his servants. These took the name of the cow pastures over which they were placed. Eventually the cow-keepers became tenants, the Lord of the Manor finding it more profitable to let than to stock and work.

The characteristic industry of the Bacupian so improved the land that during the reign of Henry VII, the crown, in order to raise its revenue, released with all the rights of copyhold the various lands of Rossendale at a greatly increased rent. The leaseholders were left in peace until the time of the Stuarts. With these kings came hard times. James the First, being sorely pressed for money, called his lawyers together to see what could be done. Professing to find some flaw in the leases granted to Henry VII, they forced the tenants to pay a fourteen years' purchase. Nor was this all. Charles II no sooner came to the throne than he, through his lawyers, enforced another 26 years' purchase, making in all from the impoverished and much wronged tenants a purchase of 40 years.

Historians say that a more bare-faced extraction of money under false pretences is surely not on record. In spite of these hardships, Rossendale grit triumphed and progressed. At this time there were nineteen different hamlets, or booths.

The earliest documents extant granting leases to private families in Rossendale date back to the year 1517, when six families of Ashworths, from the neighbouring parish of Ashworth Chapel, settled here. So rapidly did they multiply and inter-marry that bynames were resorted to for distinction, such as Ernest o' Dick o' Bob's, etc. Some of these bynames remain with us today. The Ashworths were followed by a puritan family of the name of Hardman, from whom the present Hardmans of the valley are descended.

The soil and pasture of our hills being more suitable to rearing cattle than agriculture, sheep farming was extensively carried on. The woollen trade having been introduced into Lancashire, found its way into the valley. The Flemings from Flanders were imported to teach us to weave. They brought with them the sabots or wooden shoes. These were found very suitable for our climate and rough roads, and we were quick to adopt and improve them. They remain with us today in various shapes as Rossendale clogs.

With the discovery of America and the introduction of cotton into England, the Rossendale Valley, and especially Bacup, whose climate was so suitable for spinning and weaving cotton, progressed rapidly. The advent of power, the abundance of water in the River Irwell, the seams of coal cropping out on every hillside, made it possible for manufacturers to produce cotton goods cheaper and better than most neighbouring towns, although the Bacupian was as stupid against the introduction of machinery as the rest of Lancashire.

The strong religious instinct in our character I attribute to the fact that Cromwell disbanded his army at Clitheroe, and a large number of his followers settled in our valley. Places of worship sprang up as fast as the mills. Even today Bacup is one of the few boroughs in England that can house its entire population in its places of worship. Its love of music dates far back. There is an entry in the records kept by Sir Ralph Assheton, the Lancashire baronet, as follows: "Christmas, 1676, paid to the Rossendale Players 10s."

Edwin Waugh many times referred to the musical side of the Rossendalian in his story of "The Barrel Organ: Old Dan the Fiddler". He also makes reference to the Deighn Layrocks. Many Psalm tunes we sing today originated among them. I could tell many amusing stories of these musicians, but time will not permit. Edwin Waugh or as he was called in Bacup, "Ned Wuff", is the poet of Lancashire. What Scott did for his native wilds, and Wordsworth for his much beloved mountains, Waugh, with humbler genius and less pretentious claims, has done for Lancashire. Some of us in Rossendale are very proud of the fact that the only monument to his memory is in Rossendale. Waugh's Well was built and opened to his memory in the summer of 1866, at Fo' Edge. It was originally intended to engrave the following lines upon the head of the well:

"There's a lonely rindling fountain
  Yonder moorland hills among;
From the heather breasted mountain,
  Tinkling drips its liquid song.
To its lovely music listening,
  Once a maiden sat thereby:
Ah! that maiden's dark eye glistening —
  It will haunt me till I die".

****

The above is the first verse of Edwin Waugh's poem "The Moorland Maid"

"Farewell to yon breezy mountain,
  Farewell to the flow'ry dell,
Farewell to the rindling fountain,
  And the lonely moorland well;
Farewell to the streamlet, purling
  Sweetly through your silent glen;
Oh farewell, the dark-eyed darling
  I shall never see again!"

SOME ROSSENDALE ANECDOTES

When the evacuees arrived at Waterfoot during the war, there were two black boys with them, and one of the reception committee, something of a humorist, did his best, in his own way, to make them feel at home. He took them into the Arcade chip shop and in his own words, "Gave 'em a good feed o' black peighs".

* * * * * * * * * * *

When the landlord called for his rent at a tumbledown old cottage in a Rossendale hamlet, he was taken aback when the old lady who lived there asked for "electric leet to be put in". "Electric leet?", he exclaimed; "at two an' ninepence a week th'art lucky to ged dayleet".

* * * * * * * * * * *

"Is this mon a trained singer?" a man asked the steward at Waterfoot 'Con' on a concert night. "Oh yes", said the steward, "He was trained at Milan". "Milan?" said the man -- "tha means Mill End".

* * * * * * * * * * *

A farmer who had married a woman not without money, was able to effect great improvements at his farm. One day he was looking round with great pride at all his new equipment and his wife said to him, "Tha wouldn't ha' had a farm like this if aw'd ha' bin beawt brass". "No", said the farmer, "an' tha wouldn't ha' bin here if tha'd bin beawt brass".

* * * * * * * * * *

ROSSENDALE BUILDINGS OF ARCHITECTURAL OR HISTORICAL INTEREST

(Being mainly the summary of a talk given to Rawtenstall Men's Fellowship Opening Meeting in 1960 by Mr. R. C. Cross, supplemented from other sources.)

NEWHALLHEY HALL Built probably in Oliver Cromwell's time, though little is known of its early history. The home of the Nuttall family for many years, the house has since been demolished.

NEW HOUSE SPRINGSIDE Formerly a farm, and built in 1691. Inside the house there is a rare beam-supporting post, the only example for many miles around of a "witch post", the carved "X" at its head being to keep away the evil ones.

LOWER CHAPEL HILL FARM Of similar date (17th century), but modernised inside. A very handsome building.

HIGHER CHAPEL HILL FARM Of similar type, but a great pity it is now derelict.

CHAPEL HILL FARM The bowl-like hole in the wall with projecting ledge was thought by the Rev. J. Marshall Mather in "Rambles round Rossendale" to have something to do with the days of Catholic persecution. The view of the speaker was that it was more likely to have been used for sheep salve, or even for cloth manufacture.

GREAVE HOUSE Stands at the bottom of Hollin Lane, and is mid-17th century or later. Further up the lane is Lower Constablelee Farm, late 17th century, and a feature of which is the lozenge shaped chimney at the corner. At the top of the lane is Higher Constablelee Farm, its effect much diminished by later alterations; its date is early 18th century.

WAINGATE HOUSE A beautiful building with distinctive Georgian features. The date is 1755.

HALL CARR FOLD The three-storied house near Fallbarn Crossing, a "weaving factory" before power looms were introduced. Built between 1790 and 1820.

GOODSHAW FOLD A 1659 house with the initials R.P.L.H. over the door. Then there is the "Spewing Duck" erected by subscription in 1858, but not working now. The derelict old hall of the Hargreaves family has recently been demolished.

LOVECLOUGH FOLD A handsome 17th century building now used as a works' social club. For generations this was the home of the Holt family, one of whom was the original owner of the printworks.

GAMBLESIDE Once a thriving hamlet, but the land was sterilised by the building of Clowbridge reservoir. There was a mansion there, the home of the Ormerods, but all that remains of this building, which was built in Cromwell's time, is a few window-heads lying in a field.

Nearby is *MEADOWHEAD FARM,* where David Whitehead was born, and *NEW LAITHE,* on the Dunnockshaw side, was the home of the Hudsons, who were staunch Baptists.

EWOOD HALL At Ewood Bridge, and dates back to 1647. There are initials C.G. and I.G., which Mr. Cross believed belonged to a family named Gregory, though could belong to a family named Garside. As the Offices of the Sewerage Board, Ewood Hall is kept in a good state.

NEW HALL, EDENFIELD This was the home of the Rawsthornes, but is now in ruins, and has been almost totally demolished. Only recently collapsed is the barn, with its unique arched "cruck" beams and enormous tie beam. It dates back to at least 1550.

BARON FOLD Another of these houses whose upper floors were used for weaving.

WAGGONER TUNSTEAD

Another old house which has fallen on evil days. Built in 1632, it was the home of the Tattersalls, and a heavy lintel stone carrying some initials and the date make this the oldest dated building in Bacup. It has a gabled porch and several long stone-mullioned windows, stone walls and a stone slate roof, with cement rendered brick extension at one end. Inside are some fine beams and a big arched fireplace, now made into cupboards. Just below Waggoner Tunstead is a farm called "Honey Hole".

FEARNS HALL This is an old mansion house, once the home of the Ashworths, and has a 1696 datestone over the projecting central porch of the original portion. It has a door heavily studded with nails; these, being purely ornamental, were known as "dead" nails -- no doubt giving rise to the expression "dead as a door nail". Its appearance is now somewhat battered, but it has rows of long, low, stone-mullioned windows on one side. An extension of 1830 was built on the site of a building of 1557.

WARTH HOUSE, WATERFOOT Built by Robert Haworth about 1800, and possessed a "shell" door head. Situated near to Seville's Bakery, this house was demolished some time ago.

ST. NICHOLAS' CHURCH, NEWCHURCH Inside the tower is to be found a stone carving of the Royal Arms of Queen Elizabeth I, dated 1561. This must be the oldest dated stone in the district.

ROEBUCK INN, BACUP This has recently been demolished (see picture), and was an old post house, beside the old pack mule route, off the main Bacup-Burnley road at Higher Broadclough. It had a double storied porch, carrying three stone finials, two tall pilasters or strip columns, and the date stone inscribed I.L. 1739. The initials refer to a man called John Lord. Inside the porch was a small recess said to be where tankards could be left while mules were being tended in the courtyard.

YE OLDE VILLAGE STORES These are nos. 2 and 4 Lord's Court, adjacent to the former Roebuck Inn. Late 17th or early 18th century. Stone walls and stone slate roof, two studded doors, and two early two-light windows above the small shop window on the ground floor.

ACRE MILL 1877 and earlier. A long, rectangular stone building, with two rows of 19 round-arched windows. Inscribed on the end wall to the east is: "James Ashworth 1877 Homo proponit deus disponit".

ACRE MILL LODGE Date stone inscribed 1864 J.A. Stone building at the south-east corner of the mill. Rusticated round-headed doorway.

ROCKCLIFFE HOUSE Victorian stone house. End pilasters, cornice balustrade parapet with urns. Projecting centre bay is flanked by canted aprons, sashes and cornices, and has a square porch of fluted composite columns, cornice, and balustraded balcony. Side wall has an ornamented upper window in centre, and flanking urns in niches.

ROCKCLIFFE WOOD House with stone walls and stone slate roof. Datestone on the projecting porch is inscribed
 H 1752. Iron railings.
T E

STUBBYLEE HALL Victorian stone house formerly the home of John Maden Holt, used since 1919 as the Municipal Offices (Town Hall). At the front is a centre porch of Ionic engaged columns, and flanking curved bays. Domed staircase.

Greetings card from about the time of the First World War.

A Greetings Postcard from Stacksteads, showing CROW TREE HOUSE where Crow Tree Avenue was built near School Street, FEARNS HALL, EDGESIDE LANE above Edgeside Park, and HONEY HOLE farm near Tunstead estate.

"BACUP TOWN CENTRE in 1926." An old omnibus emerges from the narrow Yorkshire Street near the old "Angel Inn" adjoining the Queen's Hotel. Townhead property on the right, the King George V Hotel on the left. Note the signpost.

AERIAL VIEW of Bacup centre, taken about 1965, looking south-west. Look carefully – many of the other photographs can be picked out from this. Recently-demolished Market Street/Plantation Street property can be seen at the top left-hand corner. (Reproduced by courtesy of the Lancashire Evening Telegraph, Blackburn).

Six services were run daily to Bacup by this horse-drawn tram, seen here near its Rochdale terminus at the Spread Eagle Hotel. Cheetham Street. Date not certain, but approximatley 90 years ago.

The tramways come to Bacup. Rossendale Steam Valley Tramways were introduced to Bacup in 1889. An early steam tram on the Bacup-Rawtenstall run.

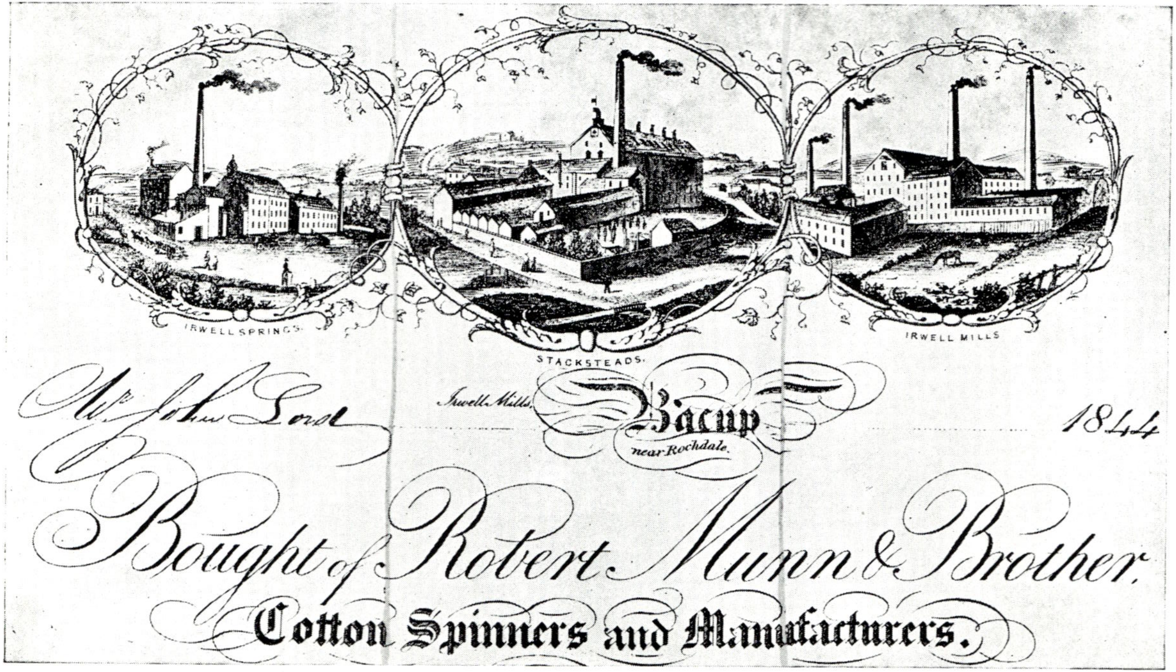

Letter-head used by Robert Munn & Brother, who built the first cotton mill in Bacup in 1824. This was Old Clough Mill; Stacksteads Mill was built in 1833, and Irwell Mill was taken over in 1838.

STUBBYLEE HALL, once the home of James Maden Holt, his sister Emily Sarah Holt, the novelist, and others of the Holt family; now the Town Hall. Situated in the grounds of Stubbylee Park and next to Moorlands Park.

Bacup tramways were electrified in July 1909. An early Rawtenstall tram from this period.

A Case of flints in the Museum of Bacup Natural History Society.

FAIRWALL FARMHOUSE 17th and 18th century stone house. An out-building is dated 1672. House is dated 1748 I^{H}D on a two-storeyed porch which has a small round-headed window. Two stone mullions, and some mullioned windows at the rear.

BROADCLOUGH HALL Home of the Whitaker family for over 300 years. Has two dated stones which commemorate re-building or extension. Over a former side door (now inside) is the date 1666 and initials I A W (John Whitaker and his wife). The second date, 1816, is now in the cellar, and denotes when the front of the hall was redesigned. The Whitaker coat of arms is over a side door -- three diamond-shapes and a horizontal bar, or, in heraldic terms -- sable, three mascles argent. The entrance front has a centre pediment, cornice, and wide entrance porch of two Tuscan columns, frieze and cornice with segmental arched doorway.

FOREST HOUSE Probably designed by John Foster of Liverpool, possibly for his own use. Date about 1828. Recessed centre with 4 Ionic columns rising through the whole height of the building to a portico. Wings flanked by pilasters with recessed central panels. Domed staircase. It was converted into a licensed restaurant at the end of 1970.

(NOTE: The Helmshore History Society and the Rossendale Arts and Antiquities Association concern themselves with other buildings of historical and architectural interest in the Rossendale Valley -- too numerous to append to this article, apart from the dates of: Tap Stone House, 1593; Great House Farm, 1600; Higher and Lower Cockham Farms, 1717; Kilnfield Farm and Todd Hall, both 17th century; Fold House (Gregory Fold), 1774; and Snig Hole Cottages, Helmshore, a good example of late 18th century work-peoples' dwellings)

The following are verses written on the occasion of the great meeting of freeholders which took place in Bacup on June 4th, 1793, to uphold the dignity of the Crown and assist His Majesty and Ministers in counteracting disaffected people who were against the Crown and welfare of England.

Chairman: Henry Whitaker, Esqr., Hempstead House, Bacup.

Rossendale Freeholders of high renown,
Stand true to your Country, the King and the Crown.
On June 4th, the large meeting attend,
And prove to the House of Hanover a friend.

Parsons came from Burnley, Colne and Haslingden;
Blackburn, Newchurch, Whalley, Holme and Todmorden.
The British flags on Bacup steeple did fly.
The French flags torn in tatters in the Irwell did lie.

The Rector of Winwick a long speech did make,
Informing the Clergy England was at stake;
Doctor Whitaker of Holme deeds and parchment did bring
To sign life and fortune in aid of the King.

The Clergy and gents to St. John's church did go,
In cockades and silk scarf, they made a great show,
Colne and Whalley singers in chorus did sing,
The old song "Hearts of Oak", and "God save the King".

When the service was over they did retire,
In front of the "Dragon" around the bonfire,
Paine's works there they burnt, and hanged Tom on a tree,
Then his effigy burnt in the year '93.

The Innkeepers all gave barrels of beer,
The rich, poor and needy partook of good cheer,
A fat oxen was roasted and given away,
Bacup people still living remember that day.

My old friend desired me to send you these verses. They were composed by a Mr. John Heyworth, of Grains Nook, near Bacup, and an old friend of Caleb's. The prospectus you sent me has gone up to Mr. Whitaker, our Magistrate. He is a relation to Caleb and that Maden Holt and Henry Whitaker, Chairman of the meeting in the verses on the other side. Caleb had told Mr. Whitaker about the paper you sent me so he sent word down to our house to see if I would lend it to him and, of course, I did so but I have not got it back, yet.

(NOTE: The above is an exact transcript of a document in Bacup Public Library, to which it was given by Mr. William Lord, of 38 Bankside Lane, Bacup, in whose family the verses had been since they were composed.)

SOME ROSSENDALE ANECDOTES

RIDIN' T' STANG

That little jingle about Ridin' t' stang went, and was done for, a felly who 'ad leathered 'is wife or bin boosing hard. The lads used to get a hand cart and with one sat on top would run through the street shouting, to where the couple lived, and shout the following:-

"Tan a ran, Tan a ran, Tan a ran, Tan, Tan,
    Wiv com this day to ride this stang,
Who for -- Old So and So, What for,
    For leathering his wife,
S heawt, lads, Sheawt ..."

which used to bring the old villain chasing after them when they made a hurried retreat.

A well known local character bought a bag of chips at Mill End, Waterfoot, and walking down Burnley Road said to himself: "Dang it -- Aw've forgetten to put salt an' aliker on 'em". So he called at the next chip shop, at Brougham Hall, and helped himself to the condiments on the counter. Seeing the look of disapproval on the face of the proprietor, he said: "Eeh well, yer'all in t'same union, arn'd yo?"

NEWCHURCH – *where four Religious Denominations had their origin.*

Up to 1511, when the church was built, the Valley formed part of the vast parish of Whalley, and its inhabitants had to go to Clitheroe for spiritual ministrations -- and finally for burial.

Legend has it that the original site was at Mitchell Field Nook -- but on three successive nights the stone that had been collected was mysteriously moved to the present site of St. Nicholas' Church on the slope of Seat Naze. This was taken as spiritual intervention, and the position was changed.

"But", comments the church's history, "may not the true interpretation be that the best building stone was to be found on Seat Naze, and to avoid the cost of transportation the church was built on the spot?

And so the "New Church" came into being -- for the first 40 years as a chapel-at-ease to Whalley, known as "The Chapel of Our Saviour in Rossendale".

Houses began to cluster around it, and a village was born. The church was rebuilt in 1561, enlarged in 1753, and completely rebuilt in its present form in 1824 when, for the foundation stone-laying there was a procession from the Boar's Head (built in 1674).

But not everyone wanted a place for religious observance. Records of the ecclesiastical court at Whalley for 1510-38 showed that one of the chief defendants was a family by the name of Marcroft from Cowpe and Boothfold. Among their "crimes" -- slander, refusing to go to church, talking during service, interrupting service, profaning festivals, making a shirt on All Saints' Day, and being notorious swearers.

Old-street (Th' Owd Gate) was always called "Kirk Gate", and all weddings, christenings and funerals concentrated there. A bridal couple, led by a man with a fiddle, would walk to church from as far as Bacup, and it is recorded that one funeral from Crawshawbooth arrived in a remarkably heavy snowstorm, and the conveyance with the coffin "had to be drawn over the top of the Boar's Head sign".

Many of the early incumbents were "absentees", and others were followers of the hounds, and kept dogs of their own.

After afternoon service, football would be played, the parson kicking off, and the pitch was from Thistlemount and back.

Notices, such as Sales by auction, were read by the Clerk from the pulpit, or standing on a gravestone outside. He would also inform parishioners of the impending killing of a beast, pig or sheep -- and orders for portions could be given to him.

Up to 1825, "rush bearing" was carried on, its function the covering of the floor of the church with rushes, a protection against the extreme cold of winter. Long after that date the time of the year was held as a holiday. A famous institution was "Kirk Fair" with its stalls and booth set up in the street. There was a cattle fair on April 29th, and one for cattle, pigs and pedlary on the first Monday after midsummer.

Newchurch, which has cradled much of the scholastic, religious, sporting, and social life of a big slice of the district, might well have been the name, and possibly the administrative centre of a united borough embracing both the present towns of Rawtenstall and Bacup.

For three centuries or more, Newchurch township extended from Bacup to Rawtenstall (these places were little more than villages), and even in later years, Newchurch School Board, set up in 1875, covered the whole of the area. But it was not to be. More progressive elements at Bacup secured the incorporation of that borough in 1882. Nine years later, Rawtenstall Borough came into being.

The "new" turnpike road reached Waterfoot from Rawtenstall in 1826, and was cut through the glen to Bacup in 1828; the railway came in 1846, although the then terminus at Waterfoot was known as Newchurch station for some time.

In 1744 a Scotsman named William Darney preached Wesleyan Methodism in Miller Barn, and 4 years later, John Wesley paid his first visit. He recorded in his diary: "A few rude people, but they kept their distance, and it was well that they did or the awakened hearers would have handled them roughly.

He came again in 1752, and in 1761 a chapel was built -- on the site of the present Thistlemount Avenue. Wesley preached there in 1766, and the place stood until 1806, when a new church was built in "Turnpike". This early Wesleyan Church was in the Rochdale Circuit, whose superintendent minister was the Rev. Joseph Cooke. He fell out of favour with the denomination, and in 1807 was invited to Newchurch by 30 or 40 people. They met in a building at the rear of New Barn, Turnpike, and in May the next year bought a plot of land for £25 on the north side of Old Street, and on it built at a cost of £500, a church opened on New Year's Day, 1809. This small bare place with its whitewashed walls was known as Cooke's Chapel. It was the start of the Unitarian Church in the district, and the present Bethlehem Church, in Turnpike, was opened on Good Friday, 1865.

There was another dispute among the Wesleyans in 1822 as to whether hand-writing should be taught in Sunday School. This was ultimately forbidden, but those who wished to continue it took a room over the home of Dr. Law in Old Street, and formed the nucleus of the United Methodists. In 1828 this sect moved to another upper room in Turnpike, and 8 years later built Mount Tabor Chapel in Turnpike. Eventually, in 1876, this was transferred to Bridge-street, and became Bethesda Chapel.

So it will be seen that four denominations which spread throughout the Valley -- Anglicans, Wesleyans, Unitarians, and United Methodists -- had their origins in Newchurch.

MORE ROSSENDALE ANECDOTES

A boy on his way to school had to walk past a farm, and shouted at the farmer on quite a few successive mornings, "Tha watters thi milk". The farmer complained to the boy's schoolmaster who threatened to thrash the boy if he repeated the offence. The next day, as the boy passed the farm, he shouted to the farmer -- "Tha knows".

Husband: "As which on uz dies first, Aw durnd know wod'll happen to t' other". Wife: "Thee speyk for thissen. Aw'm gooin back a' living' at Bacup".

A Rossendale pawnbroker had a parrot, which, when the shop was crowded on a Friday night, used to sing out: "one at a time, please". One night the bird got out of the shop and flew into the trees at "Sparrow Park". Some rooks were nesting there and they all flew at the parrot, pecking at his feathers. Amid all the hub-bub it could be heard screaming out: "One at a time, please".

A tackler decided to be in fashion and get a gas fire. He was very pleased and told his friend how much he liked it. His friend told him to suspend judgment until he had had it longer. Back came the reply: "Well, Aw've had it three weeks now, and it hasn't gone out yet!"

Once, when Accrington were playing Rawtenstall, Bill Finney, a great stone-waller, was bowled by a bowler called Haddock. The headline read: Finney bowled Haddock - no fluke about it.

ROSSENDALE AND ROSSENDALE FOLK

To begin with, our areas form part of the backbone of England, although most of our uplands fall far short of the sea-bed limestone-upheavals of north-west Yorkshire and of Derbyshire, with the Lancashire-Cheshire plain between. None the less Rossen-dale and Roch-dale are nigh each other. Their names mean something from old times, and their people form part of the living backbone of England.

We will take a peep then, and only a peep, at patches of each area's history from about eight-and-a-half centuries ago; premising first that during the fifth and sixth centuries Britian had been invaded by Saxons from North Germany, and by the Danes; also that in 1066, on the death of the Saxon King Edward the Confessor, Harold was elected in his place. Whereupon Harold's brother Tostig along with Harold Hardrada, King of Norway, invaded the north of the country, and the Saxon king called for armed forces against them.

Now at this period there was a Saxon thane or noble, Gamel or Gamul, who held lands in Rossendale, also in Rochdale, including its Recedam Castle. Gamel summoned his retainers and joined the king's army assembling at York, the engagement of the opposing forces taking place at Stamford Bridge (hence called "Battle - Bridge".) The conflict was severe but the Saxons won, September 25th, 1066. Henceforward the history of our two dales became largely collateral.

William Duke of Normandy, had visited England in 1051 and formed designs upon it; so now he, with a great fleet and army, began his invasion in 1066, and ultimately became Conqueror.

One of Gamel's boundaries north-westwards became known as Gamelsyde, modernly corrupted into Gambleside (a little above Crawshawbooth), and Rossendale became enclosed as Forest-land under severe forest laws, in order that Royalty might enjoy hunting the abundance of wild animals – deer, wolf, boar, and smaller creatures of the chase. Yet, after all, no Norman or any other king, though keeping control over all the venison, ever came to hunt there.

Gamel seems to have had a son Orme, who later had holdings in the Forest, and who for facility in the chase or other rider's reason, made a considerable clearing, ridding, or royd (on the Towneley side, I think), and it is notable that that Clearing, Orme-royd, led to descendants of that name who at Gamelside, built a little mansion which was added to twice by Ormerods till there were three gabled parts. All that structure is now gone to ruin. The old brewhouse, altered, became a temporary Baptist chapel.

Skipping now over about 400 years we come down to the time when King Henry VII ordered the dis-foresting of Rossendale and the destruction of the larger wild animals so that land might be "letten" to those who would occupy it and pay rent to the King. Down to that time most of the official men and their families had been drawn from the Clitheroe Castle district.

But in the time of Edward IV there is recorded the coming, from the Rochdale area, of half-a-dozen families, even from Ashworth Moor into Rossendale. These people were not necessarily related to each other, but were registered in Norman style as de Ashworth, from Ashworth. The number of Ashworths today is very great, but I believe not a few of the older descendants crossed over the hills back to Rochdale. In fact the population on each side is very mixed, and as Rochdale is contiguous to the Yorkshire border whether via Blackstone Edge for Halifax way, or via Bacup, Todmorden, and the Hebden valley, intercourse and interchange have been steady and ever friendly even with the "Yorkshire-bites".

Now be it borne in mind throughout the old-time changes, that while trees were on the ground for felling and the building of barns, etc., and stone was abundant, lime had to be brought all the way from Clitheroe to the forest ground and to Rochdale, in sacks or panniers across the backs of troops of galloway ponies.

Those ancient tracks are mostly traceable to this day, a portion being still known as "Limer's Lane". Some of the limers owned quite a number of animals. Another point to be remembered is that blocks of lime (already burnt at Clitheroe) were not only costly but in transport over miles of rainy uplands the lime might get "slaked" en route. Hence blocks of limestone were brought to be kilned near where building was to be carried on: hence also, here and there to this day remain such site-names as "Kilnfield"; or, in a dene or hollow where some enterprising man had regularly practised as a "kilner", his spot might become called "kilner deyne".

Now a summary paragraph or two on "the folk" of both areas. I do not attempt in the least to furnish a list of the leaders of thought and action amongst them, but rather indicate, from the touches of history already given, that the people must have been a hardy, adventurous sort through generations: hard-working, shrewd, freedom-loving and generally commendable. In Rochdale the Co-operative movement, now spread over the country, had its birth; I as a young man in the town for two or three years round about 1860 used to visit its library, etc. Local inventions in machinery of many kinds led to productive works on a great scale. Rochdale with a large share of comparatively flat area had considerable physical advantages over Rossendale with its hills and generally narrow valleys, but while the large town has grown more easily into the highest of municipal enterprises, with its stately town hall, its various schools, great free library, art gallery, and much besides, we on our side have succeeded in following up to no mean extent; and aim at further advance.

In both areas music had been a vogue among the people, especially in connection with the churches and Sunday-schools; James Leach, of Rochdale, and the "Deighn Layrocks" of Rossendale being early instances. Musical development leaned later to the formation of bands, like Goodshaw and Irwell Springs. Amongst all their toiling, both communities had always had plain men and women with a sense of humour.

To revert to the two rivers of the dales; let Rochdale remember that its main stream is a mere tributary (as it approaches Radcliffe) to our Irwell, which, however, admits it peaceably and so helps to float it down by the cities of Salford and Manchester to the Mersey in order to give the Roche a chance of reaching the mighty Atlantic.

MORE ROSSENDALE ANECDOTES

A man who had been given up as dead suddenly sat up in bed and said, "Aw'm noan deead yet tha knows". "Shut thi gob", said his wife; -- "T' doctor knows best".

Early Datestones in Bacup — the first 12 of over 200

IT·1632·IE·12

Waggoner Tunstead, Stacksteads.
Former farm. John Tattersall and family.

IAW:1666

Broadclough Hall, Bacup. Inside.
The Whittaker family. In 1559 a James Whittaker of Broadclough was the first in the list of Greaves within the old Forest of Rossendale. Another James Whittaker was Rossendale's first magistrate in 1824. A Whittaker lived here until 1923. A relation, the Rev. T.D. Whittaker, of Holme Chapel, wrote the celebrated 'History of Whalley'. + 1816 inside

1672 IHAHRH IH

Fairwall Farm, Greens, Stacksteads.
The Hoyle family lived here for two centuries until 1770. The last was John Hoyle who left the property to his daughter Dorothy, who married John Whittaker of Broadclough.
+ 1748

IT
IA 1673

Brandwood Cottages, Waterbarn, Stacksteads. Built into a wall. From the barn of Brandwood Farm. James Townsend and probably his sisters Isabel and Anne. Townsend Fold near Rawtenstall was named after this family.

in relief 1632   JL L 381 HMRH incised

Lower Top o' th' Bank Farm, near Maden Rec, Bacup

HH IH 1683

Cottage, Rakehead, Stacksteads.
Former farmhouse. Maybe Hoyle or Hardman family

JR 1687   faint

Dawson Barn, High Meadows, near Golf Club House, Bacup.
Former barn.

HAH
RM·
1688

Parrock Lumb Farm, Sharneyford.
Inside the porch.
"Mr. Heap ... a churchman ... so nearby Heap Hey, Heap Barn Farm."

16:IMH:89

Lower Hultock Top Farm, The Square, Bankside Lane, Bacup

A
EEOA
I 1696 M

Fearns Hall, Stacksteads
The Ashworth family. Edmund and Oliver Ashworth of 'Fearnes' were Overseers of the Poor for the Newchurch area. + 1725 inside + 1830

L
I E
16 97

Higher Broadclough Farm, Bacup.
John Lord. The Lord family owned much property in the area including Dykes House Farm and the old 'Roe Buck Inn'.
+ 1737

K E Y

Date on the stone. Site of datestone and district. Date on the 1683 datestone.

1683*   H / I M   3 Top Farm, near New Lane, Oldgate.   1711 + 1908

asterisked date means datestone NOT found – maybe buried, moved or destroyed.

Initials on the stone, maybe owner (e.g. John & Mary Haworth).

Another datestone on the building or nearby. See 1908 for details.

F.S. means foundation stone.
Old means building demolished.
Former means building standing but having another use.
Dates not marked with an asterisk (*) have been found during the period of search and research 1965 – 1971. Some might now have gone. Others may come to light.

John B. Taylor.

DATE	INITIALS	SITE OF DATESTONE & OTHER DATESTONES
1697	T B	Barn, near Heald Top.
1702	R S H A H	Stubbylee Hall. + 1736, 1809, 1872.
1704	E L L I L H	Greens Nook Farm
1706	I H I	Lee Farm, 17 Old Meadows.
*1709	R J E H	Old Deerplay Inn.
1725	G A S	Fearns Hall, Inside. + 1696, 1830.
1729	I L	Dykes House Farm, Broadclough.
1730	E W A	Shops Yorkshire St. Tod Rd. + 1872.
1731	E A	Nat. Hist. Museum, Yorkshire St., Tod. Rd. Inside. From?
*1733	R L E	White House, 32 Rockliffe Road.
1736	E L	Fearns Sch., from near Windy Gate, Brex.
*1736	I H E	Stubbylee Hall. + 1702, 1809, 1872.
1737	I L	Higher Broadclough Farm. + 1697.
*1738	I L I	6 Lane Head, Blackthorn Lane.
1738		Slack Gate Farm, near Fairview Rd., Mettle Cote.
1739	I L	Roe Buck Inn, Higher Broadclough.
1739	R L I	Greens House, Tod. Road. + 1766, 1770, 1815, 1832.
1739	I O	Barn, New Barn Farm, Stacksteads. + 1889.
*1740	I P	Two cottages, Four Lane Ends.
1741	I L M	Higher Slack Farm, Britannia. + 1782, 1859.
*1741	J A	4 - 6, Lower Newgate.
1746	A T E	Huttock Top Farm, off Bankside Lane.
1747	O P	Nat. Hist. Museum, Inside. From Crow Tree House, Rook Hill Rd.
1748	I H D	Fairwall Farm. + 1672.
1751	J H A	10 Fairview Road, from Tong Hall, off South Street.
*1751	J M	Lodge Lane Farm, near Bankside Farm.
1752	T H E	Rockliffe Wood House, Wesley Place Lane.
1753	R L	Farm, Old Meadows Road.
1761		First Methodist Chapel in Rossendale, Lanehead Lane.
1766	I M	Greens House, Tod. Rd. + 1739, 1770, 1815, 1832.
*1769	I L M	Door Stones, near Yorkshire St., Tod. Road.
1770		Greens House, Tod. Rd. + 1739, 1766, 1815, 1832.
1770	I H A	Drainpipe head, 'White Horse', Yorkshire St., Tod. Rd. +1907.
1773	I A M	Nat. Hist. Museum, Inside. From 1 Lane Fold.
*1774	J S S	Walmersley Farm, Britannia.
1774	T H E	16 New Line, from Lumb Hall, near St. Saviour's Sch.
1776	I J L	Ivy Cottage, Bankside Lane.

SUPERSTITIONS, BOGGARTS AND WITCHES

There are legends and stories in plenty about the activities of the Devil in Rossendale, but very little has been written about the supernatural powers of boggarts and witches.

Samuel Bamford, in his book, "Life of a Radical" refers to a witch, In a conversation with his friend Doctor Healey, he said, "There's a fine leet i' th' welkin as th'witch o' Brandwood sed when the devil wur ridin' o'er Rossenda'." Then many years later Edwin Waugh made references to the Prickshaw Witch, and in one of his articles referred to the bull-baiting ground at Hammaton Green, Bacup, as being near the old "Witchin' Hoile" -- now occupied by the Corn Mill Yard. The following story about two farms on the moors round Deerplay seems to indicate a lingering belief in the existence of witches nearer our own times.

A Tale of Two Moorland Farms above Weir

A thieving cat was taking the cream in the night from one of the farms. This was not their own cat, and the puzzled farmer and his son stayed up one night to watch for any intruder.

In the middle of the night, the dairy door was pushed open, and a cat came into the dairy and jumped on a stone shelf. The farmer and his son threw pots and pans and everything they could get their hands on at the cat, and it jumped out through the window and vanished as quickly as it had appeared.

On a neighbouring farm, the farmer happened to wake up in the middle of the night and found that his wife (not for the first time) was missing. So he kept awake to watch for her return. Eventually she crept into the bedroom with her arms scratched, her face bleeding, and black eyes, as if she had been badly bruised by stones.

Was she a witch?

* * * * * * * * * *

The only reputed ghost is the one at the Railway Inn, Waterfoot, described by those who have seen the apparition as "a tall middle-aged lady in a long grey dress", but there are many stories and legends about the Devil, who was reputed to live in Hell Clough, and also about boggarts or poltergeists. "The Tong Boggart"was the subject of a play which used to be performed by local dramatic societies. This was set on "Tong Castle", a house in Tong Fold, built in 1751, and now demolished, and of which a photograph appears elsewhere in this Miscellany.

The history of Tong Fold is shrouded in mystery, and Thomas Newbigging, referring to the belief in witchcraft and in the existence of evil spirits which was at one time very prevalent amongst the working class in Bacup, remarks in his "History of the Forest of Rossendale": "The doings of the notorious Tong Boggart are familiar to almost everyone in Bacup, and few but have heard rehearsed the story of his unearthly howlings and knockings that kept the neighbourhood in a ferment of terror for weeks together".

Mr. R. G. Neale has written about superstitious beliefs in our own time as follows: "When I lived in a community of quarry workers and drift pit workers at Rakehead on the side of Hailstorm Hill in the Stacksteads district of Rochdale, 1930 to 1940, belief in the doom crow was very common. To see a single rook or crow in flight was regarded as very bad luck or an omen of disaster. If you are alone when you see it, it is best to turn back or disaster will befall, if on the other hand you are with a companion and direct his attention to the bird and make the sign of the cross in spit on the nearest stone, you will ward off the evil results both for yourself and your companion.

Rossendale mill-girls who walked from the hillside hamlets to work in the valley had a jingle about seeing magpies:

One for sorrow,
Two for joy,
Three for a letter,
Four for a boy;
Five for silver,
Six for gold,
Seven for a secret
Never to be told.

ELIZABETH ALICK (1884 to 1938)

I have just been privileged to read a typescript volume of poems by one Elizabeth Alick, who in a poetical sense might be described as a Rossendale rose who blushed unseen.

Departing this life in 1938, she left behind her no world-shaking masterpiece, but the unquenchable flame of her faith -- a flame which will kindle a beacon-light in the hearts and minds of those who read and understand.

The sincere simplicity of her work is further characterised by a feeling of haunting sadness, and a sense of unutterable loneliness, induced no doubt by the cruel caprice of fate, which rendered her a helpless invalid in the prime of her life.

Elizabeth Alick lived in the little valley of Cowpe, and during the latter years of her infirmity, she could do little but gaze through the window of her cottage, where she lay like a bird with a broken wing.

And of the birds she says:

"Their supple ease to scorn my bonds,
Their beauty mock my cruel scars,
I lie and beat my hopeless bars
With frenzy's fever-withered hands.

But some dark evil holds the key
I cannot think that He whose word
Has winged the happy heedless bird,
Would forge this chain of death for me.

My yearning senses grieve and grope,
I *will* believe that God is hope!"

Here in her picturesque native valley, she lived, and as her appreciation of natural beauty expanded, so her poetical instincts matured to develop into a constant preoccupation.

That she bore her tribulation with great fortitude and patience is amply evidenced in the general feeling of her work. And if there is an occasional lament, there is little trace of self-pity.

Far from becoming embittered in the contemplation of her prison-like existence, she accepted with gentle resignation the cruel shackles which pinioned her body, to acquire a compensating nobility of thought of deep and wonderful understanding.

". . . and then it seemed
That all the blessings life could give
Had on my spirit beamed".

Such was typical of the spirit which animated the thought-forms of this remarkable woman.

And when again the fragrant summer breezes blow, I shall turn my footsteps towards her native valley, knowing that any such fragrance will now have a special significance.

I shall think of one, who herself unhonoured and unsung -- sang with honour throughout her considerable sufferings, without ever striking a discordant note. And until I am able to understand, I can only speculate on the wonder that she was able to sing at all.

MORE ROSSENDALE ANECDOTES

The landlord was a kindly man and in spite of rate increases and drastic price rises for repairs, he had not increased his cottage rents for several years. Eventually, however, he came to the conclusion that the rents would have to go up. He called at a cottage occupied by an old lady, and said, "Aw'll ha' t' raise yor rent this week", to get the reply, "Eeh, that's good on yo',"cos Aw corn't".

A Rossendalian who had lived many long years in Australia came on a sentimental journey to his native valley. Many of his contemporaries had departed this life, and he went into the cemetery to look at their gravestones. He stopped at one which read "J. Maden, the beloved husband of Anne Maden", but underneath it referred to a second husband and underneath again a third. Just then a woman came up to the grave with some flowers. He recognised her as an old sweetheart. They got into conversation and he said, "Aw used to think a lot abeawt thee. Aw nearly axed thi to wed mi". "Did ti?" she said. "Look wod tha's missed. Tha'd ha had thi name at top o' that gravestone".

THE FAMOUS WHITWORTH DOCTORS

He came into that valley between Bacup and Rochdale in the early 1760's, an ordinary enough looking young fellow who, one day, would enjoy a national reputation and royal patronage.

He was in his twenties, a blacksmith by trade and farrier by natural inclination. His education was limited, he possessed no qualifications but he had studied botany, was wise in the use of herbs and drugs and was, without any argument, a most dexterous bone-setter.

John Taylor chose to settle at Whitworth, then an obscure village in a wild hilly region. He soon established a thriving practice with horses and dogs, and folk, marvelling at his successes with dumb animals, began to consult him about their own disorders, for there were no doctors in the district.

His fame travelled far beyond the valley. Before long, hundreds of suffering humans were trudging or trundling along to Whitworth to seek, and often to find, a cure for their various maladies. The transition was a natural one. John Taylor of the horny healing hands became a renowned "Bone-setter and Surgeon". He never lost his partiality for his original patients, however, and "yond hoss", having been come "a lung while", would always be treated before the humans. Dr. John never minced his words nor polished his manners for the highest in the land.

In time he was joined in the practice by his brother George. They bought Whitworth House, not far from the Church, an impressive place by contemporary standards. There was a wooden contrivance at the front for securing horses during operations. George and James Taylor, Dr. John's two sons, later joined the famous team of "Whitworth Doctors" to whose shrine of healing came multitudes of cripples, hosts of pale-faced paupers clad in coarse grey, and others of all ranks, cancerous, ulcerous or severely afflicted. They were afforded rude shelter by the villagers who lived on dry oatcake, milk and potatoes, rarely tasting fresh meat.

All made instantly for the surgery where there were never less than fifty and often more than a hundred patients waiting. There, no attention was paid to circumstance or rank. The nobleman with an impressive carriage and a purse of gold took his turn with the calloused artisan and the barefoot beggar. Nor did the gruff but essentially honest Dr. John vary his fee according to the patient's ability to pay. The standard charge for all was eighteenpence a week, including medicaments and treatments. Those who could not pay were never pressed but a subscription box was passed round to make up the deficit.

The doctor's methods were hair-raising by present standards. Arthritic patients were told to rub the handrail of the stairs for long periods to loosen locked joints. Mis-shapen feet were bullied into specially made metal boots. A misplaced hip would be remedied by a smart thump from Dr. John's well aimed knee. (An aristocratic lady who suffered this indignity was vastly affronted, but cured!) Bone-setting was crude beyond telling. Apart from traditional boards and splints, patients were often tied to the iron railings outside and a flying kick would remedy a bad setting.

Medicaments were simple but effective. Sweating and straining, the doctors' wives compounded them in bulk, by rule of "thumb and finger". Glauber salts were bought by the hogshead. Salves were boiled in large furnaces, then flung on to a wet floor and cut up and rolled into small sticks. Pills were rolled by the thousand. Diet drink for purifying the blood was concocted by the gallon. Snuff made from powdered Assarabesca grown in the garden was "of wondrous virtue for the head". There were "blisters" and "plaisters", a spiritous liniment called "Whitworth Red Bottle" and a horrifying caustic powder called, simply, "Keen".

Keen indeed was this drastic substance which corroded healthy and diseased tissues alike, giving rise to the most excruciating agonies. It was common to pass sufferers by the wayside groaning from the "Keen" though it was within their own remedy, when endurance gave out, to apply a relieving "plaister". Stoics preferred the quick remedy to a prolonged series of short treatments and bore the pain for hours a day, realising that the cure continued only whilst the "Keen" was operating.

Dr. John rarely visited patients in their own lodging. "Arise, take up thy death-bed and come and see me at the surgery" was his maxim though, on a few occasions, he travelled considerable distances. Once, he was summoned to Cheltenham to attend upon, no less than, a Duchess! He diagnosed swiftly, bundled the lady's husband and family out of the sickroom, and dealt unceremoniously with the offending abscess. In gratitude, the Duchess recommended Dr. John to George III who was staying in the vicinity with his family. He was summoned to attend the Princess Elizabeth and her unspecified "head complaint" (sinus trouble, probably) which a generous allowance of home grown snuff relieved by sending the young lady off into gales of sneezing. During these royal proceedings John Taylor so far forgot his lowly origins as to slap the Queen Consort familiarly on the back, remarking: "Thou art a farrantly (good looking) woman to be the mother of such a set of straight backed lasses". The Queen, not at all offended, retorted that she had once been "as straight backed a lass as any of them!".

Long visits, however, were chiefly left to young Dr. George, a fine bone-setter who rode his horse throughout the country for that purpose at 1/- a mile inclusive. His brother James took over the horse department at Whitworth.

The Taylors, gruff, untidy, snuff-taking and tobacco-chewing characters were keen sportsmen all, and kept their own pack of hounds. Without warning they would escape the foetid atmosphere of the dressing room to be off after the hounds and gulp the sweet fragrant air. They were wealthy in the extreme. John was reputed to have amassed a fortune of £30,000 which, at eighteenpence a week, suggests a staggering number of patients treated.

Certainly Whitworth's growth from those remote village days can largely be attributed to this, the most outstanding medical family ever produced in this island. Conventional doctors tried to blacken the reputation of "Doctor" John and loudly trumpeted his unsuccessful cases, calling him a "quack" and a "horse doctor". He knew, he laughed, he shrugged his great shoulders and cared not. Of the stricken crowds at his doorstep he would demand of them who had been treating them. "What makes all you come to Whitworth if you have good doctors at home, eh?" he would taunt, knowing that half the sufferers had been given up as "incurable" by the conventional practitioners.

One lady had come a hundred miles with cancer of the breast.

"What art *thou* come here for woman?" he bellowed. "Not all the doctors in England can cure thee. Thou may go home again and dee".

This the lady positively refused to do and, with a spirit equal to his own, demanded that he try his hand, declaring: "I can bear what you inflict. Let it be kill or cure, I can but die at last".

"Thou art a brave lass", was the reply. "Then I will try, and God prosper us both". So it transpired. After six months of torture the lady went home cleared of her cancer and lived healthily for thirty years more.

What has not been generally publicised is the influence which the

Whitworth Doctors had on Blackpool in the 18th century, then a ragged collection of fishermen's hovels strung in haphazard fashion along the cliff tops. It was not yet a pleasure centre but a resort for the stricken and afflicted who travelled to the coast, on the recommendation of the more progressive doctors and with the utmost difficulty and discomfort, to take the sea water treatment. This involved drinking copious quantities of sea water, with what devastating results can be imagined, and being ducked under the waves regularly and energetically, by the professional "dipping women", not, as instinct would dictate, in the heat of noonday, but in the cool of evening, the colder light of early morning or, better still, in the needling winds of autumn. It had to be undertaken when the pores were tightly closed "to prevent the blood from flying to the head".

This could only have been an ordeal to a generation indoctrinated in the belief that water was a dangerous commodity which must be kept from contact with the human frame. Nevertheless, the first sea-bathers, daredevil or desperate to a degree, went home proclaiming an improvement which was probably due to a thorough cleansing, inside and out, for the first time since the midwife departed.

In a rising air of improvement there were added to Blackpool four good hotels, a few new properties and public bathing houses (hot or cold sea water, according to choice), barns and cottages converted to the use of sleepers and lodgers, and a desultory stage coach service in the height of the season when four hundred bathers were simultaneously crammed into the resort.

Chief attraction in this sun-kissed, wind-tossed place of few amusements, not a drop of piped water and mediaeval notions of sanitation was, undoubtedly, the presence of the Whitworth Doctors who, cashing in on the current health craze, had established a secondary practice in Blackpool. That it was presided over personally by Dr. John in 1788 we learn from the carefully preserved letters of Catherine Hutton of Birmingham who sojourned there for a prolonged spell with her invalid mother during that season.

"The success of the practitioner has rendered this village a collection of hospitals", she tells us, "almost every house lodging the maimed or diseased and some being erected expressly for that purpose. No patient is visited in his lodgings if he is able to attend at the house of the doctor ... the first comer being served first".

On an average day the doctors treated 140 persons and "on Sunday", continues Catherine, "they bleed the patients gratuitously". Ghoulish visions are conjured up by her deft description of the proceedings. "This is conducted by three persons while the patients sit round the room. One opens the vein, one follows with a basin", (presumably to catch the blood), "and the third binds".

The doctors' seaside charges were 2/- per week, "including operations, applications and medicines and at going away a patient is supplied with a large quantity of specifics of all kinds, if he choose to take them, for the sum of 6/- to 8/-.".

Wealthy Dr. John, who could likely have bought up the whole of Blackpool, lived frugally and slept in the cottage surgery in the privacy of a sort of box pew compartment erected in one corner.

He was still curing cancers. Catherine Hutton tells of the fellow lady guest who had undergone the swift treatment by "Keen" of which, apparently, there were two sorts, red and white. She had endured the pain for up to three hours daily by which means "the cancer was totally eradicated", though, Catherine reflects, "her constitution seems to have received a shock and perhaps she had acted wiser if she had taken a longer time to remove her disorder". Thus relieved in mind and body, however, the lady settled herself to enjoy the rest of her stay and, by foisting her young daughter on to obliging strangers and shunting her submissive husband off to bed early, she indulged herself by staying up late playing cards. "Perhaps she has vanity and no feeling", was Catherine's crisp comment on this, yet another of Dr. John's successful cases.

He was still hated by the professionals. "Well, John Taylor, you go on killing as usual, I suppose?" Thus he was greeted by the famous Dr. White of Manchester. "Aye, but at sometimes a cheaper rate than thou does", was the blunt reply. Yet John Taylor was honoured and his descendants after him, by the tens of thousands who had sought their aid.

Dr. John Taylor died in 1802 at the age of 62 and he rests in Whitworth Churchyard along with his wife Mary, brother George, son James and others of that famous healing team whose progeny entered the profession by more conventional means, practising variously at Manchester and Todmorden.

Family portraits were destroyed, unfortunately, when a grandson's house was ransacked during the Todmorden Riots, but at Whitworth you can still ask for Taylor Street and Cripples Walk. You may even track down the famous Whitworth Red Bottle!.

Not a bad memorial to a young blacksmith who strode into that valley two hundred years ago.

AN OLD MAN'S MEMORIES

Towards the end of the 18th century, one John Heap came from Nelson to Brex, near Newchurch-in-Rossendale, as a farm labourer. After living a short time at that place, he was married to Betty, the daughter of Richard Heyworth, farmer, a native of the district. They were blessed with four children, three sons, William (my father), John and Robert, and a daughter who died in infancy. My father was born Oct. 25th, 1800, during "Barley Time", so called because of the miserable harvests which prevailed for many years and barley was the best food obtainable. When the change to better food came, large numbers of the population died owing to the long privations they had endured. Uncle Robert was born in 1803 and died at Oldham in 1856. My mother was born. May 21, 1807. She was the daughter of Lawrence and Betty Lord, natives of Bacup. There are many families of Heap at Nelson, and Lord at Bacup, at the present day.

I, Moses Heap, was born May 8th, 1824, at Doals on the Cliviger Moors, near the rise of the river Irwell, and two miles from Bacup. My parents were married on Thursday May 8th, 1823. We were a numerous family, there being eight sons, four of whom died in infancy, I being the eldest. There were also three daughters. When about three months old we removed to Dog Pits a short distance away, a little later to Weir near the moors, after that to Old Meadows. On July 26th, 1828, we removed to Salisbury, near Lumb.

My father was a jenny-spinner, that is, he worked one of the old-fashioned type of spinning machines. They had about 100 spindles and were turned by hand. It was a good trade until the advent of the Spinning Mule, which had more spindles and was worked by steam power.

In a few months we removed to Lumb (proper), and had not lived there very long when our house fell in. It had been constructed on this wise. There were two houses adjoining the mill, two rooms on the first storey were in use as living rooms in each house and the upper rooms were used as a warehouse for the mill. They were used also for the weak, with three or four beds for the children to sleep on, who were orphans and taken from the workhouse by Mr. G. Haworth, master, to work for him, a practice which was very common in those days and much abused. This accident happened on a Sunday afternoon during summer. People were just returning from service at the chapel. It if had occurred three hours later probably we should have been killed as the beds were piled up with the debris. It was caused by the upper rooms being filled with all kinds of lumber until the rotten beams gave way. My father and mother had gone to Brex to see Uncle John who was dying; they had taken my brother with them, therefore when the crash came I and my sister went to tell the sad tale. Our little furniture was no worse but I remember we had to sleep in the mill amongst the cotton.

Some time later a worse calamity befell our little family: on February 21st 1833, my brother James was drowned. This was a great trouble - he was only four years old that day, and was interred at St. Nicholas Church, Newchurch. At that time it was customary after the funeral for a minister or sexton to give notice to the mourners which public house they were to retire to. I suppose this was as they thought to cheer one up a little and drive dull care away. There was not much work at this time for the printing press, for if a sale was to take place in the neighbourhood, a notice of it was read out by the sexton standing on a gravestone or the Church or Chapel wall, sometimes in the building. Indeed everyone was very poor and as we say from hand to mouth. People lived under what is known as the Truck system, which happily has been done away with. The employee had to buy all his necessaries from his master, thus a master held a whip over his worker's head in the form of extortionate charges. It was the same if we only wanted a little meal or treacle, etc., but one had to be careful not to overspend the wages.

An old man and his wife once went to buy in for the week, and the pay for hand-loom weaving had been very bad for some time. The old man said "Let's have a aw've a peaund o' swine's greease to mek a sad-cake wi for't tay". But the wife holding up both her hands replied in rebuke and astonishment "Eh, Aw've a peaund o' swine's greease un noa Rooavins i' th' heause! Nay, Loll, thad'll never doo un noa Rooavins i' th' heause!" -- so the sad cake had to wait o' th' Rooavins coming.

Jams and jellies were things unknown. I have many a time along with my mother and other folk waited on a Monday night until midnight for the carrier arriving from Burnley with provisions. I often think now of the dark and dreary times we had in those days. Very poor keep or living, and 12 hours to work each day, sometimes more. I remember being carried on father's back at five years of age to work. Even as I got older, the nights of winter were dreadfully long. Some had candles, others who could afford it lamps, just as their work would allow. Gas, paraffin, incandescent or electric lights were never dreamt of.

In order to keep awake in the factory, an effigy, the full size of a man was made of cotton, and when required this was carried round on a man's back through the mill to waken up the youngsters.

Sunday Schools were conducted in an altogether different manner to the present day. Most of the education one received was at the Sunday School. The boys had to write one half the day, and the girls the other half. When the time was up, the Superintendent came in and shouted "Finish your lines". That being done, he would give the order to collect the books, the rule and plumett (that is a piece of lead about four inches long to rule with instead of pencil). Spelling was considered a great feat, for the best speller always went to the top of the class.

Clogs were in general use weekday and Sunday alike. Very few were fortunate enough to have a pair of shoes to put on. I remember father bringing home my first pair of shoes, which I took to bed lest someone might run off with them before morning. Some boys wore "thrums" for a cap, that is, the bottoms of warps joined in the shape of a turban, and girls generally wore a handkerchief over their head. Some would have on a rough pinafore to cover up even worse clothing.

I remember we used to think we were highly favoured when we got some mint tea and toasted cake, or when father came home from his club at Newchurch and brought a quart of peas or mussels and cockles.

Some of the people living in those far-off days were very quaint characters -- as well as superstitious, which trait got grafted into the children, for education was almost Nil. They lived such lonely lives amongst the hills, scarcely ever going more than five miles from their native village. No wonder the awful tales told in the firelight on a cold winter's night would have its effect on the young ones. Fairies, wizards, witches -- "Billy with the Wisp", "Jack with the Lantern", and "Jenny Greenteeth".

The houses had little furniture in them, the money earned went in provisions and these were very scanty. Many a time our family of father, mother and three or four children had to join at the porridge dish with treacle and water instead of milk. In summer we gathered nettles and sour-docks for mother to cook for eating. On a Saturday night towards 7 o'clock when all work was finished and the Bobbin wheel taken away, the house would be cleaned up, the floor was washed with a long mop, then it was covered with sand, afterwards scrubbed over with a large stone at the end of a long pole. Carpets were unknown in those days.

On Sept. 8th, 1830, King William IV was crowned. All the scholars walked in procession down the road as far as Hargreaves Arms, where each one was treated with bread and cheese (each scholar carried a small gill pot), and a gill of home-brewed ale. I was six years old at this time, and well do I remember the treat we had that day, for such things were real "red-letters" to us. The Hargreaves Arms just mentioned was kept by a publican named William Clegg.

At this time not a building stood along the roadside, but it was meadow-land from Lumb to Water, a distance of 1½ miles, now it is all built on each side of the road. A great deal of hand-loom weaving was carried on in the homes, both cotton and woollen goods. Some of the woollen weavers sized their own warps by the roadside between the two places mentioned. On a fine day it was very common for the warps to be stretched out and someone spreading the size on with a brush from a can. But many of our musical friends were so fond of singing and fiddling that their looms would be idle until about Tuesday night, then they would work night and day to get their allotted work finished before Saturday.

About the year 1832 an Act of Parliament was passed to limit all mill and workshop hours of work to 12 hours. I was eight years old then, and after three years of work was passed for short-time working by Dr. Crabtree, of Newchurch, who was the first factory doctor in Rossendale.

Bull-baiting was a common practice in Lumb. A ring was fixed in the ground, and another through the bull's nose, to which a rope was attached. The rope was put through the floor ring, and drawn tight, thus bringing the beast's head to the ground. Then dogs were set on it in turn. They were often pitched to a great height in the air by the bull. It was a cruel sport, which has happily been made illegal.

We only remained a little over twelve months at Lumb, then we removed to Bank Lane, Shuttleworth, near Ramsbottom. On May 8th, 1834, my tenth birthday, we went to live in a house in the part called "Bye-road", and the next door was a beer house called "Red Lion". My father was a Jenny Spinner for Mr. John Pilling (son of the Rev. John Pilling, minister of the Baptist Chapel, Goodshaw, for 42 years.) I was a billy-piecer at 2/- a week. My sister Betty was a jenny piecer for two jennies. This small mill was next to Twine Mill and is now used as a Bleach Works. The original mill was three stories high. In the bottom room were two jennies, containing 100 spindles each, a weighing machine, stores, etc. In the second storey was one Carding Engine, one Billy with 60 spindles, which required four fulltime piecers to mind 15 cardings each. Also two (Devils) in the same room. In the third storey was a pair of mules with 400 spindles. Goods were carried to Manchester on wagons. From our mill the goods had to be taken on a truck by two men to Shipperbottom the appointed place, where the wagons received them. The two men for removing the goods to that spot, a long mile and over a rough road, on their return with the empty truck each received the magnificent sum of 3d. You may be sure it was thankfully received as 3d could not be picked up very often in those far-off days. Whilst here, meal for porridge became more plentiful, which made us feel more settled in the place.

Soon after we came to this place, my father had his footing, that is, it was a custom for a "new hand" at a factory to pay a certain sum of money for drink by way of a start at the new mill, but my father could not stand it, not being used to ale, and not having much to eat at our last place, it was too much for him, for a pint of ale made him fairly drunk. Whilst we lived here, the great Temperance movement commenced; by this reform, a person was allowed to have a certain quantity of drink in moderation, as the Scriptures tell us --- to be temperate in all things, but it was soon found out that if some folks got to taste, they could not stop until they had made a "beast" of themselves. Therefore it was agreed by a party of seven Preston men that all should be total abstainers, which meant they were neither to Touch, Taste, nor Handle.

Morality was at a low ebb in the district, which was made worse by the influx of large numbers of navvies from other districts, working at the building of a reservoir, hence a lot of drinking and fighting, which went hand in hand. I have seen men on a Sunday morning before 7 o'clock, fighting without any clothes on, and at Whitsuntide, about a score of young men always went to the Kersey Moor races on Monday for the week on fighting intent -- but on their return they were not quite so lively. To show the spirit of the place, I knew one old woman who had a son who was a terrible fighter, and he delighted in the job, not for spite, or ill will. She used to say that she would rather carry his bones in her apron, than that he should be beaten. As I have said, a great deal of immorality prevailed. A great many men and women with families were living together unmarried. But a few years after this a church was built, and the Rev. Mr. Hughes, hearing of the state of things gave notice - that all those persons unmarried, if they would come to the church, he would marry them for nothing. The consequence was a large number of weddings took place.

As for weddings in those days, there were no grand carriages to ride in, to and from church. If they had any money, they would spend it to decorate themselves. I have seen 14 couples walking in procession to be married. The men wore tall hats, decorated with ribbons, and the women were also decorated in the same way. Leading the wedding party was a fiddler, playing all the ditties he could remember, and bringing up the rear was a man carrying a basin filled with ale and rum, and letting anyone on the way have a drink.

But the time was approaching when our little family would have to make another move. Mr. Pilling, the master at the mill where we worked, had taken the Bridge Mill, Crawshawbooth and he gave his workpeople the privilege of removing to Crawshawbooth and working for him there. We removed on May 16th, 1836. We were soon more in touch with the busy throng at our new residence. My father still followed his old employment, and I mine. In those days Crawshawbooth was altogether different to what it is now (1904). In 1836, the principal mills were Bold Venture, ... Higher and Lower Folly -- named after the clough which supplied them with water, with a quarter of a mile separating them, and the Bridge Mill. The Sunnyside Printworks was the most important. About 300 Block Printers were employed, sometimes on both day and night shifts; there were only six or seven machines. Labourers' wages were very poor. Able-bodied men working in the bleach and dyehouse averaged about 10/6 per week,and strong lads 3/- a week for 12 hours a day. The Printworks was worked by Butterworth and Brooks (who became 1st Baron Crawshaw). An old friend (James Riley) had the princely wage each week of 10/6d, and he was the Engineer and Fireman with a wife and four children to keep. These were the kind of wages that would not stretch to more than thin porridge.

On June 28th, 1838, was the Coronation of Queen Victoria. The scholars walked in procession about 2 o'clock with two bands of music, and banners flying in great profusion. Each scholar had a medal attached to a piece of blue ribbon and hung from the neck. On arriving at "All Saints Church", Goodshaw, a service commenced, but as we were nearing the time for the sermon, Mr. Boddy, the clergyman, discovered that he had left his sermon at home, so by way of filling up the breach he gave notice for the choir to sing two hymns whilst he went home for his notes. The hymns sung were, "Before Jehovah's Awful Throne", and another one to the "Old Hundredth" tune. Now Mr. Boddy was a lodger at Miss Haworth's, Crawshawbooth, opposite the National School, and to his dismay when he arrived there, he found the house locked up. Miss Haworth had gone to Mrs. Butterworth's, Sunnyside House, to await the arrival of the scholars. So Mr. Boddy was obliged to enter the house through a window in order to get his notes. As he entered the church on his return, the last verse of the second hymn was being sung. The day was a hot one, and the race there and back had very much exhausted him, taking all the vim out of him, as he entered the church through the back door and went straight to the three-decker pulpit, and got through the sermon with some difficulty. When the service was over, we fell into our ranks again, and visited Sunnyside House and Crawshaw Hall, where we received oranges, etc., and returned in procession to the school for coffee and buns.

On Wednesday, July 4th, 1838, there was a great flood, called "Cowpe Flood". It happened at 3 p.m. quite suddenly, and the torrential rain made the river rise to an enormous height. People at work in the mill below had to run for their lives. The river was bridged over by the mill, and when the torrent came rushing down all the middle of the factory was carried away. My father and I visited the scene of destruction the following Sunday. At Hareholme the bridge had stood not the slightest chance and had totally disappeared. A boiler and engine cylinder were washed down, and I saw a water-wheel still hanging to one wall of the mill. Besides great damage to property, a large number of sheep and cattle were washed away. It was said the cause of the disaster was a "cloud burst" on the top of the hill, which sent the water down each side, so that at Spotland Bridge (on the Rochdale side of the hill) the storm was quite as bad. The High Water mark of July 4th, 1838, is still to be seen on the wall half-way up the second storey windows of a house.

There were as yet no railways, and anyone going from home had to do the journey on foot. The roads in some parts were mere tracks, and in others were covered with large stones to make the road firm.

We had three or four stagecoaches which made the journey between Burnley and Manchester, with stages about ten miles apart for the change of horses. One was the "Mail" coach, with a guard sitting behind dressed in a "Livery" suit, and who occasionally blew a loud blast on a horn to give notice of his approach. The fare from Crawshawbooth to Manchester was 2/6d. In our village lived a very stout man, and on one occasion he wanted to go the journey. On the arrival of the coach he asked the guard what he would take a fat goose for to the city. "One shilling" was the reply. "Here goes then", he said, and immediately mounted the coach. The man's name was Goose.

In 1840, the mill stopped several weeks for repairs. My father took advantage of this by walking to Blackpool, unknown to us all, nor did anyone know his whereabouts -- only, when last seen, walking up the old lane towards Boggart Cote (Sunny Bank) above Stoneholme Mill, very early one morning and carrying a bundle under his arm. I found out afterwards he had only 6/- in his pocket on leaving home, and in order to make this last out, he resorted to a farm-house at Marton, with a man named Whiteside, living on Porridge and milk all the time, and the few loaves he took with him. On his way home he came through Chatterton, near Ramsbottom, called at my grandmother's, and being late, she wanted him to stay till morning, but he would not, and came home tired and worn out. When passing through Horncliffe Wood, he got over the wall and laid himself down on the grass and fell asleep, but to his surprise was awakened by a heavy shower of rain. On arrival home, I think mother did chide him for going away in the manner he did.

Not far from Dunnockshaw, up the hillside stands a farm -- Bank Farm. This was occupied by a man called Peter Pickup, who worked the Hambleton coal mine. Old Peter was a cunning sort of man, he always kept a gun by his bedside, perchance anyone should disturb his sweet repose. However, one night he heard a noise in the house. The old man went down the stairs, gun in hand, expecting to meet the burglars. He called out, "Who's there?", once, twice, three times, (Then bang went the gun). Immediately a calf bawled out. Peter cried, "Eeh! Aw've shot t' cauve!" He had a passage between the house and the shippon or cowshed, as most old farmhouses had in those days, and somehow the calf had wandered through into the house. Well, Tom Healey, Organist at Goodshaw Church, got hold of this story, and made a "catch or ditty", but Peter went and paid Tom a sum of money not to let it come out, for he did not want the "Cove" being sung around the countryside like "Old Sye" had been.

The Rev. J.M. Mather, in his "Rambles round Rossendale", vol. 2, calls me an old Deaner, although I was born at Doals, over the hill. and came to reside amongst them at four years of age. When I was about 20 I came in contact with all the members for a good number of years, and I was acquainted with several generations of its singers. On looking over my diary I find that at Water school, on May 19, 1847, a selection of music was given from "Judas Maccabaeus" and the "Te Deum". Also at the Mechanics Institute, Bacup, on Good Friday, 1849, Handel's "Messiah" was performed, and at the house of John Hargreaves at Newchurch, the night before Good Friday, in 1849, a selection was taken from "Judas Maccabaeus" and the "Messiah". I also attended a performance at the same house on December 31, 1849. At the Water school, January 5, 1850, Handel's "Te Deum" was performed. Now at these gatherings no great singers were engaged, they were simply meetings of old musical friends, chiefly those known by the name, "Deign Layrocks". These notable singers worshipped at the Baptist Chapel, Lumb, and to see Lumb at its best was to be there on the second Sunday in June, a date well known throughout Rossendale. On this day crowds came from far and near. We first hear of them in 1745, when John Nuttall and his friends began to meet in each other's houses to practise music. Shortly afterwards he began to preach. Then they built a chapel at Lumb. But in 1760 they removed to Goodshaw, as this place was more central for the surrounding villages. John Nuttall was minister here for 45 years and died in the year 1792, aged 76 years.

On June 28, 1856, I, Moses Heap and Ann Jackson were married at St. John's Church, Shuttleworth, and my wife being a singer there, the choir were present. I remember they sang "All among the barley" -- afterwards we went to Southport for three days. We lived at Crawshawbooth after our marriage. The following October I went to work at Russia Mill, Newchurch, then we removed to Acre Mill, where we resided about six months, then the mill stopped. My wife was confined on May 14, 1857. The child was named Joseph, but only lived about three weeks, and was interred at Shuttleworth Church. On Fair-day, Whit-Tuesday, 1857, we removed back to Crawshawbooth.

About this time, the Padiham weavers were on strike for an advance of wages. They had the Rev. Dr. Verity, a clergyman of the Church of England, speaking for them in various places. I remember him coming to speak in the White Bull Square, Crawshawbooth. About 20 years after this, I had him recommended as a clever Doctor, so I went to consult Mr. Verity. I told him about hearing him speak at Crawshawbooth. He had a black shining cap on his head at the time. "Oh yes", he said, the weavers got their price. The cap he had on was his Crimean Cap, where he served as a staff chaplain for 18 months, leaving a Curate in charge while he was away. Mr. Verity said that the weavers told him their case, which he thought was only just and right, but said he, there are a lot of parsons with a snug easy living, that will not say a word, while they are the very men who ought to speak. But, said he, for standing the weavers' friend, he had had a great deal of persecution.

About 1860, Co-operative Manufacturing Co's were rather wildly speculating in manufacturing concerns, and forming fresh companies. Large numbers of store members withdrew their savings and deposited them for shares in the newly-formed companies, saying they would pay a better "Divi", but the majority before very long regretted the rash act. Amongst the number, Britannia Mill, built about 1852 or 1853, and also the Victoria Mill with the same date. The Britannia Mill was formed into a company with £5 shares, and soon all were taken up. I had 4 shares in this. Before long every penny was lost. The Britannia Company was afterwards formed into three separate companies, but all with the same result. Many persons were unable to secure shares in the Britannia Company, and so the Stoneholme Mill Company was formed. This Mill was built as early as possible. When it was completed, their money was done. The American Civil War was commencing, so there was a dark outlook for them. Cotton could only be brought over at great risk of capture, or set on fire, hence the price of it rose as high as 2/6 per pound. Many were made bankrupt. Robinson & Holden of Goodshawfold told me that in three weeks they had lost over £800. Whilst this dark cloud was hanging over the land, the Stoneholme Co. decided to sell the mill. It had cost £18,000 and sold by auction to the Globe Spinning Co. for the sum of £8,500. There was a lot of hard-earned money lost by these firms going down.

It was also a hard time for the operatives. Soup kitchens and "dole" centres were established for meat and clothing. Able-bodied men worked on the roads for 9d or 1/- a day. Others had to work on the "Great Height" at 2/- per day. Some old men went to school with a slate on their back. My old friend John Tims went in this way and I think they got 9d a day. (Some years later, my friend went to live at St. Annes, and two of his sons were drowned in the lifeboat disaster during a great storm on December 9th, 1886. The wreck was the "Mexico", and there is still a lifebuoy to be seen in the Southport Library, on which the name "Mexico" is still visible.) Young women and girls were sent to a sewing school. This was done to keep the people alive, as most had nothing to fall back upon, and they could not afford to starve.

During 1876, I commenced to travel with yeast over the hills to Water, Dean, and as far as Deerplay, calling at the farmhouses etc. en route. I did this journey for 16 years week by week. I must have walked thousands of miles on these journeys. Spring, Summer, Autumn, and during the snows and frosts of winter, when shoes and trousers have been frozen hard like boards, and the snowdrifts higher than the walls and hedges. I have actually walked over a five-barred gate of a field without seeing anything but snow. Perhaps it lasted a month or more before it all melted, but fog was the worst. While crossing the boggy moss on the hill-tops, I stopped at a farmhouse for a few minutes one day, it was foggy, and the night was gradually closing in about 4.30 p.m. in November. When I left, the farmer's wife would have crossed the field with me, but no, I said I could find the stile. Well, off I went with confidence, but I got from the track, and keeping on as I thought in the right direction, but all I was doing -- I was just circling the field; at last I saw a light in a house-window nearby, it was the same farmhouse, and it had taken me two hours to accomplish it. However, the farmer lit a lantern, and went along to set my feet on the right track. But when the spring and summer came round, these troubles were forgotten. To hear the songs of the wild birds on the moors, in the quietness, where one had the opportunity to think a little of what is going on, instead of being always in the midst of the burly-burly of life... It was on these journeys that I met so many of the old singers of Dean. Many of them I knew in my youthful days. Now and again, from one or another during chats, bits of history or experience would come out.

I visited the Preston Guild on Wednesday, September 6, 1882. It was a splendid sight, all the various trades, etc. in the town being represented in the procession. The Guild is carried on for one week (each day), and is only held every 20 years, having been carried on in Preston for hundreds of years.

During 1898, a tea-party and re-union of old teachers and scholars was held at the Baptist Church, Lumb. I wasn't aware of it till some time later, when a friend gave me the following piece of poetry, which was recited at the meeting by one of the teachers:

"A Welcome to owd scholars"

To all th' owd scholars sitting here,
Aw gie mi earliest greeting.
Aw hope yo' all ar doin' weel,
An' fairly likin' t' meeting.
It does mi a lot o' good to see
So monny weel known faces,
Aw use to see in years gone by
O' Sundays in the'r places.

There's two owd names aw'l mention first,
Ther two yo' all weel know,
Ther's Moses Heap fro't Crawshawbooth,
An' John Barcroft fro't Green-Law.
Them two, wi' parson Ashworth's son,
Are first on't book, they sen,
An aw' feel sure we all extend
A welcome whoam agen.

There are owd friends yo'll all agree
An' yet aw morn't forget,
The Madens and the Buckleys
At come to this school yet.
An' neaw aw'll touch o' th' younger end
For names they are not wanty,
Aw'll call em whod they're best known by
An start first wi' Jim Jonty.

Ther's Sally, o' owd Bobs, Lucy o' James's --
Deyne Layrocks, sure enough;
They used to sing i' th' choir here,
An' so did Jimmy O' th' Clough.
We'n then four brothers John O' Sams,
A An' Gregory lot fro't Carr,
Tho' one o't latter lot aw thinks
In foreign lands afar.

MOSES HEAP (1824 to 1913), local diarist and musician.

Bird's-eye view of THE GLEN or THRUTCH – a tight squeeze for road, river, and rail – looking towards Stacksteads about 20 years ago. Note how Baxter's brewery chimney at Glen Top has been raised to avoid the unusual air currents in the Glen.

GLEN BOTTOM. Note the dove-cotes on the rock ledges and "Glen Inn" with raised chimneys and bait stables.

GLEN TOP, showing on the right Glen Top Brewery, the old Stables, and "Glenville". The houses along Booth Road lead to the tree-hidden Fearns Hall on its slight prominence.

FEARNS HALL, Booth Road, Stacksteads, about the turn of the century. Note the changes -- fence, gateposts, gates, trees, cement rendering, door knocker. Originally the porch was a single upper storey on two pillars.

BRIDGE STREET about 1905, taken from near the Mechanics' Hall. The "George and Dragon Inn" and the "Bull's Head Hotel" can be seen on the right, St. John's Church visible in the background. Note forms of transport and dress.

TONG HALL or TONG FOLD, off Tong Lane and South Street, demolished December 1959. Note the dove-cote over the double-storeyed porch. The datestone 1751 with the initials of John and Anne Hoyle was preserved. According to Major David Halstead it is said an oak beam had a date of 1600, but was covered with lime.

Greetings card from about the time of the First World War.

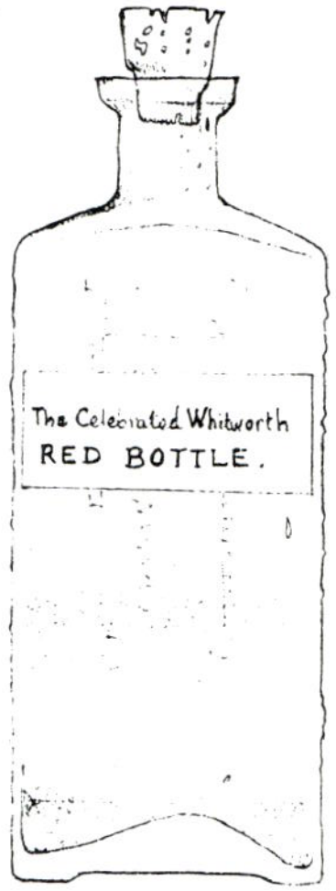

The recipe was confirmed by Mr. Nuttall of Maxim & Nuttall, chemists at Whitworth, who used to mix it. The bottle had a white label, and was printed in red.

Ingredients of the above:

- Camphor
- Compound Tincture of Lavender
- Oil of Thyme (Origanum)
- Logwood
- Methylated Spirits

The old ROE BUCK INN at Higher Broadclough just before demolition in 1971. It once had a bowling green at the rear. The datestone 1739 refers to a John Lord who owned much property in the Broadclough area.

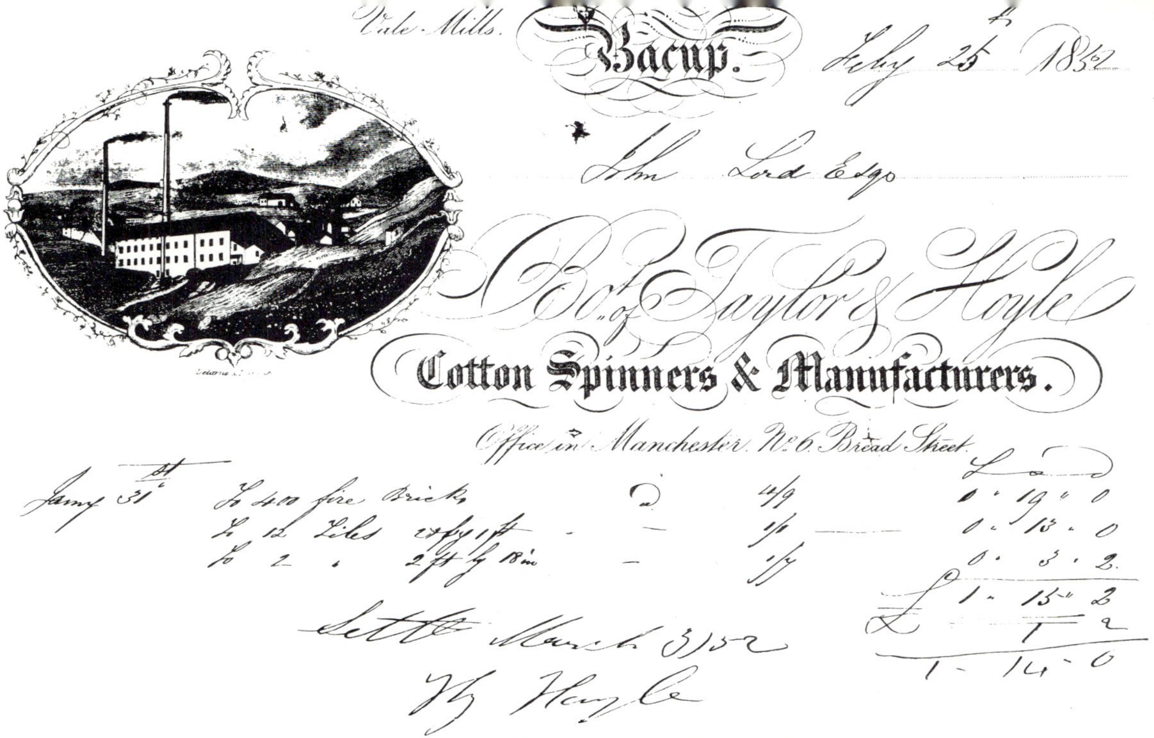

Vale Mills. Bacup. Feby 25th 1852

John Lord Esqre

Bot. of Taylor & Hoyle

Cotton Spinners & Manufacturers.

Office in Manchester No. 6 Bread Street.

				£ s d
Jany 31st	To 400 fire Bricks	@	4/9	0 . 19 . 0
	To 12 Tiles 2ft by 1ft	—	1/1	0 . 13 . 0
	To 2 " 2ft by 18in	—	1/7	0 . 3 . 2
				£ 1 . 15 . 2
				1 2
				1 . 14 . 0

Settled March 3/52

[illegible] Hoyle

An early cotton-spinning company's bill dated 1852, showing Vale Mills. Another example of headed notepaper of over 100 years ago.

EDUCATION DEPARTMENT.
Form 146 (a).

Registered Number { 2140

This Certificate must be carefully preserved by the parent.
In the case of any Child commencing as a Half-timer before obtaining this Labour Certificate, the Parent and Employer become liable to immediate prosecution without further notice.

SCHEDULE III.

School District of THE BOROUGH OF RAWTENSTALL.

LABOUR CERTIFICATE.

When duly filled up and signed on this side by the Teacher, this Form must be presented at the School Board Office, accompanied by a Registrar's Certificate of Birth, or Statutory Declaration of Age, at the time appointed for the purpose.

AGE AND EMPLOYMENT.

Date of Birth from Registrar's Certificate
—o—
Day 21
Month May
18 83

I certify that Clara Blackburn,
residing at Crawshawbooth,
was, on the 9 day of ~~May~~ June 1896, not less than ~~eleven~~ 13 years of age, as appears by the registrar's certificate [~~or the statutory declaration~~] now produced to me, (¹) ~~and has been shown to the satisfaction of the local authority for this district to be beneficially and necessarily employed.~~

(¹) Strike out what follows if the child is qualified for full time employment.

(Signed) John Bailey
~~(²) Clerk to the (³)~~ Attendance Officer.
for the above district.

(²) or other officer.
(³) School Board or School Attendance Committee.

W. B & L (135a) 61588 50000-8-95

PROFICIENCY.

I certify that Clara Blackburn,
residing at Crawshawbooth,
has received a certificate from A. Sharpe Esq.,
one of Her Majesty's Inspectors of Schools, that he (*or* she) has
(⁴) reached the V Standard.

Date of Inspector's Schedule Certificate.
—o—
Day 23
Month Feby
1895

(⁴) "reached" means passed in reading, writing, and arithmetic, in the standard mentioned, or a higher standard.

(Signed) G. L. Littlewood
Principal Teacher of the Crawshawbooth Wes. School.

or (²) Clerk to the (³)
for the above district.

Dated the 9 day of June 1896

Labour Certificate granted by the Rawtenstall School Board under the Education Acts 1870-1880, authorising the bearer to work as a "half-timer" in the local mill.

Then ther's "Jack Dick" un "Dick Dick",
But aw've fergetten some,
But never mind, aw gie yo' all
A welcome back to th' Lumb.

Before aw bid you all "Good Neet",
Eawr parsons aw mun mention,
Aw think the good they all ha' done
Deserving eawr attention.
Then here's to all a reyt good wish,
Whether yo'r poor or wealthy,
An' hope yo' all ar' doing weel,
And feeling nice and healthy.

By Nemo.

On January 30, 1903, I received a few lines of poetry from my old friend James Riley, Accrington. It is as follows (refers to a phonograph):

Well, Moses, old Friend, your letter to hand,
I see by its reading, you have got a fife band,
I suppose it can talk, whistle and sing,
If you all join in chorus, there'll be a fine din.
What wonderful things we have seen in our time,
Does it ne'er make you wish to start life anew
And see what there'll be in two thousand and two,
T'will perhaps be as well to wait the Lord's time,
May the Cloud and the Pillar, a light to us shine.

The last entry in the Diary reads, "June 11, 1904, General Baden-Powell, the hero of Mafeking, S.A. paid a visit to Accrington to open a new Drill Hall". Here the Diary comes to a close, at the ripe old age of 80 years. Moses Heap in July 1909 removed with his family to Southport, and died there April 24, 1913, having lived 21 years after the death of his beloved wife, and was interred in the family vault at St. John's Church, Shuttleworth.

COWPE VALLEY

A little rugged valley, high and green,
The sport of many a tempest, hale and keen,
Yet, from thy deepest dell, to sunniest crest,
We love thee - who were reared upon thy breast,

Who, in his boyhood, bore the bracing sting
Of thy harsh winter, and thy healing spring,
Who -- running to the little village school,
Across thy velvet meadows green and cool.

At dewy morn, with eager, hurrying feet --
Felt full upon his forehead, keen and sweet
The frolic of thy tearing wind -- with nip
That brought the glowing red to cheek and lip.

Who pointed pencils on thy window-sills --
And brought his half-pence to the village tills --
Who hied for Rooley Moor, with picnic fare,
Light as a bird and lithe as any hare.

Who, truant maybe to his mother's will --
Followed the fleeting hounds o'er moor and hill;
Feeling a full-grown man, at noontide joy,
But creeping home at dusk -- a fearful boy.

Who sought for bracken in thy shadiest nook,
And wet his feet in every rattling brook;
Who sleighed thy sloping meadows through and through,
And steered his kite beneath thy summer blue.

Who wore the halo of thy sunny skies
Upon his head, or in the guileless eyes --
Of his far youth, needs never to be told
How well it wears -- that little rim of gold.

A little rugged valley, high and green,
The sport of many a tempest -- hale and keen,
Yet, from thy deepest dell to sunniest crest,
We love thee -- who were reared upon thy breast.

TH' OWD DAYS (At Bacup End ut Valley)

I often think ut days gone by when I were but a lad,
O'er t' village, wheer I use to live an' all t' good time I had,
Wheer winter-time browt "sledgin' neets" deawn yon owd "Joiner's Broo",
Till t' local farmer chased us off an' towd us weer to goo. ***
At t' other end ut village there stood Beulah Sunday Schoo',
I use to goo theer every week wi' all t' good pals I knew.
Wheer Superintendent made us goo to t' Chapel -- I con tell,
Unless we had an "Excuse Note" -- (we'n written eawt eawrsel).
We often took a walk through t' park, or reawnd bi "Gawmless End",
Or else, we'd trail up Deansgreave yon, an' o'er bi t' delf we'd wend,
At Sunday neet we'd goo to town, in hope to find some fun,
'Twer -- ice cream in Chris Riding's shop, then -- eawt to t' "Rabbit Run".
We trailed abeawt up Burnley Road an' reawnd bi St. James Street,
An' theer we'd stop, an' laugh an' talk wi' lasses on t' same beat,
But if it rained, we'd crowd into some shop door-hoil a-while,
An' mony a future life were planned in gradely mating style.
I've known it too, when I wer young to walk reawnd by Blackwood,
Then kick a ball on Stackstead's Rec, an' get wom full o' mud.
No "messin'" then, 'twer straight to bed, "Yo'll get no tay to-neet!"
An' theer I laid, neath blue washed walls, brass knobs an' candle-leet.
Ay, what a life, it wer for sure, an' yet such happy days,
Although we had no radio ner tele' to win praise;
But progress has bin made sin' then, conditions weel improve,
Except for t' human element, their feelings in t' same groove
For pain an' laughter, grief and joy, all human beings feel,
Thus, what a blessing it would be, if folk would but reveal --
The truth o' livin' weel today is proved by ONE who cared;
For t' secret o' true happiness is -- another's trouble shared.

(*** -- The late Jack Crowther, of Britannia)

TOP O' GREENS

I was out of breath,
When I reached my favourite spot
At the top of the hill.
From the foxhole I felt like Gulliver,
Pondering my model village world
With eagle eyes, The Rossendale Valley
Seemed to me infinite.
As crowned by its wise old hills
Which reached ruggedly --
Concealing their untold secrets
To kiss the lips
Of the impenetrable sky
The low-lying and polluted clouds.

The microscopic population
Scurried endlessly to and fro;
As ants, in their timeless worlds,
Their blood as familiar to the Valley
As the Irwell which fed it
As it meandered as a strand
Of the Valley's cotton
To link the huddled settlements
Between the hills and scrub
As beads on a rosary
And was metamorphosed as a glow-worm
As it was captured momentarily by the sun
And the moorland streams as sparkling crystals.

The sun -- like me
Had fought to find its freedom
And through the moorland beige
That set the cotton grass
And hare-bells nodding
In fairyland harmony,
And the shadow of the opposite hills
Waving across the meadows,
Like stroking a rabbit's fur backwards.

I idly began counting the factory chimneys
Which loomed phantom-like
Throughout the Valley as sticks of incense,
. . . there were twenty-seven!

PRESENTED TO MARTHA AND JOHN ORMEROD

Dear Martha and John, I thought that I would
  Write a few simple lines unto you.
But my pen is so bad and my ink is not right
  That I find it is not good to do.
However I'll try and I'll scribble it o'er,
  And make is as plain as I can,
But before it should puzzle your brain very sore --
  Just bring it to me for to scan.
But perhaps you will say what this writing's about
  That Hepzibah has thought fit to send.
Its concerning our wedding, I've not the least doubt,
  And of that we shall hear in the end.
You are right, my dear Friends, and allow me to say
  That I feel very well satisfied,
To see you so happy and cheerful today --
  Your wishes seem all gratified.
May you always be happy and cheerful as now,
  And prosper in all that you do,
In sickness, in health, in pleasure or woe,
  The right path may you always pursue.
You both have seen fit your kind parents to leave,
  And your fortunes to blend into one --
May you give them no cause nor a reason to grieve
  And to wish that the tie was undone.

And now, my dear Martha, a husband you've got,
  Be kind to him, open and free,
Be good tempered and courteous, whate'er be your lot,
  And trust him wherever you be.
And likewise to John, I say, take your dear wife
  And cherish and love her sincere,
Mid losses and crosses and turmoils of life
  Be her guardian and friend ever near.
May you pray unto God Who your union doth bless,
  To grant you His favour and smile.
All through life's chequered scenes -- His footstool address,
  That your hearts may be kept from all guile.

It may be the Lord will His goodness extend
And bless you with offspring so dear;
Should that be the case, on His Spirit depend --
Strive to bring them all up in his fear.
And may they rise up to be useful and wise
And to you joy and comfort afford,
Tender-hearted, obedient and always be like
Olive branches encircling your board.

And now my dear Friends, 'tis my prayer and desire,
That your corn and your wine never fail,
But pray to the Lord that your hearts He inspire,
Or your efforts will never prevail.

And when you have suffered His will here below,
And finished your mortal career,
May you stand full equipped and ready to go
When your Lord says "Ye blessed, come up here".

And now my dear friends, what shall I say more,
Words cannot express what I feel,
I wish you both well a thousand times o'er
And leave Heaven the rest to reveal.

From your Friend Hepzibah Nuttall.

MEMORIES (1)

Sometimes at quiet Eventide
  When thoughts unfettered flow,
Unconsciously my heart returns
  To days of long ago.
Back from the unforgotten past
  Comes like a vivid dream
The memory of Life's fair dawn,
  Sweet as a vanished dream.

Ah, sweet remembrance of the Past,
  Though sadness thou dost bring,
Though thy sweet song is ever fraught
  With a deep mournful ring,
I love to call thee back anew,
  And fancy thou art real,
Though I can never feel again
  Just as I used to feel.

I used to hear a gentle voice
  Calling me from my play,
When chilly grew the closing hours
  Of childhood's happy day;
But, ah, the light may dawn or fade,
  I hear no longer now
The music of those tender lips
  That kissed my childish brow.

I used to gaze with simple faith
  Into a lovely face,
Lovely to me because its smiles
  Were full of tender grace;
But now that face so strangely pale
  With its sweet love-lit eyes
Seems like a memory of Spring
  Beneath the Winter skies.

Ah, Childhood! thou wert sweet to me.
  On thy bright winsome morn,
But soon thy radiant light was quenched
  Leaving the day forlorn.
Thy star, a mother's love, had sped
  Into the far unseen,
And I was left to mourn its loss
  And dream "what might have been".

MEMORIES (2)

The murmurous music of a silver stream
   That softly glides upon a golden bed:
The slow and changeless chanting of a dream
   That lulls the soul when busy day is dead.

The breathing moisture of the meadow-bloom:
   The faint exhaling of the fragrant hay:
Cool airs, that cull their sweetness in the gloom,
   And draw the fragrance from departing day:

The gentle radiance of the setting sun
   That tints the tender greenery with gold:
The many beauties, merging into one:
   The shadows linking, as the light grows old.

Ah, tender memories of scene and song!
   Ye send your subtle influence so near,
That half my senses to the past belong,
   And wander ever with remembrance dear.

Creator of my childhood's dear delights,
   The voice is hidden in the whisp'ring calm,
And in the spirit of reposeful nights,
   Thy gentle soul is breathing out its balm.

But with the memory of thy shining eyes
   Returns the longing I have lived to still:
My eyes are lifted to the lonely skies,
   My hands outstretched towards the silent hill.

And with a bitter anguish in my call
   I cry aloud across the moaning sea,
My love I cannot live without thy soul,
   Come back beloved: oh, come back to me!

BONNY OWD BACUP

There's no special beauty abeawt it, 'tis true,
No squares or big buildings to rivet the view,
Dame Fortune upon it casts monny a frown --
But oh! all the same, it is Bacup old town.

Friendly owd Bacup, drowsy owd Bacup,
Dreamy owd Bacup, the town o' mi heart.

When aw wur a youngster aw'd lots o' friends theer,
An oalus geet fro' 'em the best o' good cheer.
Ah! the hours aw spent wi' 'em wur pleasant and breet
An' aw felt a new lad as aw trudged whoam at neet.

Friendly owd Bacup, drowsy owd Bacup,
Dreamy owd Bacup, the town o' mi heart.

If owd navvy Jackson wur livin' today
He'd stare to see trams runnin' up Bacup way.
He oalus said Bacup wur only half made --
That he'd finish it off when he bowt a new spade.

Friendly owd Bacup, drowsy owd Bacup,
Dreamy owd Bacup, the town o' mi heart.

Aw've sin monny places sin aw wur a lad,
Aw've formed monny friendships -- some good and some bad,
But give me the hills wi' the heather so brown,
An' the lads an' the lasses o' Bacup owd town.

Friendly owd Bacup, drowsy owd Bacup,
Dreamy owd Bacup, the town o' mi heart.

Whenever fro' Bacup aw see an owd face,
Me heart jumps wi joy nearly eawt o' its place;
We strowl to th' next pub, an' we set eawrselves down
An' we talk o' breet days spent in Bacup owd town.

Friendly owd Bacup, drowsy owd Bacup,
Dreamy owd Bacup, the town o' mi heart.

THE STILL SMALL VOICE

I heard the rustling of the leaves,
The gentle whisper of the breeze,
I caught the fragrance of the flowers,
Amid the cool and shady bowers,
    I heard God's still small voice.

I heard the rippling of the brook,
I heard the cawing of the rook,
I saw the little lambs at play,
And children romping blythe and gay.
    I heard God's still small voice.

I saw the lightning flashing bright,
I heard the thunder's voice of night,
I heard the swishing of the waves,
And 'mid the rocky mountain caves
    I heard God's still small voice.

I saw the silvery moon at night,
I saw the twinkling stars of light,
I felt His presence very near,
And heard Him whisper soft and clear,
    "My little flock, you need not fear".

HEARTACHE

I heard a little woodland bird
  Lift up his voice, so strong and clear:
Then for the echo waited he
  But not a sound could hear.

I saw a child -- a pretty maid,
  Some daisies gather from a mound,
Then with a little scornful foot,
  Trample them to the ground.

Of all the bitter wants and woes
  That cause the heart its keenest pain,
Naught seems to me so sadly sad
  As love, that loves in vain.

COME, BILL, LET'S SPEND ONE LONG, LONG DAY

Come, Bill, let's spend one long, long day
Among the ling and heather,
An' summon back fro' th' misty past
Breet days we've spent together.
Let's tak a trip to Murky Earth
(Wheer fowt we monny a battle),
An' see if Farmer Tum is still
Among his pigs and cattle.

Good Tum! Aw'd loike once more to see
Him tend those useful creatures --
His fat old sow, an' old milch cow --
That breetened up his features;
His shippon an' his styes, no deawt,
Are theer as reet as ever --
But poor owd Tum, aw fear mi mich,
Has crossed the Jordan river!

We'll strowl along to Crawshawbooth,
An' on to th' Bull and Butcher,
Wheer thee an' me once on a toime
Geet booked wi owd "Jack Scutcher"
An' then we'll strowl round Deerplay Bar,
Wheer oft we've walked wi' th' lasses --
Why, Bill, it seems but yesterday --
By th' mon, heaw quick toime passes.

An' when owd Sol sinks in the west,
An' song-birds cease to twitter,
An' moon leets up owd Cribden's breast
An' th' stars aboon us glitter.
We'll end eawr strowl at Lolly Mill
Wheer th' lads are olus jolly
An' o'er a glass o' Baxter's beer
Talk o'er eawr youthful folly.

Let other bards in loftier lays
Laud other scenes an' faces --
Aw love a hill we call Seat Naze,
An' folk around its bases;
More dear to me's owd Rooley Moor,
Wi' th' Moor Cock on its heather
Than Alpine hills or Apennines
Or th' job lot put together!

There's the chap with the "Can't", and the chap with the "Won't",
And the chap who's betwixt, more or less;
There's the chap with an "Aye", when it ought to be "Nay", and
The "No", when it ought to be "Yes".
There's the chap who's too weak to get up when he's down -- too
Bluffed to strike back when he's hit,
And the chap who bobs up when he ought to stay down; and the
Chap who does nothing but sit.
There's the chap who is brave when there's nothing to fear, and
The chap who's afraid without shame.
But the world wanting men has no patience with these -- what it
Want is the fellow who's game!

What it wants is the chap with the "Can" and the "Will", and the
"Get up" and "Hustle" and "Do";
And the chap who "comes back", with a smile on his face, when the
World thinks he's beaten clean through:
The chap who'll back down, when he knows he is wrong, and the
Chap who'll stand firm when he's right,
And the chap who keeps faith, when he pledges his word, and will
Back up his stand with a fight;
The chap who forever puts right above wrong, and honour o'er
Riches and fame;
Yes, he is the chap that the world's looking for -- the trustworthy
Fellow who's game!

THE REAL DELINQUENTS

We read in the papers,
We hear on the air
Of killing and stealing
And crime everywhere.
We sigh and we say
As we notice the trend,
"This young generation
When will it all end?"
-- But can we be sure that it's their fault alone
When maybe the most of it's really our own?
Too much money to spend,
Too much idle time,
Too many movies of passion and crime,
Too many books not fit to be read
And too much evil in what we hear said,
Too many children encouraged to roam
By too many parents who won't stay at home.
They don't make the movies
They don't write the books
That paint a gay picture of gangsters and crooks.
They don't run the bars, they don't drive the cars,
They don't make the drugs that addle the brain,
It's all done by older folk all greedy for gain.
Thus in so many cases
It must be confessed
The title "delinquent" fits older folk best.

MUSINGS BY THE GRAVE OF THE OLDEST INHABITANT

Quite near to Bacup centre lies
  Secluded, hid from human eyes,
An open space, but little known,
  With weeds and thickets overgrown.

Here now repose for evermore
  The folk who once in days of yore
Assembled here to praise and pray
  In church and school across the way.

If these memorial stones may tell
  The kind of men that 'neath them dwell,
A simple folk they would appear,
  Devoid of envy, pride or fear.

No marble monuments abound,
  No scrolls or angels fly around,
Nor is the simple mind perplexed
  By classic quote or Latin text.

No striving has there been to build
  The loftiest tomb with cherubs filled,
For all, 'cept one, recumbent lie,
  In rows aligned, with face to sky.

This upright stone distinction gains,
  Mark well the wonder it proclaims,
That one should walk her Lord before
  A hundred years and then three more.

Be not deceived: we have not yet
  The one who lived the longest met.
Another still the claim can boast
  Of matriarch of the sleeping host.

Not many know the woman's name
Who so long cheated nature's claim,
But here in stone in letters neat,
We learn the details of this feat.

'Tis Mary Harrison whose span
Exceeded that of normal man,
Who yielded not the vital spark
Till eight years past the hundred mark.

The Maden family of Greens
She served as nursemaid in her teens,
And there she still sustained her role
When God above required her soul.

In seventeen ten she made her bow
Upon this earthly scene, and now
Her death, one fifty years since past,
We celebrate, in verse, at last.

(This poem won the 1st Prize in the Local Section of a Poetry Competition organised by Bacup Public Library in February 1968.)

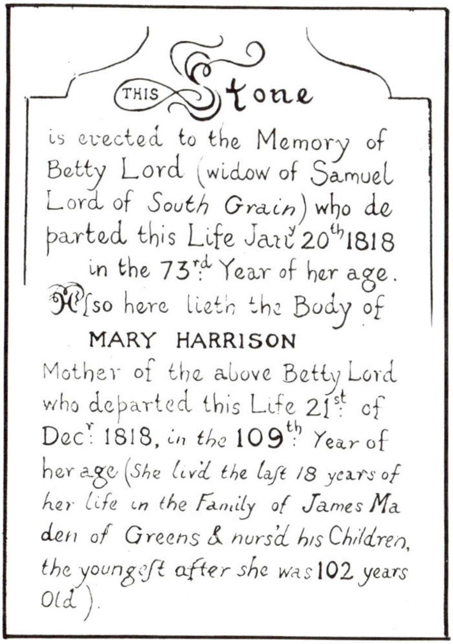

CHILDHOOD

Ah yes, it was a happy time!
    Summer and Winter, both were glad:
We cared not for the heat nor gloom,
    For we had naught to make us sad.

It was the time when all was love:
    When all was music, mirth and play:
It was the time when joyous song
    Filled all the long and sunny day.

It was the time when kisses fell
    Like plenteous dew upon my cheek:
The blissful hour when loving smiles
    From gentle eyes were ne'er to seek.

My childhood was a happy time,
    For I was born where life was free.
Brothers and sisters eight were we
    A wild, unfettered company.

My childhood was a sunny time
    For I was born where life was bright.
Nature, arrayed in loveliest garb,
    Dwelt there in all her wondrous light;

The meadows where we used to play,
    The gleam of sunlight on the rill,
The shadows from the giant trees
    I see with eyes of gladness still.

And often when at work I sit
    In duller regions of today,
Their beauty on my inner sight
    Comes flashing like a silvery ray.

Our playgrounds were the moors and hills,
    The lonely glens we sought for shade,
And sometimes when my fancy roams
    Adown some cool and quiet glade

I seem to hear, as oft I heard
    Peals of light laughter ringing clear,
Like some sweet half-forgotten song
    It falls upon my inner ear.

Ah yes, it was a happy time!
    For we had naught to make us sad:
We cared not for the heat nor gloom,
    Summer and Winter both were glad.

But even sweetest, loveliest dreams
    Must soon or late attain their end,
And even Childhood's pleasant road
    Must sometime lead us to the bend.

The sweetest melody of earth
    Is but a short, unfinished lay,
Passing with all our vanished charms
    Into the land of yesterday.

A SONG OF ROSSENDALE

Aw landed at owd Waterfoot,
   One day in May this year,
An' theer's ne'er a "pub" or licensed club
   But aw sampled whoile aw'r theer.
An' its ho for the jolly chums aw met
   An' its ho for Baxter's ale --
There's never a place on the earth's broad face
   Loike merry owd Rossendale!

Aw seed owd faces that aw know'd
   When aw wur a gay gossoon;
An' monny a street that has felt mi feet
   In clogs as weel as shoon!
Aw seed the green hillsides again
   O'erlooking th' verdant vale,
What aw climbed wi joy when aw wur a boy,
   An' lived in owd Rossendale.

An' Tum, an' Jim an' Hugh an' Joe,
   They marched me everywheer;
But aw knowed as mich abeawt th' owd place
   As onnyone livin' theer!
An' th' lasses, bless 'em! heaw they smiled
   To see me strong an' hale --
Aw yerd 'em say "Heaw weel he look --
   Th' owd Bard o' Rossendale!"

Aw'll save mi brass, an' aw'll goo again
   Some day afore so long!
Mon, aw loike to be amang owd friends
   An' to yer a good owd song.
Meanwhile aw'll think aw'm wi you still
   An' th' owd "Free Press" won't fail
Fro' time to time to print yo a rhyme
   Fro' th' Bard o' Rossendale.

WINDBELLS

"One day", I used to say; "there will be time
To see these wondrous places in my book:
I, too, shall go to Samarkand, or climb
Some shining peak whose ridges overlook
The scented Vales of Kashmir. I shall bring
A beaten silver box from Mandalay,
A bowl of jade, and rubies by the string
To please a Tartar princess in Cathay!"
So dreaming, I forgot Time does not wait.
For now there is no road to Samarkand,
And closed against me is the glittering gate
To Kashmir and Cathay. The things I planned
Are far beyond my reach, as lost to sight
As that elusive peak I never found . . .
But magic names like "windbells" still delight
My every sense. Must I be always bound
By circumstances to a northern clime?
And yet the swallow, nestling in the eaves,
Comes back each year at his appointed time --
So potent is the spell that England weaves!
Who knows what dreams would taunt me as I stood
Beneath the tamarind and deodar?
Why barter harebells in an English wood
For rustling grass on coasts of Malabar?

THE BELLS OF ROSSENDALE

(Respectfully dedicated to the members of the Palatine Club, Waterfoot, and spoken for the first time at a "Rossendale Night", November 19th, 1921.)

Hark to the Bells of Old St. Nicholas,
  As they call to evening prayer;
Softly fall their gentle voices,
  O'er hill and valley fair.
You fill my heart with memories,
  Of childhood's happy days;
As I listen to your greetings,
  Sweet Bells of Rossendale.

There you swing in your belfry hoary,
  Mellowed by the hand of time;
Pealing forth that oft-told story
  Of the Saviour's love divine.
Your holy message cheers me,
  On life's rough and thorny way;
As I listen to your greetings,
  Sweet Bells of Rossendale.

Your chimes ring out loud and clear,
  O'er dene and moorland wide;
They rise and fall in the summer breeze,
  Sweet bells of eventide.
They bid me hope for greater things,
  In the time that is to be;
As I listen to your greetings,
  Sweet Bells of Rossendale.

I have heard the great St. Peter boom,
  Where the yellow Tiber flows;
I have heard the sweet-toned Angelus
  In the valley of the Rhone.
Bud amidst my many wanderings,
  There's none so dear to me;
As the music and your chiming,
  Sweet Bells of Rossendale.

ROSSENDALE THRUTCH

(The Hell Clough Legend)

(An impromptu -- slightly amended -- written during an afternoon visit to that place, June 21, 1930)

Rossendale Thrutch was once a lake,
And there the Devil his bath did take --
At least that's what they say.

At early morn he splashed about,
Amusing himself by catching trout,
Or in some other way.

But fear arose in his black heart
When, as he saw, with a dreadful start,
The water running away.

To mend the breach at once he went
To old Hell Clough, on a purpose bent,
With apron strong and wide.

He filled his clout with rocks and stones,
With lumps of earth and elephants' bones,
And went to stem the tide.

Leaping and jumping, on he went,
But before he reached the new-made dent,
Something terrible happed.

He'd almost gained the flowing Thrutch,
When lo, because of running so much,
The strings of his apron snapped!

Down to the earth with thund'rous sound,
Tumbled the stones and built a mound,
A landmark there to make.

Visitors yet this spot are shown,
Where people still hear the Devil moan,
And his voice with anger shake.

Now, we can ride in a motor car
(We, who have gathered from towns afar)
Through the bed of this notable lake.

A lot of happy Lancashire folk --
Authors and lovers of quip and joke,
Out for their quarterly wake!

(Note: In the Proceedings of the Geologists' Association, vol.LVIII, part 4, 1947, pages 340-344 there is an article on "The Age and Origin of the Thrutch Gorge". This was written by the late Vernon Dean of Accrington and F. Hodson, F.G.S. (now a Professor at Southampton University). It shows that the gorge (now known as the Glen) was cut as an overflow channel at the end of the Ice Age when the Irwell was diverted from its original source (more to the north) by glacial drift obstruction.

MORE ROSSENDALE ANECDOTES

The high-spot in John Ashworth's year was his visit to Wembley for the Cup Final. He went down to London on the Friday, stayed at the Regents' Palace, and then on the Saturday morning strolled up Regent Street, along Oxford Street to the Marble Arch and up the Edgware Road. The year before last he was passing a pet shop in the Edgware Road when a parrot in a cage shouted to him, "Aw know thee". John was captivated and went into the shop to buy the parrot. The shopkeeper said the bird wasn't for sale, but it had laid some eggs that week and he would sell John an egg if he liked. He said he would put it in a box packed round with cotton-wool and John could incubate it when he got home. Last year John went to Wembley for the Cup Final as usual and followed exactly the same programme. As he was strolling up the Edgware Road there was the self-same parrot in the pet shop and as John was passing it shouted, "Aw know thee", whereupon John shouted back, "Aye, Aw know thee, too, thi fayther wor a duck".

A Waterfoot butcher had given "Owd Mily" some potted meat, and a woman in the shop offered to give him some bread and butter so that he could make some sandwiches. She got the reply: "It's good enough beawt bread".

THE BRITANNIA COCONUT DANCERS

Every Easter Saturday, the Britannia Coconutters dance their way through the streets of Bacup, starting off at 9 a.m., and wearing out a full set of clog irons in the course of the day's dancing, during which they cover about 65 miles, entirely within the borough boundaries!

The first "Coconutters" were a Stacksteads group called the Tunstead Mill Troupe, which was formed in 1857, and celebrated their jubilee fifty years later. Another troupe were the Lee Mill dancers, one of whom, Mr. James Mawdsley, moved to Britannia in 1903, joined the Working Men's Club there, and was instrumental in the formation of the Britannia Coconutters.

With their blackened faces, black jerseys, red and white kilts, and white stockings (which are all reputed to have come from the Moorish sailors, via Cornwall), the "Nutters" are a gradely sight, and their shining black clogs make a typically Lancashire consummation. Their head-dress consists of white turbans decorated with coloured feathers.

The dances performed by the "Nutters" are supposed to be pirate dances which were brought over to Cornwall by Moorish pirates. Some of these sailors settled down in Cornwall, and became employed in the local mining industry. As mines and quarries were opened in Lancashire in the 18th and 19th centuries, several Cornish men came north bringing with them not only their knowledge and experience of mining, but also reputedly bringing their dances to Bacup. In particular, two Cornishmen who came to work at Whitworth Quarry (some three miles from Bacup on the road towards Rochdale) are supposed to have started the dances in this area. The dances spread throughout Rossendale, and at the turn of the last century there were at least four groups of Coconut dancers in the Valley. It is from the Tunstead group that the Britannia Coconutters are descended. Their ritualistic dance dates back more than a hundred years in Bacup.

Their two dances are the GARLAND DANCE (during which each dancer carries an arched garland decorated with red, white and blue paper flowers), and the COCONUT DANCE. The Garland Dance is a Spring ritual dance, connected with the renewal of vegetation. The Coconut Dance is unique in this country, the dancers tapping out rhythms on wooden discs or "nuts", which are fastened to their hands, waists, and knees. The origin of the dances has not been traced officially, but it is known that they were performed in feudal times when the rushbearing carts took the rushes to the Lord of the Manor, and the "Nutters" danced in front of them. The dancer with the whip, known as the "Whiffler" or the "Whipper-In", preceded the dancers, and it was his duty to lash out with his whip to drive away the forces of evil.

The costumes and clogs used by the Britannia Coconutters are made locally. Music is provided for their local performances by a section of the Stacksteads Band, and on their travels further afield by an English concertina. Their music is copyright but has never been published, and the Nutters have visited Arnhem (Holland) in 1956, and Ireland. In 1952 they achieved the best result ever by a British team in the International Eisteddfod at Llangollen. Out of 17 entrants from all over the world, the Britannia Coconutters scored 80 points to reach fourth place in a festival which no British team has ever won. (The first prize went to the Yugoslavian folkdancers of Serbia with 96 points, 2nd were the Orlyk dancing group from the Ukraine with 91 points, 3rd were an Austrian group with 82 points, and the Nutters shared fourth place.) In 1964 they did even better, and came 2nd.

The "Nutters" were the First Prize-winners at all the Carnivals in Lancashire from 1922 to 1939, and have appeared many times at the English Folk Dance & Song Society's Festival at the Royal Albert Hall in London, where they first appeared in 1931. More recently they have had several appearances on television.

The "Nutters" raise about £200 for charity every year, and maintain a very high standard in their dances.

Some twenty years ago, Bill o' Bow's wrote a special dialect poem as a tribute to the Britannia Coconut Dancers on the occasion of the retirement of two long-serving members, Mr. Arthur Bracewell and Mr. Mark Pilling. The former was responsible for the re-formation of the "Nutters" after World War I, and the latter was a member of the "Nutters" for over 20 years.

At Cecil Sharpe House, the headquarters of The English Folk Dance & Song Society, Mr. Derek Froone received a replicative dance troop, crafted in wood and fashioned by Mr. Norman Wilkinson; the red and white costumes worn by these small figures were designed and executed by Miss Margaret Waller.

EAWR NUTTERS

(History of the "Nutters", in Lancashire dialect)

Eawr Nutters are comin', they're dancin' in t' street,
   Ther's crowds standin' watchin' all havin' a treat,
In red and white costumes, wi' faces all black,
   An' t' coco-shells beatin' a-crack-a-jack-crack.

Th'owd Lancashire clogs are tappin' eawt t' tune,
   An' youngest to th'owdest familiarly croon;
For year after year it's bin handed deawn,
   This melody played when they're dancin' through t' teawn.

It coom first of all, well, so Ah've bin towd,
   When th'owd Cornish miners invaded eawr fowd,
Areawnd Wit'orth valley an' o'er Tunstead way,
   'Til 1907 showed a Jubilee Day.

Fifty long year o' Folk Dancin' in t' street,
   Fro' mornin' 'til midday, 'til lat' on at neet,
Fifty long years sin' Tunstead began,
   A team wer then formed up at good owd Britann'.

But when Nineteen-fourteen brought war to eawr land,
   Th'owd "Nutters" were "scattered" an' had to disband,
An' though 'twer accepted, th'owd team's had its due,
   Still, t'melody lingered in t' minds of a few.

For mony long years it lay dormant, an' then - -
   A one, Arthur Bracewell, geet goin' again,
He reawnded t' lads up, at first but a few,
   An' that would, Ah think, be in t' year '22.

But "Time" is our Master, keeps flingin' us ills,
   We try hard to feight him wi' potions an' pills,
An' though t' spirit's willin', eawr flesh is but frail,
   Owd age in its turn tells a lame sort o' tale.

’Twer thus, Arthur Senior turned reawnd to his lad,
“Tha’ll tek on this task, son, tha will so, by gad!
“We waint ha’ no laikin’ wi’ wark neaw in seet,
“So labour an’ lead ’em to dance ony street”.

Sin that day, eawr Arthur’s bin Leader, as weel - -
He’s done Secretary, an’ grateful we feel,
He set an example in service bi t’ mile,
An’ echoed his faything by dancin’ th’owd style.

His troop neaw have danced througheawt owd Rossendale,
In Lancashire, Midlands, o’er hills and through vale;
At Royal Albert Hall, seven times they’ve appeared.
While Harringay ’rena, again loudly cheered.

Their record’s a good ’un, -- they’ve prizes by t’ scoore,
An’ one thing we’re proud on, o’ this Ah feel sure --
Placed FOURTH ut Llangollen, in t’year ’52,
Five points aboon rest of eawr British Isle’s Crew.

Fro’ Blackpool to Lytham an’ Newcastle, too,
They’ve danced for t’ young students ut their “Rag-rag” Doo,
Th’owd band’s allus wi’ ’em in close harmony,
An’ what abeawt t’ “Brass”? Why, its for Charity!

A reight worthy callin’ a noble response,
An’ t’ Nutters remember wheerever they dance,
All t’ poor an’ all th’ aged, all t’ sufferin’ an’ t’sick,
May such, long find comforts through th’ efforts ut wick.

Eawr Folk Dance Society had a film made,
To show to each country when visit they paid,
Heaw this gradely dance troop, unique in itsel’
In harmony laboured, tradition to tell.

At Cecil Sharpe Heawse displayed soon there’ll be --
A grand replicative dance troop theer to see,
While Miss Margaret Waller created all t’ togs,
Eawr own Norman “Wilkie” did fashion all t’ clogs.

But neaw Fayther Time calls another to rest,
  A mon who has danced twenty-one years ut best,
Eawr member, Mark Pilling, we'll miss him fro' t' cast,
  Long may he recall happy mem'ries ut past.

Yet, though Mark's retirin', he's noan bi hissel,
  We're loisin' another, it pains me to tell,
For eawr Arthur Bracewell has served us so weel,
  His absence, Ah know, we cornt miss but feel.

Then best thanks to Arthur an' Mark too, this day,
  We've seen through their efforts success com' eawr way,
An' while we would wish 'em Good Health an' Good Cheer,
  They'll allus be reight gradely welcom' reawnd here.

May you long be spared to think on this neet,
  So happy wi' friends an' good neighbours in seet,
An' as you reflect in your mem'ry's e'e,
  May success bless "Nutters" in t' days yet to be.

Eawr Nutters are comin' they're dancin' in t' street,
  Ther's crowds standin' watchin' all havin' a treat,
In red an' white costumes wi' faces all black,
  An' t' coco-shells beatin' a-crack-a-jack-crack.

MORE ROSSENDALE ANECDOTES

A boy who used the word "Gradely" was reprimanded by his teacher. He gave the lad a dictionary and asked him to find the word "gradely" in it. "Well, can you find it, boy?", said the teacher shortly. "No", said the lad, "it isn't a gradely dictionary".

A boy went into a general shop kept by a deaf old man, and said: "A Quarter o' coffee". "What sort o' toffee?" said the old man. "Nod toffee, coffee", said the lad -- "wod they mek tay wi'".

GAWMLESS END

Soon after leaving the village of Britannia, and beginning the gradual descent down Shanter Brow, one can see on the steeply rising hillside the castle-like structure widely known as "Gawmless End".

Originally built as "Old House Farm" during the eighteenth century, we are reliably informed that the present-day structure was rebuilt in the nineteenth century on the site of the former building.

It was then decided to incorporate the addition of a rather substantial *windbreak* against the prevailing tempestuous elements of wintertime -- which winters, statistics tell us, were particularly severe during that period of time.

Accordingly, the massive gable-end was constructed to simulate the frontal appearance of a castle complete with battlement embrasures.

Although it must be one of the most ornamental "Windbreaks" in existence, yet, because of its utilitarian purpose it cannot be wholly accepted as a *Monumental Folly* of the type usually associated with cranks.

On one occasion, an interested stranger, on making enquiries, was jocularly informed that he was now gazing at "Shawforth Castle". Needless to say, his subsequent investigation was most disappointing. Every ready with his endless resources of good-natured banter, it was practically inevitable that the local native should appropriately name it GAWMLESS END.

MORE ROSSENDALE ANECDOTES

A local man claimed that his cat was the best mouser in the Valley, but when his friend was "camping" him one day the cat slept peacefully on the hearthrug, although a mouse came out from under the fireplace. The friend took him up on this, but got the reply: "Eeh, that's one of eawrs -- tha' should si what happens when a stranger comes in".

WAUGH'S WELL

Waugh's Well was opened in the summer of 1866. Mr. Jos. Chatwood had a large hand in the proposal, and Mr. Thomas Brooks (the late Lord Crawshaw) supplied the stone for the tablet and other stonework about the well.

Mr. John Spencer, F.G.S., F.R.A.S., then manager for Butterworth and Brooks, got the work carried out and a celebration was subsequently held at Fo' Edge Farm, Mr. Brooks bearing the cost of a generous lunch. The occupier of Fo' Edge at that time was Bill o' Johnny's (Taylor), whose wife Ann (named as Owd Ann in the early pages of "Tattlin' Matty") was a capable woman and a good cook.

It was originally intended to carve the words of Edwin Waugh's poem, "The Moorland Maid" on the tablet, but this was never done, and the inscription was simply "Waugh's Well, 1866". The Easter of 1881 found "Bob o' Dick o' Giles's" (Ashworth) of the next farm ("Slacks") building up the stonework and fixing the flag-seating about the Well. After a few years, "Dick o' Giles's", a worker at the Fo' Edge quarries, followed four of his sons -- the above-named Bob, and Tom and Dick and Ned -- to Maine, U.S.A.

Waugh makes many references to Rossendale in his books. His poem "Little Cattle, Little Care" was written whilst at Fo' Edge. And in his sketch, "Owd Cronies", Waugh relates how Owd Jane is trying to tell a story, but stops to say, "Here, come, if we're ɑ' gooin' to talk at once, like Rossenda' churchwardens, I'll wait a bit till ther's a better chance".

The well was renovated and largely rebuilt in 1966 by Mr. Wilf Baldwin and Mr. Harry Sagar of Rawtenstall (members of the Pennine Paths Protection Society, Rossendale), and a bronze head of Edwin Waugh (modelled by Mrs. M. Lord of Newchurch and cast in phosphor bronze by Mr. Bonzor of Rochdale) was incorporated in the structure as well as a memorial plaque to Ward Ogden, a great Rossendale rambler. A crowd of 450 people watched Mr. Harry Craven unveil the renovated well on July 16th, 1966.

Note: When the Lancashire Authors' Association visited Rawtenstall in 1930, Alderman W. Hardman, who welcomed them, traced the connection of several local people with "Old Ann" who lived at Fo' Edge when Waugh's Well was opened in 1866. Mrs. Hoyle, the wife of the Rawtenstall sanitary inspector, was a niece, and Mrs. William Whittaker, who was present in person that afternoon, was one of Old Ann's grand-daughters. Alderman Hardman also said that on one occasion when Mrs. Hardman (his own wife) broke her arm whilst playing with a sheep at Ringleton Fold, she was taken to the "Whitworth doctor" by Old Ann.

HIGHER HILL (Cowpe)

Across wide meadows and the yielding soil
Of upland wastes -- the keen, delicious wind dd
Of solitary moorland, clean and kind,
Sweeping the sordid taint of irksome toil
From brain and brow: by narrow winding streams,
And fields of waving bracken, green and tall --
Where the wild moor-cock sends his eerie call
Into a silent arcady of dreams --
By pathless plains and rugged steeps we go
To probe the placid deeps of thy delight:
To feast upon thy calm -- beloved height --
Leaving the toils of traffic far below;
The few, grey sheep upon thy barren sides
Make Solitude complete, and loudly -- shrill
The piping curlew cries -- from hill to hill
Bridging the murmurous quietude that bides
Mile upon mile -- until at last we seek
The lonely lake, that in thy bosom lies --
A rippling mirror of the cloud-rent skies,
Deep-rimmed in russet moorland, bare and bleak.

MORE ROSSENDALE ANECDOTES

A follower of East Lancashire cricket team for sixty years remembers a match at Rawtenstall when George Tribe was Rawtenstall's professional, and Jim Smith the East Lancashire professional.

Little Joey Middleton came in to bat for Rawtenstall, and one old lady on the terraces saw that he was about to face Jim Smith, who stood about 6 ft. 5 ins. She said: "What a shame ... it shouldn't be allowed".

Knowing that Joey was one of the best amateur batsmen the League has seen, the East Lancs follower remarked' "Well, you know, he has got a bat to defend himself with". The old lady's only reply was to slap his face.

REPLY IN VERSE

"That terrible Rossendale Valley, where poor Anthony Greenwood is the M.P.". "The wild, bitter little towns of North Lancashire" -- Ray Gosling in "The Listener", quoted in the "Rossendale Free Press", Saturday 30 March 1968.

Aw yerd tell o' a feller
As coom through Rossendale,
An' then 'ee wrote to Th' Listener
Wi' sich a weary tale.

This terrible owd valley,
It's wild and bitter, too.
Just heaw mich did 'ee see on't
When 'ee were drivin' through?

Mooast likely 'ee'd a taxi
Or private car to ride,
'Ee'd just go dashin' up th' main street
An' glance eawt to one side.

'Ee 'appen didn't notice,
Behind eawr shops an' mills,
Behind eawr rows .o' heawses
Them everlastin' hills.

'Ee's never bin to th' Fo' Edge,
Nor forrad to Waugh's Well,
An' sin' the glorious beauty
O' moorland, dale an' fell.

'Ee's never toiled up Turnpike,
Climbed onward to Seat Naze,
An' hearkened th' curlew callin',
Watched sheep an' cattle graze.

An' 'as 'ee bin up Deerplay,
An' tramped theer heawr bi heawr,
An' gazed deawn th' length o' th' valley
As fur as 'Owcombe Teawr?

'Ee's never walked to Goodshaw,
Or o'er bi th' Gambleside,
An' known the peace an' quiet
O' Swinshaw's countryside.

Or deawn bi th' Limey Water,
Sin th' Quaker Meetin' Place;
It's humblin' if the best of us
Meets history face to face.

'Ee's never stood on Cribden,
An' felt theer, gazin' deawn,
The fierce pride o' belongin'
To "th' bitter little teawn".

'As 'ee ne'er talked to th' natives?
(They don't all eat their young)
'Ee'd learn as they're all preawd
O' th' stock fro' which they're sprung.

'Ee'd larn as they 'ave courage,
An' salty humour too,
I' short, they're gradely fooak,
They're jannock through an' through.

So 'ee con 'ave 'is Fleet Street,
Or some place just as grim,
'Ee doesn't need to pity us,
We're reight ill off for 'im.

MORE ROSSENDALE ANECDOTES

The Mayoral chair of a town in Lancashire was occupied by a personage who was well known for his liberal generosity. Among others that sought relief from him during his term of office was a well-known local character known as "Talkin' Tim", and he asked for the loan of two or three pounds to buy a donkey and cart, and set up in the rag and bone business.

"Well, Tim", said the Mayor, "if I lend you this money, how are you going to pay me?"

This was a poser for Tim, but a sudden thought struck him, and he blurted out: "Well, your worship, if you're kind enough to lend me th' brass, aw'll tell thi what aw'll do --aw'll call th' donkey after thee".

BRITANNIA COCONUTTERS performing their Garland Dance on Easter Saturday.

BRITANNIA COCONUTTERS performing their Coconut Dance – in the Square near the "Red Lion", Whitworth, at the 1971 Whitworth Festival.

WAUGH'S WELL, Near Fo' Edge Farm, in the dilapidated state it was for many years before its renovation in 1966.

WAUGH'S WELL, after renovation 1966, with side seating, new lintel stone, bronze head of Edwin Waugh and the poet's dates – 1817 to 1890, and a memorial stone to Ward Ogden, naturalist and rambler.

TERMS OF

MISS HAMER'S SCHOOL,

IRWELL COTTAGE, BACUP.

	S.	D.	
Young Ladies under Eight years of age	*6*	*6*	*per Quarter.*
Do. from Eight to Eleven	*8*	*6*	,,
Do. above that age . . .	*10*	*6*	,,
Weekly Boarders . . .	*£3*	*0*	,,
Day Boarders	*£1*	*10*	,,

A QUARTER'S NOTICE REQUIRED PREVIOUSLY TO THE REMOVAL OF A PUPIL.

Miss Hamer's School was an early private school in Bacup, but so far enquiries have failed to locate the site of either the school or Irwell Cottages. (original in Bacup Library).

Bacup's Road, River and Rail Walk 1968.

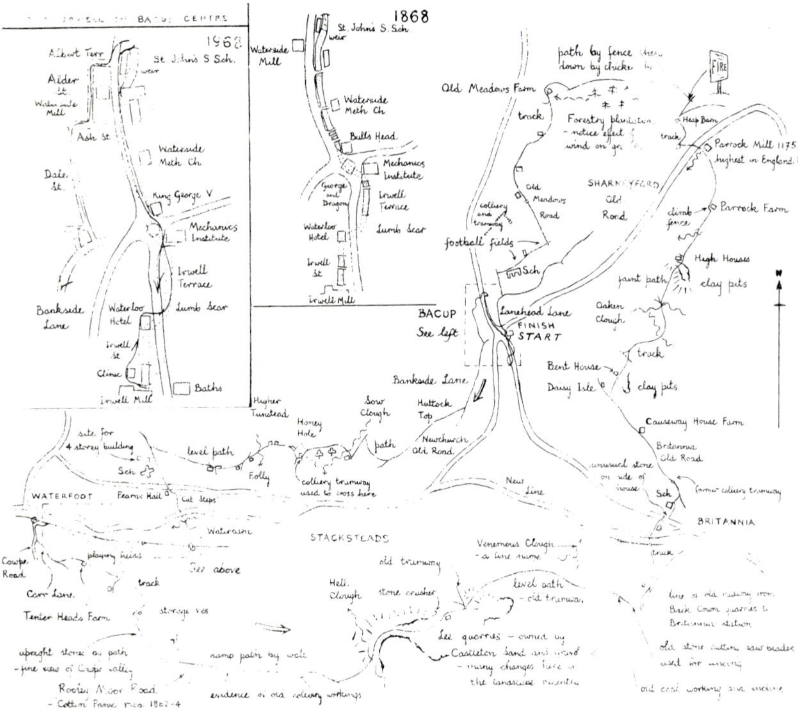

Sketched by John B. Taylor for the 4th Bacup Boundary Walk, showing the relative positions of channels in Bacup town centre in 1868 and 1968.

Greetings card of STACKSTEADS, depicting five familiar scenes, taken about 1960.

The RIVER IRWELL at Carr Bridge, Broadclough. Burnley Road is to the left. Taken about 1920.

DOG PITS MILL and Cottages, off Burnley Road, above Higher Broadclough, taken from near the bridge over the river Irwell about 1900. Only the foundations are now to be seen.

Holme Nook, a quiet part of Stacksteads (Postcard photograph from about 1920).

The recently demolished PARROCK MILL at Sharneyford was billed as the highest mill in England at 1175 feet above sea level. Originally produced cotton, finally chickens. (More in the foreground is the ground where Sharneyford Methodists used to play cricket. The boundary on the left was at the top of the slag heap!)

LOWER CHANGE, Todmorden Road, about 1910. The garden of "The Greens" on the left, and the road on the right.

PILGRIM'S CROSS

On the wide expanse of moorland stretching from Helmshore to Holcombe on the north side of the Irwell Valley, there is a stone monument on the site of an ancient pilgrim's cross or whowell.

The cross was erected prior to 1175 and is named in charters of gifts of land in Holcombe Forest in 1176 and in 1225. In 1662 King Charles II gave the Manor of Holcombe to General Monk, Duke of Albemarle, through whom it has descended to the present Lord of the Manor.

Nothing is known of the removal of the Ancient Cross, but its massive socketted foundation actually existed until 1901. The splintered remains of the cross were seen however by Rev. J. Marshall Mather, as the following quotation (taken from his essay, "A Pilgrimage to a Confessor's Grave", written before 1888 shows:

> "Two men -- so the story runs -- while in a state of intoxication laid wagers as to the possibility of its removal. Toward it they together directed their staggering steps, the one whose wager necessitated the trial of strength seizing the upright stone, and wrenching it from its socket. It fell, and was splintered into many pieces, *some of which may still be seen lying around* ".

The Pilgrim's Cross was once a place of prayer and rendezvous for pilgrims on their way from Lancaster to Whalley. In the days when travellers always faced danger from bandits, they would give thanks to God for their safety.

MORE ROSSENDALE ANECDOTES

Joe had persuaded Mary to take an evening stroll with him. He was shy and couldn't think what to say, but after a time he said: "It's a nice neet!", and relapsed into silence. Then, after a time he observed: "T'moon's breet". Another long silence. He racked his brains to think of something else to say, then his face lit up as he pointed to a row of cottages. "Mi gronfayther built them cottages", he said.

After a long walk, he asked Mary if he could go out with her again, and she replied, "Aye, but not until it's a nice neet, an' t' moon's breet, and thi gronfayther's built another row of cottages!"

GRAVES IN GARDENS -- TO MAN, DOG, HORSE AND CANARY

It is usual for most people if they are buried when they die to come to rest in a cemetery. There are in the Rossendale Valley however four inscribed graves which, by accident or design, are separate from any churchyard or cemetery.

At Edge End Farm, above Constablelee is the pillared tomb-stone of Thomas Haworth who died in 1800 -- it is thought as a result of falling from his horse or overbalancing whilst seated on a gate behind the farm. Part of the verse says:

"Reflect when thou my grave dost see
The next that's made may be for thee".

Another grave now forms part of the pathway up to Orchard Terrace, near the "Black Dog" in Crawshawbooth. Originally on four pillars, it states -- with spelling mistakes -- that:

"Hear was intered the Bodey of James Haworth of this Place who departed this life 2th Jenuary 1772 Aged 63".

This grave is of an ancestor of James Haworth, a Quaker who lived in the "Mansion House" shortly before it was demolished.

Behind the new houses near the "Red Lion" at Higher Cloughfold is the pillared grave to an innkeeper, James Ormerod, who died in 1817:

"When we this good man's life explore,
We cannot but allow,
Whate'er this place might be before,
'Tis consecrated now".

-- It now forms part of a hen-pen!

A fourth grave is in the front garden of Carr House, Lomas Lane, Balladen. Under a carved skull and cross-bones is the simple statement:

"The Remains of Richard Ashworth Here rest in Hope. He was born Feb.22 1677 died May 28 1751".

Richard Ashworth was the Baptist minister at Cloughfold for 52 years. For a number of years before he died he had to be helped into the pulpit because he had become completely blind.

Turning from man to his best friend the dog, Rossendale has a number of gravestones to dogs.

The most famous is Lovely's grave, high on the side of Cowpe Lowe and not far from Lowe Lodge. It is the burial place of an 18-year-old bitch called Lovely, which died in 1873. The poem on the stone includes a stone-mason's error:

"On the the 12th of May,
They laid away,
One that was loved by many,
She hunted rats and was kind to cats,
And birds she sought out many."

Stories about the dog vary. Some say Lovely belonged to a quarry-man and went up into the hills to work with her master each day; others believe it belonged to a barber in Waterfoot and would follow anyone with a gun; whilst others say it was an inmate at the "San-Doyle" beer house at Sandy Bank.

The rhododendroned grounds of Lea Bank almost hide two graves -- two of Craven Hoyle's dogs. The inscriptions are "Sally Nov. 2. 1910" and "Leita May 2. 1916". Most ex-pupils of Lea Bank School know where to find them.

At Ewood Hall, in the garden, is a stone with the carving "Topsy died March 18th 1883 aged 10". This was the fox-terrier of George Turner Hardman, a fine and favourite dog which he used to show.

A memorial stone to a horse is built into an outhouse at Peers Clough Hall, Lumb. "In memory of Sally 20.6.58". Sally was Constance Brooks' horse which strangled itself with a tether rope.

At Fearns County Secondary School, but originally at Stubbylee Hall, Bacup, is a loose fragment of a gravestone to a canary which died 12th Oct. 1869. Part of the "flowery" inscription reads:

"Spring woodland flowers form a grateful shade,
Around the tomb where poor Canary's laid,
Sweet violets they tendrils intertwine,
With creeping cowslip and with fragrant columbine".

Recently there have been erected other gravestones to dogs and a variety of animals in Rossendale. These are at Sunny Bank Farm, Crawshawbooth, which has become well known, even far afield, with the setting up there of a pets' cemetery.

THE HARE ON THE ROAD

(Seen near Ewood Bridge, December 1954)

From under a fence he came -- out of the dark secret ditches which border many of the Pennine moorlands. A swift unexpected intruder, bounding from invisible tracks with such intensity that our conversation ceased abruptly in the quick need for exacttime-braking to avoid "death on the road". "A fox!" we called simultaneously, as the powerful head-lights gold-sheathed him. "A hare!", we exclaimed, now identifying his graceful bobbing movements and admiring his remarkable physique as he paused for about ten seconds in the froad beam of light on the road.

Remarkable and superb he was, with a certain dignified unawareness of highroad perils, which likened him to some pedestrian secure in his "human rights" on a zebra crossing. There appeared no mesmeric panic; no hypnotic surrendering to strong unaccustomed light; but just that brief halting with head and front paws up; eyes warmly vivid in the lamps' fierce glare!

One sixth of a minute -- a few more bounds, and on the opposite shadowed sidepath he half turned towards the car with a comical swaying movement, almost like a curtsy; then disappeared in the dark silences of the wild uplands: captive only to his instinctive needs; his dependence on his own kind!

Less than half-a-minute had elapsed since his unwitting intrusion; but his untamed charm and vigorous form -- gold-drenched in the searching light, caught the imagination, and created a permanent picture of beauty. Conversation seemed banal now. On the screen of a scurrying man-machine had been flung a reminder of the old allegiance to Nature. He had come from the secret haunts of unknown creatures; to return to the broad acres of freedom and liberty: the realm of the timid, the fearless; the victors and vanquished !

"A wonderful animal!" exclaimed the traveller in the corner. "Magnificent!" said the car driver: "And such an easy target! Yes!" he repeated: "Such an easy target! -- but -- but --" and his voice trailed away to silence. BUT! Surely that curtsying gesture on the sidepath was a graceful salute to a man who also loved life and liberty!

Within the kingdom of impatient man
    He stays his course, and halts his freedom's plan --
His zest for life where secret creatures go;
    His kith and kind -- and in the highway glow
Reveals his perfectness: his instincts checked until
    Some urging hunger claims his ardent will
And swift to answer Nature's ancient cry;
He leaps man's fence -- his cloak, the moonless sky!

ON T' MOORS O' ROZZENDALE

Aw've tramped o' t' moors o' Rozzendale
  Fer mony a year, thi ne'er ged stale.
Aw've faced th' owd wind fer mony a mile
  Wod memories ! -- it's bin worth-while.

It's t'way Aw'm med, Aw ged a thrill
  On owd Cowpe Moss or Hailstorm Hill,
When waatchin' t' curlew wheelin' reawnd,
  Or hearkenin' t' snipes'quare drummin' seawnd.

Aw'm allus swell wi' local pride
  At t'seet o' bonnie Cribden side.
Or when at oal areawnd Aw gaze
  Fro' Balladen or t' top o' t' Naze.

It's grand o' t' tops ut breyk o' t' day
  To see yon swoopin' tewits play;
It's grand i' t' dark up on yon heights
  To see th' owd valley's twinklin' lights.

Wod better ner to tek yor ease
  Wheer t' purple grasses wave i' t' breeze;
Or leyn agen an owd stone stile
  While t' larks are singin' up o' th' Hile!

Aw'll thramp o' t' moors o' Rozzendale
  Until Aw'm owd an' wake an' frail,
An' then Aw'll read owd Edwin Waugh --
  He sung ther praise i' words ut glow.

OLD BLOOMERIES FORMERLY IN ROSSENDALE

(This extract is taken from a paper read 4th April, 1872, by James Kerr, and included on pages 57 to 70 of the Transactions of the Historic Society of Lancashire and Cheshire, new series, volume XII, under the title "On the remains of some old bloomeries formerly existing in Lancashire")

Bloomery is the name given to the open-air furnace, formerly in use in this and other countries, for the reduction of metallic ores by means of wood-charcoal. The term is derived from the Saxon, *bloma,* a mass or lump, referring to the form taken by the smelted metal, and is still in use among iron-furnace men, though in a somewhat modified sense; the name "bloomery" being now given to the first forge through which iron passes after it is smelted, while the term "bloom" is applied to the mass of iron when it has passed through the "bloomery", or, in other words, has undergone the first hammering.

A bloomery formerly consisted of a low cupola, constructed of clay or stone, the fire in which was fanned by the wind, through apertures left for that purpose, the amount of air admitted being regulated by the opening or closing of the apertures, in accordance with the strength of the breeze, or the intensity of the heat required, for the various stages of the roasting and smelting processes.

The remains of this class of primitive bloomeries are found in all parts of the country. In the Forest of Rossendale these included (a) one discovered on the north side of the turnpike road at Millar Barn Meadow-road, opposite the Newchurch railway station; (b) one at "Cinder Hill', on the left of Red Brook, north-west of Holcombe-Hill, and about two miles from Ramsbottom; (c) one on the farm of Priestbooth, about three miles from Bacup, on the Todmorden road, situated at the upper extremity of "Sunder Clough" gully; and (d) at Smithy Croft, Rakehead, near Stacksteads railway station, on the left bank of the Irwell.

This last belonged for many successive generations to a family named Ashworth, who carried on there the trade of working cutlers, and whose descendants frequently received the distinctive designation of the Cutler-Ashworths, occasionally individually named: "John Cutler", "Edmund Cutler", etc.

The old tradition, as related by Mr. Edmund Ashworth, of Fairwell Farm, Brandwood, in his 79th year, is that "during the Wars of the Roses, (1450-1485), a man of the name of Ashworth, by trade a cutler, came from Sheffield, and established upon Smithy Croft a forge and workshop", the remains of which, along with an abundance of "clinkers" (scoriae), were often seen ... until some years ago, when the croft was entirely broken up by quarrying operations. The tradition goes on to say that the cutlery business was continued here by this family until they became the owners of Boars Greave, in Cowpe, to which they ultimately removed. In West's *Antiquities of Furness,* the names "Smithy" and "Bloom Smithy" are frequently given to old bloomeries there, and they are also called "Forges".

The traditions that the Ashworth family were cutlers, and resided in the vicinity of the croft on which their smithy and forge are reputed to have stood, is supported by a lease of lands let to them by the authorities of Whalley Abbey, for nineteen years, on 8thMarch, 10th Henry VIII (1518). In the Coucher Book of Whalley, the same persons are named as holding the same lands ("Brendwoode and Cowhope" -- now Brandwood and Cowpe, on part of which stands Smithy Croft). Three leases, two issued in 1561, and a third in 1608, designates the tenants as "John Assheworthe of Greens, cuttler", and "John Assheworthe, his son, cuttler"; from which we see that the Ashworths of Greens, which is in the same locality with Smithy Croft, were *cutlers* from before 1561 to after 1608.

The Cutler-Ashworth tradition, intimately connected with the Rossendale bloomeries, is supported by the above documentary evidence, for a central part of at least a century, there being in 1518, seven families of them distinctly named as tenants of the lands on which Smithy Croft stands, and in 1608 at least two, father and son, both cutlers, holding Greens and Elle Bank in the same locality.

* * * * * * * * * * * * *

MORE ROSSENDALE ANECDOTES

During the war, a local ne'er-do-well had to join up, but he was soon home again. He had asked an officer for a "chow o' bacca", and when the indignant man replied: "Don't you know I'm a major?", our character rejoined with: "Eeh, arti? Tha's getten' a good job. Aw'd stick to it if aw were thee".

WHERE LOCAL HISTORY FINDS A HOME

Call of duty apart, I cannot remember when I paid a visit to the Museum and Art Gallery in Whitaker Park, Rawtenstall. It's all wrong; and especially for one not at all averse to using valuable hours of a holiday visiting "stately homes" and soaking up the history of people in whom one takes only a passing interest.

A party of sixth formers from the Caldy County Grammar School near Hoylake came to Rawtenstall to visit the Museum and the Library in their practical work on Lancashire Textile history as part of their "A" Level G.C.E. syllabus. Their visit coincided with Rawtenstall Museums Week in 1968.

At Rawtenstall any large scale activities were precluded on the grounds of economy, but it was decided to publicise the Museum by issuing a catalogue of what the Librarian and Curator, Mr. Jon Elliott, calls "the better known Rossendale Room".

I have always found this the most interesting section in a museum, which incidentally is housed in a former "stately home", which like so many others in the Valley has passed into the service of the public.

The house was built nearly 120 years ago and was the former home of the Hardman family, who owned Newhallhey Mill and were engaged in the woollen industry.

In 1901 the house as part of the bequest of the late Richard Whitaker passed into the ownership of the town to serve the generations which followed as a museum and art-gallery.

Mr. Whitaker was the town's first Freeman. The casket and scroll which was given to him when he was made a Freeman remains a lasting memorial of this great benefactor and is one of the interesting exhibits of the Rossendale Room.

This room is a treasure trove of proud memories. That fact emerges very quickly from the catalogue. -- Portraits bring back memories of the men who established Rossendale as an industrial community, with emphasis on cotton in the days of the Industrial Revolution, and with footwear moving into the major position at the turn of the century.

Among the cotton men there is David Whitehead, the founder of the group which bears his name and is now international in its fame.

In the portraits of members of the Hardman family there is a reminder of the eminence at one time of the woollen industry in the town.

Footwear is well represented with specially commissioned portraits of the men who were pioneers -- men who carried proud names like Rothwell, Hirst, Hoyle, McLerie, Parker and Brooks. And not forgetting the man who perhaps became the most famous of them all -- Sir Henry Whittaker Trickett.

Another portrait demanding a second look is that of Thomas Newbigging, who came to the local gas undertaking as engineer and stayed to achieve fame as a local historian. His "History of the Forest of Rossendale" has long established his position as a leading authority on the Valley.

Pat Stephens, another local historian, takes a worthy place there too, while the humble have not been ignored with portraits of John Mackenzie, the match seller, and Betty Treacle, a Crawshawbooth eccentric.

Other paintings have had their inspiration in the many historic buildings -- the Friends Meeting House, the Old Unitarian Chapel, Hareholme Mill and the Old Mansion House at Crawshawbooth to name just a few.

Photographs bring the general scene more up-to-date though in this respect the main collection of photographs, prints, etc. is housed in the Reference Library.

A Neolithic flint arrow head is evidence of people living in the Valley more than 4000 years ago. That interesting piece of archaeology was the subject of one of my earlier articles.

We take pride in our musical achievements. One of three plaques won by the Rossendale Male Voice Choir at the International Eisteddfod at Llangollen takes its place among many relics of the men who started it all -- those unique musicians of the late 18th and 19th centuries, the Deighn Layrocks (Larks of Dean).

Just walk around and you will see exhibits that bring back memories of the days of the turnpikes and toll bars; of the old Rossendale Hunt; of great events like the Boer War and the Great War. So many in fact that the best advice is to go and see for yourself.

Mr. Hargreaves Wilkinson was appointed the first Curator in 1905. His years of service were long enough for him to be in control in my early days as a reporter. He was quite a character and I remember him for many things -- if only for the reason he gave for his good head of hair.

Others who followed him were Mr. H.C. Caistor and Mr. H.I. Hunt, and, of course, Mr. Elliott. Each in their way have been able to capture the pride of local achievement. And in every respect they are considerable.

OUR TOWN

There's folk as say that Bacup's
   A dull and dreary town,
But 'ow's it dull and dreary
   Wi' such beauty all around?

There's some as never see beyond
   The edges of their nose,
But tek a look round th' district
   And exercise thi toes.

First, go to th' top o' Deerplay,
   And on a fine, clear day,
They say you can see Blackpool,
   Forty miles away.

Then climb and see the Cenotaph
   Standing there on th' hill,
And say a prayer for th' lads who're gone
   But whose mem'ry lingers still.

Then go on a little further
   And you'll be surprised to see
The beginning of the Irwell
   Which goes on to the sea.

Come back o'er th' road and tek the path
   That branches to thi right,
Look down upon th' Weir Village --
   Isn't that a lovely sight?

Then walkin' on down Burnley Road
   You'll come to Broad Clough Hall,
It really is a picture
   Amongst the trees so tall.

Whilst on your left, the Irwell,
   Now very plain to see,
Goes laughing over th' rocks and stones,
   And flows on, merrily.

Another day, perhaps you'd like
   To walk up to Britann',
There's much to see fro' Rochdale Road,
   And much for you to scan.

Look t'ards New Line and there you'll see
   Ross Mill, a big, fine mill,
And there's St. Saviour's Church on th' bend,
   And th' quarry there, on th' hill.

Go o'er th' owd Road and tek a look
   At beauty all around,
Go past the school, and Thorn Estate,
   And back into the town.

Next, tek a walk up Bacup "Rec",
   I know that it's a pull,
But there's no air that's purer,
   So get thi lungs all full.

And stop and watch 'em golfin',
   Or sit and watch 'em bowl,
And there you'll find sweet peace o' mind
   And contentment for your soul.

Then carry on down th' meadows
   And come out at Sowclough,
You can go on up th' 'Oney 'Ole,
   If you haven't had enough.

Go over th' Waggoner Tunstead,
   And drop down i' Fearns' Moss,
By Fearns' Hall, go down th' Cat Steps,
   There you can catch a bus.

Or cross o'er th' road, o'er th' iron bridge,
Where now the Irwell's wide,
Go past the end o' Brand Wood Road,
And up, past Chapel Side.

Go past the tip that's up Rakehead
And on into Hell Clough,
That's up at th' top o' Cutler Greens
If you've still not had enough.

Then carry on, past th' cemetery
It isn't very far,
Past th' top o' th' park, into New Line,
And out by th' Reservoir.

Or if you feel you'd rather
Go up to Sharneyford,
Walk up until you come to th' well,
And come back o'er th' owd road.

Perhaps you'll hear the Christ Church bells
Ring out from their bell tower,
So stop, and rest, and listen
And spend a quiet hour.

And thank God for the beauty
That you see all around,
Then carry on, Dark Lane, Greensnook.
And on, past th' Cricket ground.

You'll feel you've had a gradely walk,
As Lane Head you come down,
And come out, just by Woolworth's,
In the centre of the town.

But if you say that you can't walk
And get up on the hill,
Just catch a bus to Park Hotel,
It's nobbut threepence still.

Go o'er the tip, and cross the road,
And go into the park,
And sit there in th' rose garden,
And forget about your wark.

Enjoy the beauty round you,
And all the lovely flowers
The colours of the Lupins
And the lovely rosy bowers.

Or go a little further,
To the children's playing ground,
The tennis, or the bowling greens,
There's plenty to be found.

Then go and look at Stubbylee Hall,
Where our Town Council meet
To have the Council meeting,
Once monthly, Wednesday neet.

And here's our chance to thank 'em
For all the work they do,
From the youngest to the oldest
We thank 'em, good and true.

But if you feel you'd rather stop
Near th' centre of the town,
There's lots of forms by th' Cenotaph,
Where you can sit you down.

Or sit in th' St. James' Gardens,
Watch the folks pass to and fro
As they go about their business,
Watch the buses come and go.

Or at th' bottom o' Rosebank Street,
There's a lovely garden there,
Wi' lots of lovely bushes
And trees wi' blossom fair.

And so you see, there's plenty
Of beauty to be found
In this little town o' Bacup
If you'll nobbut look around.

So when you hear folks grumbling,
And trying to drag us down --
Stand up, and tell 'em straight
You're proud to live in such a town.

DON WHILLANS

Don Whillans doesn't smile a lot. He's a joker who delivers all his best lines with a straight face.

Like for instance when he turned to Dougal Haston at the dead end of the road to the summit of Everest. They were just two blobs of struglling humanity, frailly hitched to the unyielding sheer face of the South West Col on the last approach to the summit.

They had been stuck at 27,000 feet for three days, waiting for a few hundred feet of rope and two bottles of oxygen to get them to the top. Equipment, help and finally hope was exhausted at the fag end of two gruelling months. The monsoons were only days away. The cause was finally conceded to be lost.

And the top blob, which was Whillans, turned to the blob below him and said, in that rich Rossendale Valley voice, of fulsome round vowels: "How about b-----off, then?" And they did.

But reflecting on the full, quarrelsome story of the international Everest expedition, on his return home, Whillans grinned through his neatly shaped beard and said: "What a comedy. I'm only just catching up on what went on.

"We started off with 31 climbers and at the end of it there were just four of us on the mountain. Some packed in and some got sick. We wondered where everybody else was. We joked that perhaps we were on the wrong mountain. When we got to Camp Six (the summit assault camp) there was one Sherpa and a Japanese climber supporting us, and they weren't going well enough to take the lead."

"Every other day there would be notes from Jimmy Roberts (the expedition leader). 'Joe Bloggs has gone sick. Jim Crow has given up. There is no support. The decision is yours.' The notes are all here in the stuff I've brought back."

"With just two more men to back us, we could have done it. But at that height two men can carry very little. One day they brought oxygen. The next day they didn't come at all. The next day they brought 200 feet of rope. At one stage if we had had just two full bottles of oxygen we would have made a bid for the top."

"It got a bit uncomfortable at the end. The weather was wild right from the start. It marooned us at one camp for ten days. The blizzard was so bad that we couldn't get even three yards to the food tent. At Camp Six it was colder than I've ever known. It was 35 degrees below zero at the camp below, and it was colder than that where we were.

The last two nights I was so perished with cold that came through the sleeping bag and the down suit that I didn't sleep at all."

Whilst he and Haston were waiting, with draining hopes, for rope and oxygen for the last assault up the face, Whillans decided one afternoon to traverse across the face just for something to do. "It was unbelievable. There was a gentle scree slope. We could almost have walked it to the top in four hours with oxygen. It was a tempting risk to try it on what we had, even though there is danger of hallucinations without enough oxygen. That's how men get lost on mountains. But then the point of the expedition wasn't just to get to the top by the easy route. The whole effort had been thrown at the so far unclimbed South West Col."

An Indian and an Austrian climber were out together. The Indian got stuck out of sight of his companion, who decided to go back to base for help. "It goes dark on the mountain at six o'clock. It was five o'clock when he got back and it was generally accepted that the Indian was an hour and a half's climb away. We shot off and made it in three-quarters of an hour. I traversed round the bend where he was hidden from sight and found him crusted in ice all over his face and part of his exposed body. He was frozen like rock. He had been exposed for a couple of hours in a wind which puts you on the border of frostbite in two or three minutes if your hands are exposed. His hands were solid blocks. It was impossible to move his hooked fingers. His eyes were frozen wide open. There was life in him but only just. He didn't know I was there. Nothing could have saved him, even if it had been possible to get him back. There was five minutes of daylight left. The only thing to do was to get the rest of the climbers back to safety. It was five more days before the storm died down. Then it took a full team seven hours to recover his body. I've seen death on the mountains many times before. There's nothing to be done. It's no use letting it upset you. The possibility of death is always there and it's never very remote in the mountains."

Whillans, 5ft. 2in. high and so stringy he looks as if a strong wind would blow him over, has a rugged, lusty body that incredibly gets stronger in extremes of altitude and temperature that gradually devitalises most men. He would still like to be the first Englishman to crown Everest. "I'll make it up the unclimbed South West Col next time ..."

WARD OGDEN

(Tribute to a late founder member of the Rossendale Pennine Paths Protection Society.)

Beneath the wide and open sky
Where skylarks soar and peewits cry,
We left his dust: he did not die --
He roams Elysian moors on high.

He fought with zeal to gain for all
The right to walk where curlews call,
To keep the moorland pathways free
For Valley folk like you and me.

Although he loved our lanes, our brooks,
Our shady woods, our wayside flowers,
T'was on the wild and breezy moors
He spent his most rewarding hours.

Sturdy and strong, rucksac on back,
Tanned by the wind on face and neck;
In winter cold or summer heat
He tramped the hills o'er ling and peat.

One time he walked it in one day
To Hawes from Rossendale all the way,
Long swinging miles o'er moor and fell
Where whinberry grows and wheatears dwell.

Beneath the wide and open sky
Where skylarks soar and peewits cry,
We left his dust: he did not die --
But roams Elysian moors on high.

HARRY CRAVEN

Harry Craven, born 4th October 1907, was a native of Bacup, and one of a family of seven. In his early teens he took up athletics and worked as bottom man to his brother Fred, who was an accomplished hand-balancer. For a time they worked with a road-show in Newcastle as the Craven Brothers Equilibrists Extraordinary. However, his family needed the money of a regular wage-earner, and so he started work in the coalpits. This did not entirely suit his health, and he later worked at Valley Supply; since January 1956 he was a guillotine operator with Howard & Hargreaves Ltd.

In his younger days, Harry was a keen cricketer and a good opening bowler for Sharneyford Methodists. The Jubilee Handbook of the Bacup and District Sunday School Cricket League records that on August 7th, 1926, he took 8 Shawforth Wesleyan wickets at a cost of a mere 7 runs. In later years he became President of Sharneyford Methodist Cricket Club.

In his twentieth year, Harry joined the Bacup "Nat"s, became Librarian, Recorder, and later Secretary, and contributed weekly lecture and meeting reports to the local press. He also began to write dialect poems under the pen-name Ross Endale.

He joined the Lancashire Authors' Association in 1937, and won the Scholes Cup with his "Draughty Heawse" in 1940. This is one of his best-known works, and reproduced in the Rossendale Anthology, though not in the present work. The poem was inspired by one of the houses known as "Old Sheephouses", formerly Allandale Terrace in Rochdale Road, Bacup.

In November 1949, Harry became the Editor of the Red Rose Circulating Magazine of the Lancashire Authors' Association, a post he still held at the time of his death on Thursday, August 19th, 1971, whilst on a visit to Morecambe.

Harry Craven was an acknowledged authority on the local dialect, and also a Vice-President of the Edwin Waugh Society of Rochdale. It must have been one of his happiest moments when he unveiled the renovated Edwin Waugh memorial at the Centenary gathering at Waugh's Well in 1966 before a crowd of some 450 people.

His was a quiet, unobtrusive personality. The warmth of his friendship, and the kindly tones of his softly-spoken voice, endeared him to many. The Editor of this Bacup Miscellany is very pleased to have this opportunity of expressing his genuine appreciation of one of the joint compilers of it, and from whose pen came some two dozen items included in these pages.

FAREWELL, OWD BRID

Farewell, owd brid, thy singing's done,
A gradely rest be thine,
Through generations still to come --
Thy name shall ever shine.

For mony years in harmony,
Tha played a tuneful part,
An' though thy singing neaw is o'er,
Thy song still stirs the heart.

Yon "Sunset Musings" o'er th' owd hills,
When Sol sank deawn to rest,
Thy "Draughty Heawse" and "Farewell Farm";
Acclaimed to be thy best.

Thy pen wer never clemmed for ink,
It fed us day by day,
And yet, unconsciously to thee --
Gave us "A lift on t' way. . ."

Although, too soon, tha's ta'en thy hook,
And left this earthly wom,
May mony a mon and mony a book --
Quote thee for years to com'.

Farewell, owd brid, thy singing's done,
A gradely rest be thine
Through generations still to come,
Thy name shall ever shine.

(Written by Bill o' Bow's as a tribute to the memory of

Harry Craven, L.A.A.)

FOREST FANTASY (Reflections on burning a piece of coal bearing a perfect fern leaf impression)

Black diamond hewn in the abysmal deep,
From scintillant seams of a million eyes,
Reveal now, the secrets of primeval sleep,
Ere smoke, thy soul-substance, belch forth to the skies;
For Man, who reclaims thee from low-vaulted night,
Extending 'neath mountains, and fathomless sea,
Ignites thee, dark fragment, and volcanic might
Erupts thro' the red mists of antiquity.

'Though myst'ry shall cling to thy ancient remains,
And darkness enshroud thee, 'tis well to define --
Thy lineage, which sprang from the wooded domains,
Bespeaking thy contact with bygone sunshine;
How green was thy grandeur that clung to the bough,
When life all-luxuriant exulted birth,
Inherent the power possessing thee now,
From giants of primal perennial earth.

When nature o'erwhelmed thee in dense tropic glade,
'Midst ravishing beauty, and colourful bloom,
Thy towering kindred -- thy tiniest blade,
Were doomed to the dungeon of stratified gloom;
No more, the proud forest of rich virgin stock,
Thou slowly subsided below the earth's crust,
Yet nurtured, and pressed to a bosom of rock,
'Til triumphant neons transmuted their trust.

In deep silent slumber thro' millions of years,
Decayed vegetation to min'ral matured,
Now thenceforth, thy origin visibly clears,
For here has a fossilised fern leaf endured;
Mute witness, it heralds thy ancestral source,
Nor could rock-ribbed strata thy life-lease efface,
Compressed in the earth mould by fantastic force,
Thy life-light is traced on thy leaf-lovely face.

And so, dusky remnant of dim deathless age,
Behold! that art risen from black lustrous bed,
Invested with forces that mightily rage,
When thy magical substance to furnace is fed;
Now, flame-fluent wonder, with miracle fraught,
The dawn of creation to sunset has run,
The primeval forest for this day was wrought,
Thy spiralling spirit reclaimed by the sun.

A LESSON FER LARNERS

Ah went in t' garden one fine day,
  To see heaw things wer showin',
A teawnsman tame, Ah'r new to t' game
  O' watchin' greenstuff growin';
Ah used to laze thru sunny days
  Wel nature kept on werkin',
Ah stopt away when skies wer grey
  And did some armcheere shirkin'.

No sooner thru yon gardin gate
  Ah faced a sea o' weedin',
Gret wavin' stocks o' giant docks
  Wer gluttoned wi' good feedin',
Ah'd ramblin' roots an' twinin' shoots,
  Heigh climbers an' low creepers,
Ah thowt -- "Owd mon, iv this goos on
  Tha'll need a *theawsan* reapers!"

An' slinkin' to mi snoozin' nook
  A vicious mood befell mi,
Owd Digger cum, an' sed, "By Gum,
  Just hearken wel Ah tell thi;
Tha'rt like a fool 'at runs fro' t' school
  An' connot run no faster,
Mi heart fair bleeds to see good seeds
  O'erwhelmed wi' ronk disaster!"

"Iv *tha* wer in a hotbed trapped,
  Wi' fella mortals seethin',
Wi' scarce a cup of owt to sup --
  An' th' air too feawl fer breathin',
To sink below this weight o' woe
  An' rot on t' lowest level ...
Neaw cornta see? Them plants'll dee,
  Tha lazy idle devil!"

He lashed mi wi' a furious tongue
Until mi brain wer' reelin',
Ah'd no defence -- it's commonsense --
'At plants have fella-feelin',
Like us, they strive to keep alive,
Tho' pinched an' poor wi' givin',
Theyn face an' form to feight life's storm,
An' th' urge to goo on livin'.

Ah sent fer Digger yusterday,
Fer weeks we'd never spokken ...
He cast his ee'n o'er t' gardin scene,
He smiled, an' t' spell wer' brokken;
"By Gum", he sed, "By Gum, owd chum,
No cabbages grew finer,
Thi peighs an' beans, an' oa thi greens,
Ar twice as big as mine ar!"

THE PEOPLE'S PEACE

Shall we again make light of victory?
Then we, no less, the common enemy!
Once more, in full possession of the field --
Achieve the means and then so meekly yield?
Or shall we, now, the lasting peace devise
For shocked and vacant minds, and sightless eyes?
That never more shall nations stand aghast,
Their vaunted symbol flags at limp half-mast,
Some of their colours ev'ry vestige drained
Some, mud-spattered, torn, and bloody stained;
While man, a sheep, by shepherd statesmen led,
Is counted in the fold of countless dead,
Yet man shall learn, ere warring systems cease,
The people's war demands a people's peace!

SONG AT SUNSET

(English Version)

I like to tramp my native hills,
    When evening shades are showing,
The lovely day has cooled away,
    At sunset's rosy glowing,
When crimson charms -- tinge upland farms
    With magic tints and shading,
And blushing, sweeps o'er harvest heaps,
    In twilight shadows facing.

Refrain: My footpath leads to yonder height
    Where fondest fancies play,
    No artist yet, -- with colours bright
    Could paint the dying day.

Fair Autumn blends her mellow hues
    With lightsome fairy fingers,
Beneath the spread of Heaven's bed
    The lovely landscape lingers,
And in a flight of sheer delight
    A skylark anthem raises,
And every trill of choral skill
    Is singing sunset praises.

As lustrous clouds diffuse the sun,
    Red-beamed to bathe deep valleys,
So wispy oars -- on sky-line shores
    Dip down from gold-lined galleys;
They gently ride the sunset tide --
    With other cloud-ships sailing,
In stately quest of harbour west,
    With dappled wake-waves trailing.

But now the night starts shading o'er
    Those bright-brushed beams of glory,
Time's fond farewell bids nature tell
    Her age-old bedtime story;
Day dimly files thro' Heaven's aisles,
    Where parting rays are glancing,
And sprinkled dew will gleam anew --
    When dawn again comes dancing.

TRICKS O' T' TRADE

"Tha tells mi, young tinker, tha'rt just leavin' t' school,
  If that's oal tha's larnt lad, tha'rt nobbut a fool,
Wi' that sooart o' thinkin' tha'll soon bi in t' cart,
  It's when tha starts werkin' thi larnin'll start; ,
To mek a fair livin' in th' hard world today
  Thers theawsands who'll stop thi, or stan' i' thi way,
An' whether Dame Fortune deals di'mond or spade,
  Tha'll ha' to get busy an' larn tricks o' t' trade".

"Neaw t' question arises lad, what wilta be?
  Tha'rt sturdy an' strong, independent an' free,
Thi forebears -- tho lackin' material wealth --
  Could stalk wi' oal t' skill of an owd tomcat's stealth;
To hunt -- or bi hunted, i' dell or i' den,
  They mostly succeeded -- an' would do agen,
Today, in a modern moore civilised glade
  It's still t' law o' t' jungle to larn t' tricks o' t' trade".

"Tho ne'er born to t' riches o' th' heigher degree,
  Tha'rt little worse off lad, fer owt Ah con see,
Tha might ha' bin pampered, an' sickly an' frail,
  But then, havin' roughed it, tha'rt hard as a nail,
Tha might ha' bin awkerd, or haughty an' cowd,
  But tha'rt gradely an' humble i' t' *commoners* fowd,
An' so fer life's battle tha stans on parade
  Wi' vict'ry to him who con larn t' tricks o' t' trade".

"A lad wi' ambition con still mek his mark
    Wi' lots o' good luck, an' a deal o' hard wark,
On life's lofty meawntain tha'll wax an' tha'll wane
    Like monny a million who've struggled i' vain;
Aim heigh if tha'rt aimin' -- tha'll find it'll pay,
    Tha'll never reych t' summit wi' aimin' hofe way,
Strive on lad, keep climbin' an' don't bi dismayed,
    But just keep on gooin' an' larn t' tricks o' t' trade".

"Thru good times an' bad times, liv' mod'rate an' plain,
    An' ne'er let thi stomach dictate to thi brain,
Fer once tha's full-feasted i' luxury's cheere,
    Tha'll feel twice as hungry when *poverty's* theer;
Bi thrifty, an' build up on what tha con spare,
    An' never bi greedy for moore nor thi share,
An' owd goat con thrive pikin' t'scantiest blade --
    Bicose he wer 'prenticed to larn t' tricks o' t' trade".

"Wodever tha does lad, get this i' thi yed --
    Tha'll ne'er mek much progress wi' lyin' i' bed,
Get up an' see t' sunrise -- thers no grander seet --
    Ner life's true perspective i' natcheral leet;
Bi grateful to Heaven, gie thanks, ner suppose
    Thers no bigger devil ner t' devil tha knows!
In't leet o' success lad, thers monny a shade,
    An' that way, Ah dar say, tha'll larn t' tricks o' t' trade".

THE BLACKSMITH'S LAMENT

The smithy stands -- a Pennine pile forlorn,
  A rugged grime-stained relic tempest-torn,
Its fissured walls pour putrid dust-streams grey,
  As crushing Time grinds on its crumbling way;
Along the sagging roof-trees crudely hewn,
  The sliding sandstone slates are sadly strewn,
Yet, still within, the lusty smith attends
  His tuneful toil, where metal-music blends.

Skilled master of a practice long pursued,
  His craftsman blood fired by his fathers crude,
The blacksmith smites the gleaming spark-drenched bars,
  While forth cascades a show'r of steely stars;
Thus has it been for generations gone,
  The old tradition passed from sire to son,
Each life a link, forged in the far-famed line,
  According to the ruling sire's design.

But fate hath claims whom none shall disallow,
  The smithy, and the smith, face ruin now,
The action of Time's acid -- long delayed --
  Corroding, cracks the coffers of his trade;
No gleam of hope illumes the dull-browed day,
  Alas! where progress strikes -- old customs stray,
New power throbs with wild exultant roar,
  Replacing that which was, and now's no more.

He turns about to view the confines drear,
  With more than faint suspicion of a tear,
His clouded sight forbids but scant survey,
  Since objects dearly loved now prompt dismay;
While rusted ruin flaunts his shining schemes,
  So leisured life induces idle dreams,
Now like a haunting tune of tender turn,
  His mind is made to grieve -- his heart to yearn.

No king, deposed, had suffered such dismay,
  Nor one who'd held a more unrivalled sway,
Than he who stands forebodingly to brood --
  His banishment, in sullen solitude.
For where the hissing forge-fire glistered white,
  Emblazoning the darling shades with light,
Now, dying embers droop their fading eyes,
  The ancient bellows stilled -- restrains its sighs.

From mem'ry's sheath each arrow of his aim,
  Unerring, flies to prideful days of fame,
And drowsy visions lull his simple mind,
  As ghostly equines endless circles wind.
A charming cavalcade of tossing manes,
  Of clattering hoofs that tune the stone-strewn lanes,
To greet old friends, in this -- the social round,
  He nods, for nodding pleasantries abound.

Come carriage teams in superb graces versed,
  Immaculately groomed on May the first,
Sleek stately steeds, all newly shod and spry,
  The lowly plodding plough-horse passing by;
Come pondrous shires with heavy measured tread,
  They, lion-maned, were lambs the children led,
Attendant he, on prim, and princely proud,
  The broken, the dispirited, the cowed.

Dear yesterday, though long thy years between,
   How near -- each distant recollected scene,
Sweet pictures from the panoramic past,
   Reincarnated in the mind-mould vast;
How soothing to the soul of dire despair,
   How moving to the heartache centred there,
O cruel fate, to leave him thus bereft,
   Unequalled in thine annals -- heartless theft.

Within the fold, midst life of modest mien,
   The House of God still dominates the scene,
A fine church-gate, whose scriptured symbols placed --
   Cathedral splendours in a rural waste;
The churchyard tombs, with iron scroll-work spired,
   Who laboured here loved every moment hired,
Thus skilled, he stubborn clings to Art's brief shaft,
   The living artist of a dying craft.

The upland farmers, turned to modern trends,
   Bring trifling tasks, as sympathetic friends,
In all their councils still acclaim his worth,
   And mindful of his sorrows quell their mirth;
Beneath the brooding canopy of cares,
   To recognise his tragedy as theirs,
Meet eagerly, an ever modest fee,
   Nor dare his wrath for despised charity.

And so his world draws to its bitter close,
   His livelihood -- to stupified repose,
Malignant growths of progress now accrue,
   To doom the era of the iron shoe;
Yet, works he wrought shall unremitting wage
   Mute war, on frailties of the future age,
When craftsmen yet unborn, attend at last,
   To marvel at the metals of the past.

SONG O' BACUP

Ah've yerd folk say 'at Bacup Teawn
Wer inside eawt an' upside deawn,
Ah've yerd 'em scoff, an' laff to scorn --
This quaint owd teawn wheer they wer born.

Chorus: Ha! Ha! Ha! He! He! He!
Owd Bacup is the teawn fer me;
Ha! Ha! Ha! He! He! He!
It's here ah'll live an' here ah'll dee.

Neaw folk who co'll a spade a spade
Say Bacup's last place God e'er made,
No wonder then 'at strangers grin,
It's queerest shop they'n ever sin.

Eawr railway station, understand --
Is happen th' only one in t' land
Wheer trains con cum' an' trains con goo --
But wheer they'n never yet run throo.

In Bacup Teawn yo'll heawses find
Built in to th' hills 'at rise behind,
When passin' snobs -- aboon heawse tops --
Con luk stroight deawn eawr chim'ly pots.

Up Ratchdal Road th' owd "Empire" stands
Wi' two greawnd floores on diff'rent hands,
Neaw Newchurch Road leads up to t' proof --
An' Ratchdal Road bears deawn fro' t' roof.

Eawr famous swimmers sarved us true,
Eawr singers an' musicians, too.
An' Bacup's famous still, ah know --
As t' place wheer nettles winnot grow.

Inside eawr hills black di'monds shine,
   Tho' t' miners here don't goo deawn t' mine,
They allus say -- to get to t' coile --
   They travel up yon coile-pit hoile.

Agen'st eawr noble grain it rubs
   To find fer ev'ry church -- two pubs,
Wheer once churchwardens feelin' stale
      Could sing like brids on common ale.

St. Swithen's day makes Bacup smile,
   Fer here we measure rain bi t' mile,
Eawr weekly rainfo'll easy beats --
   That farce o' forty days an' neets.

Then let us do eawr Teawnship preawd,
   Let's sing its praises long and leawd,
Cling tight to t' teawn wheer yo wer born,
   It might get swilled away to-morn.

LAUREL -- CROWNED

She cherished long-loved legacies
   With questing thought,
Consorted with sweet harmonies,
   And nobly wrought --
In measures dainty and refined,
   The fragrant treasures of her mind;
Profusely, from her bounteous bower,
   Proud poesy burst into flower,
Until, inspired by vistas fair,
   Pale fancies blossomed orchids rare;
Life's pulsing pleasure, time-fulfilled,
   The tuneful grove is deathly stilled . . .
Farewell, sweet songstress laurel-crowned,
   Well tended was thy earthly ground!
Grant patriot zeal its prideful place,
   Mark well her constancy - and trace --
Her fleur-de-lis and emblem dear,
   The Red Rose, bloom of Lancashire!

OWD WEYVER LASS

Fer eighty yer hoo's sowjered on,
Wi' brush an' shovel, pot an' pon,
Hoo's lavished eawt a lifetime's skill
Fer t' maisters deawn at t' cotton mill;
Thru slump an' boom, thru foul an' fair,
Gret faith eawtshone her dark despair,
'Til neaw contentment com's at last
To wekken her fro' t' neetmare past.

In th' early heawrs o' wint'ry dark,
When life seemed nowt but bed an' wark,
Poor bits o' childer trailed thru t' gloom
To t' weyvin' shed -- an' t' clatterin' loom;
To slave in t' world o' waarp an' weft,
(Hoo's lots o' bitter mem'ries left!)
But time relents -- soft smiles re-trace --
To mellow her long-suff'rin' face.

Hoo'll sigh no more fer t' days long gone,
When t' fam'ly's fulsom' porridge-pon
Wer browt to t' boil bi neet an' day,
Fer supper, brekfast, dinner, tay;
Wi' lobscouse happen once a week,
Or sometimes -- chep beef -- tough as teak.
Hoo's chowed som' gristle in her time,
An' thowt them marra-booans prime!

These pampered puppet-folk today
A coorse like hers could never stay;
They'n progressed far, an' yet Ah feel --
They don't know when they're doin weel!
Wild youth rebels: its com' to pass
Too little wark fer too much brass.
Preawd Rome once fell fer such as this,
We're perched on th' edge o' th' same abyss!

If Ah could have a medal struck
Fer life-long sacrifice an' pluck,
Ah'd symbolise in t' brode design
Her deathless spirit -- an' divine,
'At never yet admit defeat --
Wel hoo could stand upon her feet,
To read:- "Forever in her debt. . ."
Forgive, owd lass, an' try forget.

CALLIN' OAL CATS

N eaw som' folk keep parrots, pet dogs, an' oal that,
    At eawr heawse we're keepin' a big ginger cat,
When t' wife's mother browt us this wild cat accursed
    Hoo'd nobbut just landed when t'shoppin' bag burst,
It sprang like a tiger, an' struck eawt at me,
    An' splashed a red tram-line fro' t' thigh to mi knee,
An' t' wife went an' stroked it an' called it "My lamb" --
    Wel, my leg o' mutton felt sticky like jam.

Wi' these jungle jumpers, Ah ne'er could agree,
    Ah don't like yon cat, an' it doesn't like me,
But wimmen con handle such crayturs wi' ease,
    They'n so much in common wi' wild cats tha sees,
If Ah bend to stroke it, it viciously strikes,
    Wi' teeth sharp as needles, an' feet full o' spikes,
A female Sir Lancelot, it's fearless an' bowd,
    An' carries moore lances nor oal t' knights of owd.

Ah land whom at taytime -- t' cat sleeps in th' armcheere,
    Ah dro up to t' table an' t' cat pops up theer,
It taps at mi leg just as much as to say --
    Ah'm givin' fair warnin' -- Ah' ve waited oal day,
Hoo gies it some catmeyt, but my meyt coms slow,
    It's not as Ah'm bothered -- just sommat to know . . .
Hoo sarves mi two chops, but Ah rarely get both
    Fer t' truth is, eawr Ginger is faster bi th' hofe.

As most cats get frisky bifoore a big storm
    Depend on 't 'at eawr cat'll run true to form,
It chases it' tail on a mad circular tour,
    An' springs oal reawnd th' heawse never once touchin' t' floore,
Last Sunday, it plagued mi fer t' best part o' t' day,
    Kept pokin' mi paper an' runnin' away,
Ah struck back wel t'wife wer upsteers mekkin' t'beds,
    It turned an' it ripped Sunday paper to shreds.

Ah've trained lots o' dogs, but Ah haven't a clue
    Fer claws sharp as razors, an' teeth 'at bite through,
Ah towd t' wife, "Ah'm beawn to get rid o' this cat!"
    Hoo flared up an' sheawted -- "Mi mother browt that,
Tha'rt same as oal yo'r breed -- tha'rt noan gradely reight,
    Thi thinkin's oal twisted -- it's never bin straight!
Eawr Ginger's like my side, that's easy to tell
    Thank God it's bin larnt to luk after itsel!"

Hoo snapped an' hoo snorted an' pulled a long face,
An' her fist swung an arc like a drum major's mace,
"Fer t'last time", hoo sheawted, "Ah'm tellin' thi flat
If tha lays a finger on my little cat . . .
Tha's browt it oal on wi' thi cruel neglect,
Ah've ne'er sin thi stroke it, what dosta expect?
It's shifted mi mice, an' it's comp'ny fer me --
So hands off eawr Ginger, or else Ah'll shift thee!".

T'cat glinted thru slanted slits crafty an' green,
Wel t' wife's risin' temper browt fire to her ee'n,
An' hoo ranted an' raved an' med such a gret row
'At Ah thowt it moore seemly fer me to sing low;
Her so'prano shrikin' so flattens mi bass
Thers times when Ah think hoo's in th' aria class,
Fact, fiction, an' fancy, hoo works into t' scheme
Until Ah'm fair weary o' t' martyrdom theme.

When t' visitin' parson sat deawn in t' cat's nook,
He prayed fro' his heart, an' he quoted t' Good Book,
"O Lord high in heaven", he'd started to tell,
"Deliver us safely from . . . 'Oh, Jezabel'!!"
Eawr Ginger had struck him, he grimaced wi' pain,
"Dear friends do forgive me, good-bye once again!"
Ah couldn't stop grinnin' -- neaw isn't it strange
When somb'dy else suffers it meks a nice change.

Com' bedtime, Ah mek a rare target in t' dark
An Ginger's a marksman fer sharpshootin' wark,
When Ah tek mi shoon off it springs into seet,
It knows 'at Ah've corns -- an' Ah daren't use mi feet,
It scythes at mi legs as Ah swing 'em i' bed
An' when it's bin vicious Ah've sin 'em run red,
An' what price my vict'ry tho t' tiger bi tamed --
If t' tamer geet helplessly crippled, or maimed?

So tell mi yo critics, wheer would yo' begin?
When Ah've drivven t' cat eawt hoo skrikes -- "Let it in,
It's rainin', eawr Ginger's fair soppin' Ah'm sure,
An' then com' to bed, fer it's midneet or moore!"
Last neet as Ah'r dreamin' o' t' fox-huntin' chase,
A rain-sodden cat-tail coom lotherin' mi face,
Ah felt so disgusted Ah shifted mi shop --
T' cat went under t' covers, an' Ah slept on t' top!

OPEN CAST

Nostalgia-fed, my loyal heart long yearned.
  Until at last, my eager feet returned,
To childhood scenes of happy carefree days,
  Where now, bewilderment and shock amaze;
My ears assailed with deep pulsating sound,
  Whose awesome shock-waves shake the very ground,
With churned-up muddy acres limp beneath,
  I walk -- a stranger on my native heath.

From fire-clay shelves along the black-seamed hill,
  The giant juggernauts disgorge their greedy fill,
They rive the earth with flashing steel-tipped claws,
  And yawning, metal-mouthed, ply clashing jaws;
Deep-dented caterpillar tracks are cast,
  Where mastodons once trod in ages past, ,
These few brief weeks of demon force deployed,
  The wealth and bloom of centuries destroyed.

With aching heart and anguished mind allied,
  I only know my grass-green world has died --
That darkling death, for which, I now proclaim --
  My deep disgust, my sense of shock and shame;
This once-lush pastureland my fathers farmed,
  Whose white-washed farmsteads milk-rich cattle charmed,
This land, o'erwhelmed, sinks to its miry fate,
  For min'ral wealth to briefly scintillate.

And now alas! disconsolate I mope,
  And thro' this monstrous morass grieve and grope,
Tumultuous then, my condemnation ran --
  Of vile and vengeful vandalistic man!
I close my eyes, inducing trance-like spell,
  To live again the past I loved so well,
In sightless concentration *blindly see* --
  Those dear sweet vistas of fond memory.

HEIGH ESTATE

(Revised Version)

No moore fer me, yon draughty heawse
Wherein Ah used to grunt an' greawse --
Ah've flit to t' "Klondyke New Estate"
An' christened th' heawse on t' garden gate,
"Sol Sunnyside", it ses on theer,
Ah'll ha' no common numbers here;
Ah'm livin' neaw i' luxury's lap,
Wi' ev'rything (but ale) on tap.

Ther's fifty families oal towd --
Bin drafted in fro' th' owd slum fowd.
Ther faces shine wi' honest pride,
Wi' t' childer's necks on t' shadda side;
Neaw if Aw tell you -- dunno laff --
Som' connot weysh, they'n coyle i' th' bath,
We're preawd as punch, an' full o' pluck --
Contented just like pigs i' muck.

Tek Missis Munn, at th' end o' th' row,
Heaw hoo's made yon garden grow;
Oalready, hoo's a pile o' tins --
Yo couldn't shove i' twenty bins;
Hoo's salmon, sardine, pear, an' chunk,
Ah've never sin such bloomin' junk,
Hoo's soot an' cinders, clinkers too --
Oal piled up eawtside "Ash View".

I' woms like eawrs, wi gadgets smart
Yo're wark's hofe done bifoore yo start,
Just press a switch -- plug in to t' main
Or turn a tap, or -- pull a chain:
An' then it's handy, don't yo think --
To kneyd yo're dough i' th' white-tile sink.
By gow! it's som' an' diff'rent here
At thirteen an' a tanner cleear.

Of oal mi neighbours, noan are blest,
Like Missis Gregg, at "Cockpit Crest",
Her felly keeps a tooathrie hens,
Inside two wire-net chicken pens,
It's puzzled me fer monny a day,
Wheer t' nest-box is fer th' hens to lay,
They sleep in th' heawse, Ah know fer sure,
'Cos th' hen-hoyle's cut in t' cubbert doore.

When scandal stirs eawr motley throng,
Just harken Misses Moody's tongue;
Hoo coms an' whispers -- "Han yo yerd --
When Widda Wesley weds her third?"
An' tho' hoo never leaves a card,
Wi' t' compliments o' Scotland Yard,
Hoo knows as much, an' could yo' look --
Ah'll bet hoo keep a Doomsday Book.

In t' biggest heawse on' th' avenue,
Nine childer form a fam'ly crew,
They'n oal bin drilled an' weel rehearsed,
In t' mealtime rule o't' "yungest first".
Com bedtime, mother mends ther togs,
Wel feyther ceawnts ther little clogs.
Thers no misfits, fro' th' heigh to t' low,
What's tight fer Freddie fits yung Joe!

A six-foot delphchap rents "Rocklee",
If looks mean owt -- he'll never dee,
By gum! yon felly has a twist,
He eits his meals -- hand o'er fist;
Wi' two fine sons for table mates,
They need no dog to lick ther plates;
In th' "Alecan Arms", th' owd chap foots bill,
But sups a quart to t' lads a gill.

Another sowl fer strong brewd sup
Is yon 'at wed John Tommy Tupp.
Hoo teks her drink like soil teks rain,
It's just like teemin' 't deawn a drain;
Wel poor John Tommy slaves in t' pit
Hoo's gettin' boozed on "gin an' it",
Hoo staggers wom -- a pint-pot queen
To t' dust an' dirt at "Dazzle Dene".

In t' march o' progress, Sammy Stub
Is t' President o' th' Henpeck Club,
His lecture theer -- (on tamin' shrews)
Appeared in t' "Lion Tamers' News",
Wi' t' trainin' fork an' sharp command,
He geet 'em eitin' eawt o' th' hand,
But when t' Club parrot screeamed – "Sam!"
He landed wom bifoore his tram.

Just opposite, lives Johnny Twist,
A reight sincere Salvationist,
When noisy neighbours feight an' fratch
This Daniel dars to lift ther latch;
In answer to som' frenzied howl,
He rushes in to save his sowl,
But when gret pots an' pons are thrown --
He rushes eawt to save his own!

Wel, sich is life in eawr domain,
We'n nowt to loise, an' oal to gain,
We'n little brass -- an' still less gowd,
But what we han, we're beawnt to howd;
Yo' credutors in t' bowler hats,
'At run yo'rsels as thin as lats --
If t' Government should stop eawr dole,
Yo'll ha' to punce us eawt -- that's oal!

(All the characters in the foregoing verses are purely imaginary)

OWD SAMMY'S BRASS

Owd Sammy wer deein', twer plain to bi sin,
An' yet wel he're living' he wouldn't give in;
He'd plenty o' money, had Sammy, but still --
He're allus too stubborn to make eawt a will;
Wi' monny a claimant to snatch his estate
He'd hearken to nob'dy, but goo his own gate.
An' neaw, when he're lyin' at death's gristly doore
His relatives thowt they'd bi seein' him moore.

Wi' ee'n dry as tinder, (fer no tears wer shed)
They panicked, an' clustered reawnd owd Sammy's bed.
Ther yeds geet together, an' wise ceawncil spoke --
"If Sammy waint *write* let's hope 'at he'll *toak!*"
They fratched, an' they frittered away o' his brass,
A process 'at cost extra coppers fer t' gas;
Fer noteven t' bowdest ther subject could broach --
Wel Sammy wer rattlin' away like a coach.

Fer theer in a coma he slumbered an' snoored
Wel they wer debatin' on t' "full sum assured".
He'd allus bin keaurful, ne'er wastin' a stitch,
They see'd ev'ry prospect o' strikin' it rich;
An' seein' as heaw they'd bi stoppin' a while
They med a gret fire, an' geet watter on t' bile.
They'd have him to weysh, aye, an' lay him away,
But just neaw his chamber lukked cheerful an' gay.

They toaked o'er his fauseness -- his life-long mistrust --
O' bankrupted bankers when banks used to bust.
His brass med no int'rest, accoordin' to som' --
He'd said he'd had th' int'rest o' savin 't awhom;
They searched heigh an' lowe, even tappin' on t' woles
A-huntin' his fortune an' scrattin' like moles,
Still Sammy slept on wi' his secret secure
Tho som' said his mattress lukked bulky fer sure!

In t' mid'st of o' t' rattle an' th' hullabaloo,
Owd Sammy coom conscious -- tho' nobody knew ...
He hearkened a while fer his yers wer still quick,
An' what they wer sayin' fair med him feel sick;
But like an owd fox, slinkin' softly an' sly --
(Ere snatchin' his feast) has to eit humble pie,
Owd Sammy lay doggo an' bided his time,
His body worn eawt, but his brain in it prime.

Like hunderd-yard runners excited an' tense,
They hung reawnd his bedside to wait i' suspense;
Brute fooarce an' rib-ratchin' effort won t' day,
An' nearest o' kin wer shoved furthest away.
Ther tempers wer risin' an' t' temp'rature too,
They boiled an' they swet in a swelterin' queue;
Just then, Sammy stirred, an' they yerd him declare --
"Nod even a furnice con burn beawt fresh air!"

Neaw som' flushed deep scarlett an' inwardly quailed,
Wel others moore freetened retreated an' paled;
"Oh aye", muttered Sammy, "Ah know why yo're here,
But never yo' bother -- yo'll o' get yo're sheere!
It's wheer do Ah keep it, yo're wantin' to know?
Shuzheaw fast Ah tod yo' yo'd think Ah wer slow,
Ha' patience a minute, an' do as Ah bid,
Just foller mi finger -- fer that's wheer its hid!"

Excited an' tremblin' ther hearts i' ther shoon,
He pointed to t' fireplace, an' altered his tune
"To blazes wi' money if that's heaw it went,
Neaw just let mi tell yo' ther'll not be a cent!
Thers bin a cremation -- a funeral pyre.
A fortune up t' chimley, yo'n set it afire!
Ah'm tekkin' it wi' mi, an' leavin' yo' beawt ..."
An' smilin' his last, poor owd Sammy passed eawt.

RICE PUDDIN'

Mi parents were two patriots unhonoured an' unsung,
   Who brought up several childer, broad o' back an' strong o' lung;
We lived, like little feightin' cocks an' feightin' we were able,
   Fro' fore to rear to rip an' tear ut everything on t' table,
An' well mi fayther struggled to maintain eawr clooas an' shoon,
   Mi mother wer' a Trojan, allus mekkin' stuff in t' th' o'on,
To visualize th' owd days agen, Ah connot help but grin,
   When mi mother made rice puddin' an' we used to feight for t' skin.

Unlike your fancy families o' crest or monogram,
   Eawr only seal o' excellence wer' set on pots o' jam.
We stuck to traycle butties like a babby sticks to t' dummy,
   To thus exist each podgy fist wer' t' rammin' rod for t' tummy;
An' if we'd no impressive names, we boasted other angles,
   We'd each a classic Grecian nose, complete with Roman-candles,
Eawr social climbin' relatives wer' never nowt a-kin,
   When mi mother made rice puddin' an' we used to feight for t' skin.

Should luxuries be limited upon eawr table toppin',
   Woe to him ut had a cough, an' couldn't eat for coughin',
We raised no Premadona, but we had a singin' kettle,
   Which sung o' tay, all t' live-long day, in t' sweetest tones o' mettle.
Poor Ma wer' so considerate, for this, Ah'll give her credit,
   "Goo easy wi' that table-cloth, your fayther hasna read it!"
'Twer one thing preychin' silence, quite another quellin' t' din,
   When mi mother made rice puddin' an' we used to feight for t' skin.

Heaw we pined for bakin' days, when extra special feeds,
   Wer' tackled wi' gret gusto, an' at record breykin' speeds,
Eawr Willie, being th' owdest lad, an' havin' t' biggest belly,
   Could eyt his weight in butcher's meight, an' then fill up wi' jelly!
Of all the things we tucked away, you never saw such gluttons,
   Each waistcoat wer a catapult for shootin' off its buttons,
But wheer we'd loist a button, we could allus stick a pin,
   When mi mother made rice puddin' an' we used to feight for t' skin.

Sometimes, due to lazy o'on, eawr dinner used to dally,
   Until, eawr achin' stomacks rowlled like thunder deawn a valley,
We'd sniff an' snarl impatiently like heawnd dogs unreleased,
   'Til puddin', Aye, an' t' taytoe pie, eawr appetite's appeased;

Neaw, had we tasted famine when this war mad world wer' queuein',
We'd have eyten t' full week's weshin' wi' a bag o' dolly-blue in.
We'd have swopped a hundred cig-cards for a dimpled double chin,
When mi mother made rice puddin' an' we used to feight for t' skin.

But time rowls on, an' childer grow, 'til parents see that day,
Th' owd whom looks like a restaurant, when t' courters com' to tay,
Wheerat, eawr hungry brotherhood can sit their prim precillas,
An' celebrate their heigh estate, an' eyt like gret gorillas.
You talk abeawt your fancy cooks, there'll never be another,
To make a better puddin' ner mi dear departed mother,
Long live these happy memories in th' minds o' kith an' kin,
When mi mother made rice puddin' an' we used to feight for t' skin.

SIMPLE PSYCHOLOGY

Ah'm owd an' Ah'm ailin'
Ah'm frail an' Ah'm failin'
Mi poor legs are trailin'
Ah connot last long.

Tu far gone fer curin'
But weel worth insurin',
Ah jus' keep endurin'
Ah never wer strong.

Mi doctor's debatin'
Wi' t' surgeon, 'at's waitin'
Tu start operatin'
Wi' t' razor-edge knife?

To Doctor Stilleter --
Ah'm sendin' a letter,
Ah never felt better
Yo'n gi'en mi new life!!!

TH' OWD FOLKS

Ah'd like to see th'owd folk weel treated,
Who've long bin dealt sich shabby deals,
It isn't they've getten near-seeted,
They cornt see so mich at their meals;
For t' pension is still nobbut meagre,
An' th' heawse rents are ever so heigh,
An' mony a lanlord luks eager
To get oal he can eawt o' t' keigh!

Awft, after a lifetime's hard labour,
Th'owd craytures han little to show,
Dire circumstance drives like a slaver,
An' t' poorest o't' poor ought to know;
Fer neawm when they getten past toilin',
An' drained o' their energies dry,
Th' State helps 'em to keep t' kettle boilin'
An' hopes 'at they've somewheer to lie.

Like sowjers who feight a grim sortie,
Eawr actions are teed to a time
Ther's some, wer' surreawnded at forty
When just in their best feightin' prime;
Wi' no chance to gie full-time battle
To save fer a helpless owd age,
Ther still scrapin' coppers to sattle -
Debts, born of a starvation wage.

The best praychers on t' practice o' livin',
Shude know heaw to give an' to tek,
It's painful to see one hand givin'
An' t'other hand snatchin' it beck;
Preawed folk seek no charity favours,
(An' t' poorest are t' preawdest o' these,)
Sufficiency - spurnin' life's labours,
Just covers a mon when he dees!

It's sarten if Darby shude sicken,
It's nobbut cowd comfort fer Joan,
No sooner is one on 'em stricken,
Ner' t'other luks haggard an' dro'n;
Wi' canker an' hardship in t' body,
They looken so pinched an' so frail,
To spin eawt ther State-granted shoddy,
They've nowt left but courage to fail.

We're oal human buildin's o' feeling,
We'n th'option to oppen th' heart's doore,
But som' are so lofty in t' ceilin'
They "Luk deawn" on folks nearer floore.
It's heigh time th'owd structures wer tended,
Ther crumblin' feawndations made seawnd,
It's time t' social system wer ended,
For one far moore hansomely creawnd.

Then let us determine to leeten,
Oal t' burdens we'n forced 'em to bear,
Bring eawt generous justice to sweeten
Th' existence injustice turned seawr;
To my mind, ther's nowt could be apter,
Ner nowt no moore welcome Ah'm sure,
Than addin' a new cheerful chapter,
To th' annals ut poorest o' t' poor.

TO A PENNINE SPRING

If I should live for *ten score years and ten,*
   I scarce could hope to see the like again.
By chance divine, I waited on thy birth,
   To see thee gush -- a spring -- from Mother earth;
How well recalled the magic of that hour,
   When Heav'n invested me with supreme pow'r,
A guileless boy, my wonder rampant ran,
   I was a God -- before I was a man!

Up thro' that rock-strewn clough of dear delight,
   My rebel feet had raced in truant flight,
Until, far-spent, and feeling heat-oppressed,
   I languished on a tufted upland crest;
While drooping cattle drowsed that sultry day,
   The plover wheeled his dizzy air-display,
Here, lilting lark-song charmed the summer scene,
   And vivid flowers splashed the verdant green.

When suddenly, from somewhere in the ground,
   I heard the faintest bubbling liquid sound,
My idling penknife aimlessly had traced --
   Deep patterns on the spot I had defaced;
A tiny muddy trickle first appeared,
   Full joyously it danced -- and slowly cleared,
A minute fountain, spilling new-born spray,
   As mutely I upon the greensward lay.

Now, in Time's annals, fifty years have sped,
   Fast flows the stream where once a silver thread,
And still I dream -- and oft re-live anew --
   The rapture of that wondrous day's debut;
When God's own floodgates opened unto me,
   Who knows? Did I supply some vital key?
A guileless boy, in Heaven's bounteous plan . . .
   I was a God - before I was a man!

AH DID WHEN AH COULD

(Believed to be one of the last poems written by "H.C.", and found among his papers after his death)

Th'owd felly coms o'er mi,
Ah'm failin' ut last,
Ah'm noan long fer this world,
Ah'm gooin' whom fast;
An' tho' Ah'm not claimin'
Ah did o' Ah should,
Ah'd just like to tell yo',
Ah did when Ah could.

Ah've slaved an' Ah've sweltered
'Til swet swilled mi brow,
Fer my trouble wer, --Ah
Could never say "Nowe!"
Ah've delved an' Ah've rooted,
Life's worst knocks Ah've stood,
But allus Ah tell yo'
Ah did when Ah could.

On monny a "pay-day"
(Yo've guessed reight, no doubt!)
Ah allus excelled, when
Ah were werkin' fer nowt!
Mi breet schemes fer t'future
Hav' bin nipt in t' bud,
It's no use repinin' --
Ah did when Ah could.

Th' owd engine kept slowin'
'Til summat went snap,
An' stern fate condemned mi
To live wi' "th' owd chap",
Nostalgia com's surgin'
I' memories' flood,
Wi' t' sorry admission --
Ah did when Ah could.

An' one o' these fine days,
They'll fotch mi feet first,
As stiff as a jawm-stone,
An' shove mi in th' "hearst";
When happen -- somebody --
'At's long understood,
'Ull freely acknowledge --
HE DID WHEN HE COULD.

FAIR MAID O' ROSSENDALE

(This ballad was originally written in Standard English by Mr. D. S. Goodbrand of Manchester, and rewritten at his request in Lancashire dialect by Harry Craven. The idea belongs to Mr. Goodbrand, in whose book "Odin's Mead", published by St. Ann's Press in 1969, the verses were first published. But the actual dialect is Mr. Craven's, and appears in Bacup Miscellany by kind permission of Mr. Goodbrand.)

When I wer young an' in mi prime
The open road wer my way,
Fer wark Ah never had the time,
An' so Ah tramped the highway;
One day did pass a gradely lass,
A-cyclin' deawn to t' factoree --
Twer yon fair maid o' Rossendale,
Yon fair maid o' Rossendale,
Yon fair maid o' Rossendale
Who cast her spell on me.

Hoo coom next morn on bird-song borne
Fer t' woods areawnd wer ringin',
Ah sensed -- an' faced -- oal dire distaste
Her flashin' een wer flingin':
"Ah'll ha' no tramp nor idle scamp".
An' off hoo peddled flauntinlee --
Twer yon fair maid o' Rossendale,
Yon fair maid o' Rossendale,
Yon fair maid o' Rossendale
Who cast her spell on me.

Ah mopped mi brow an' made a vow
To stop mi rough wayfarin',
No moore to laze but mend mi ways
An' live a life worth sharin';
Fer t'lass wer rare beyond compare,
E'en tho' hoo snubbed mi haughtilee --
Twer yon fair maid o' Rossendale,
Yon fair maid o' Rossendale,
Yon fair maid o' Rossendale
Who cast her spell on me.

As a roadman rough an' mighty tough
Ah tackled hard wark gaily,
To swet an' strain an' laff at pain
If Ah could see her daily;
Tho' never born to scan wi' scorn,
Ah felt hoo scorned mi low degree --
Twer yon fair maid o' Rossendale,
Yon fair maid o' Rossendale,
Yon fair maid o' Rossendale
Who cast her spell on me.

As a farmlad next wi' muscles flexed
Ah hoped Ah'd soon impress her,
But Ah blocked her way wi' a looad o' hay
Which did nowt but distress her:
Hoo tossed her yed which plainly said,
"Tha's made mi late fer t' factoree" --
Twer yon fair maid o' Rossendale,
Yon fair maid o' Rossendale,
Yon fair maid o' Rossendale
Who cast her spell on me.

As a postman then Ah tried agen
To breyk her stubborn fetters,
Ah knocked post-haste an' allus placed
Big kisses on her letters:
"Ah'll wed", hoo said, "no dunderyed",
An' yet Ah thowt hoo smiled at me --
Twer yon fair maid o' Rossendale,
Yon fair Maid o' Rossendale,
Yon fair maid o' Rossendale
Who cast her spell on me.1

Now in t' wintertime, wi' t' frost an' rime
O'erwhelmin' fate entrapped her,
Her cycle did a sudden skid
An' in mi arms Ah wrapped her;
Her een shone breet wi' t' lovelorn leet,
An' then Ah kissed her tenderlee --
Now yon fair maid o' Rossendale,
Yon fair maid o' Rossendale,
Yon fair maid o' Rossendale
Rides tandem-style wi' me.

SUNSET MUSIN (G) S

Ah like to thramp mi native hills
   When scarce a breeze is blowin',
An' th' heat o' t' day has cool'd away,
   An' t' sunset's rosy glowin',
When crimson charms tinge th' upland farms
   Wi' magic tints o' shadin',
An' t' blushin' yield o' th' harvest field
   In t' twileet starts a-fadin'.

Fair Autumn blends her mella hues,
   As wond'ringly Ah ponder
On t' beauty spread o'er Heaven's bed,
   When t' sun is sinkin' yonder.
Wi' t' liltin' lays o' t' layrocks praise,
   (No feathered choir moore fittin')
Ah'm mute among their Evensong;
   Ah'm soarin' as Ah'm sittin'.

As lustrous cleawds in t' gilded west
   O'erhang deep purple valleys,
So, wispy oars on t' sky-line shores,
   Dip deawn fro' gowd-lined galleys;
They gently glide on t' sunset tide,
   Wi' other cleawd-ships sailin',
In stately quest o' th' harbour west,
   Wi' dappled wake-waves trailin'.

When th' Artist Hand starts shadin' o'er
   Yon breet-brushed beams o' glory,
Time's fond farewell bids Nature tell
   Her age-owd bedtime story.
Day dimly files thru Heaven's aisles,
   Wher partin' rays are glancin',
An' dewy weet will sprinkle neet,
   Til' dawn agen comes dancin'.

A QUAINT OLD DOCUMENT

"Received the 7th day of May 1743 of John Lord of Broadclough, by us, Laurence Lord and Elizabeth my Wife, the Sum of Forty five pounds for Stock and the farther Sum of Two pound and Sixpence for Interest, making in ye Whole Fourty Seven pounds and Sixpence, which said Sum is in full of all Accounts, Debts, Claims, Dues, Demands, Sum and Sums of Money whatsoever, from the beginning of the World to the Date hereof, as witnefs our Hands

Witnefs hereto

Henry Lord	Lawrence Lord
James Lord	the mark ʘ of
	Elizabeth Lord

May the 7th 1743

Then Received of John Lord aforesaid by Laurence and Elizabeth Lord the sum of ten pounds four shillings in full of all accounts Debts, Dues and Demands whatsoever, from ye Beginning of the World to the Date hereof as witnefs our Hands

Witnefs hereto

Henry Lord	Lawrence Lord
James Lord	the mark ʘ of
	Elizabeth Lord

* * * * * * * * * * *

It goes without saying that there must have been a great preponderance of people bearing the surname Lord, which perhaps was not surprising in view of the intermarriage patent during that period. The reader will also note that Elizabeth, if not illiterate, was unable to sign her name, and made her mark by drawing a circle with a dot in the centre.

LANCASHIRE NEET ARTISTES, January 29th, 1972. Back row: Ron. Schofield (barely in picture). Tom Harry A. Howard, George A. Wormleighton, Ronald Y. Digby, Mrs. J. Townsend (Joan Pomfret), Mrs. M. Lord, Mrs. Hague (pianist). Front row: The Mayoress (Mrs. A. Howarth), Mrs. mary Kershaw, Mrs. Harry Craven, Clifford Heyworth (Bill o' Bows), Mrs. A. Ridgeon, The Mayor (Councillor A. Howarth).

Some of the fair maids o' Rosesndale at Bacup Recreation Ground about the turn of the century. This used to be a regular Sunday afternoon occupation, but the presence of the band suggests a special event.

Brandwood Farm, near Waterbarn, taken about 1900. (the photograph is worth comparison with the present Brandwood cottages). Note the altered windows and the gas lamp. The window near the lady is now bowed and copper canopied. The barn is now demolished and the datestone put in a nearby wall.

BRIDGE STREET looking between the George and Dragon and the Golden Lion towards the Conservative Club. Date about 1910. The Conservative Club lost its top storey in 1964. The castle-like wall protects the open river Irwell.

ST. JAMES STREET looking towards the Mechanics' Institute and Townhead property. Taken about 1910, note Barnes' draper's shop on the left. The shops and houses on the right stand where the present day bus stop and St. James Gardens are.

BACUP has suffered almost more than any other town during the Cotton Famine; and though that now is nearly over, it has left many of our Manufacturers bankrupt--seven of our mills idle; and most of our poor loaded with debt. In the midst of all this the walls of our Church, the principal one in a population of 18,000, have given way; and though props have been applied, it is yet in such an unsafe condition that the Bishop has directed the galleries to be closed; and few of our once large congregation like to venture inside it. Many go but seldom anywhere, and many to dissenting places of worship, of which there are some nineteen in the town.

The old site is not available, and the only site suitable is an expensive one. It is offered to us at half its value, by John Whitaker, Esq., of Broadclough, Bacup, and a subscription--altogether £600; our only wealthy Church Manufacturer has also offered a handsome sum, and other subscriptions of £100 and less are promised. The poor too are ready with their small but earnest help; but we cannot see our way to more than £1,500 towards a required cost of some £5,800.

Above two-thirds of our population are dissenters. No Church was built here from the Reformation till A.D. 1789. A Baptist Chapel was built A.D. 1692, the fruitful source of some dozen more in the surrounding district. The Baptists indeed are comparatively more numerous here than anywhere else in England. They have six Chapels in the town, with accommodation for about 3,200; whereas if our Church were usable there would be only Church accommodation for 2,170 for the whole town and neighbourhood. It is proposed that the new Church be entirely free.

Bacup Parsonage, 1866.

A plea from Bacup Parsonage, 1866. The old Parish Church collapsed and was replaced on the same site by the present St. John's Church at a cost of £15,000

NEWCHURCH ROAD near Tunstead Church, taken about 1910. Buildings from the right -- Coronation Buildings, Beaconsfield Club, Railway Tavern, Commercial Inn.

SCOTCH JIMMY – "MAYOR OF STACKSTEADS"

"Ah wonder if yo Stacksteads fooalk
Know yo had once a Mayor,
Who with full "Highland Dignity,"
Did fill yo're civic chair.
'Scotch Jimmy' were a freeman reyt,
He never paid his rates.
Bud neaw un then he made his way
To th' 'college' eawt o' th' gate."

(Verse 3 of a poem by "Shepster" entitled "Another Bit o' Owd Bacup." The Notice says: "STAND FOR CHARLEMAGNE." The date is unknown, but the picture may conceivably have been taken for a Victorian carnival, perhaps Queen Victoria's Jubilee).

JOSEPH PICCOP

Mr. Holt of Loveclough had a farm labourer named Joseph Piccop (Pickup). He was born, lived, and died at Loveclough. He had a wife and six children, some of his descendants are living at Crawshawbooth at the present day.

Piccop was baptised and sent out to preach by David Crosley. After the latter's death in 1744, Piccop became the Minister at Ebenezer Baptist Chapel, Bacup, as Crosley's successor; at that time very few places of worship could afford a minister of their own, as they were all very poor -- hence ministers had a great deal of travelling, many a time after walking 20 or 30 miles would perhaps have 2/- or 2/6 for his services.

One day Piccop had half an acre to mow (Lancashire measure) and after he had done that he walked all the way to Manchester, a distance of 20 miles, and preached to a large congregation at night. Then a walk home again during the night. Mr. Piccop was much in request at "Cold House Chapel", Tib Street, Manchester, which at that time was the only place of worship for the nonconformist there. Members had to come from this place to Bacup to be baptised by Piccop in those days. "Cold House Chapel" was demolished in the year 1900.

Mr. Piccop often went to London on a begging tour, and a good many anecdotes are told about these visits to the metropolis. Mr. Piccop at times preached against the prevailing fashions and customs of the world. He took the liberty of doing so whilst in London, particularly against the dress of the ladies.

Mr. Piccop did not make a very genteel appearance. He carried little of the parsonic dignity of some of our modern preachers, in his exterior.

Such was his popularity in London, that a congregation would have assembled at five o'clock in the morning to hear him.

A certain gentleman who had been very pleased with the discourse, in thanking Mr. Piccop hinted that he had exceeded the usual time, saying that he ought to have noticed his watch. Mr. Piccop in his rustic simplicity informed him that he'd never had a watch in his life, upon which the gentleman drew his watch from his pocket and presented it to him, declaring that he should not be without any longer.

Joseph Piccop died of cancer in 1772, was about 70 years of age, and was interred inside the Ebenezer Baptist Chapel, Bacup.

BEFORE THE RESERVOIRS CAME TO GRANE

Go over the Grane beyond Haslingden at any time and it is certain you will see the motorist who has pulled on to the grass verge and is enjoying the beauty of a lovely scene. Especially where he can overlook the reservoirs that provide their own atmosphere of Lakeland charm.

Those reservoirs were achieved at a price -- the doom of a village which in its day had been a thriving community with the people employed in cotton mills, stone quarries and farming.

Only a few ruined buildings remain as tangible reminders of an earlier settlement, though St. Stephen's Church is interesting in that in 1926 it was removed stone by stone and re-erected a mile nearer the town of Haslingden.

In the days when it was an established village, Grane was a stimulating place in which to live. A place where you would find more than a fair share of "characters".

Some of the more notorious have already found their way into the history of the district. They were the whisky "spinners", the crafty men who devoted their lives to dodging the Revenue.

It would seem that the illicit distilling of whisky was continued in some of the remote parts of Grane and Musbury for most of the 19th century. But this is not their story -- that is one to be told at much greater length to do it justice.

I am thinking now of the law-abiding villagers and one who in his day knew them well -- and wrote about them -- was a former Mayor of Haslingden, the late Alderman W. H.J. Cowpe, He was a clothier and could say that he and his father in 60 years could never remember having made a bad debt with a Graner. They were very thrifty, hard working and honest. And also they had a very keen sense of humour. Nearly every family in the Grane had a nickname by which they were better known than their own.

One row was known as the "Biggins" -- Scandinavian for buildings -- and the nicknames of eight families living there were "Kailey", "Dougle", "Fatty", "Fudge", "Mush", "Coil Bob", "Laddy", and "Doddy Hoil".

One of the wittiest was known as "Scenning Tom". He worked in the quarries at Hutch Bank where the wages were paid on Saturday noon.

By Friday he and his mates had exhausted their credit at all the four pubs in the village. It was warm and they were thirsty on this particular occasion. Tom had the bright idea of raiding the children's money box. -- All he could get was 2½d. In those days beer was only 3d a quart and less than a quart was no use. So he gave a jug to one of his sons, telling him to go to the Wellington for a quart of ale but on no account to let the landlord see his money until he had got hold of the jug filled with beer.

And he added: "When tha's getten owd, tha mun put this 2½d deawn and walk eawt. T' landlord ull call thi back and seh 'Here lad, tha' art a 'openny short'. Tha mun turn reawnd un tell *him*, 'Nay awd man, it's thee uts a 'openny short'."

One day at the Wellington Tom was having a drink with the driver of the engine working on a railway line from the Grane siding. Tom asked him about the engine and the speed it could do. He was told about 20 miles an hour, whereupon he said he would race the engine from the top of the siding if he got 30 yards start.

Knowing that Tom could not run a mile in six minutes let alone two, the driver accepted. The race was fixed for the following Saturday afternoon, and the village turned out for it. When the driver had got steam up Tom took his place not alongside the engine but in the middle of the track in front of the engine.

The driver dared not run over him, so Tom trotted home an easy winner. -- Paying up somewhat reluctantly, the driver complained that he "had been had", whereupon Tom said he wuld give him a chance to get his money back. This time he would race his whippet, provided the animal "runs the same way as me".

The start was made at the Wellington with the dog owner at Little Edwards, the finishing mark. When the signal was given to start, Tom turned round and ran backwards. The dog could not run the same way and though it finished a long way in front, it had not fulfilled the conditions. Tom had won again.

Another character was "Ginger" who was known as the biggest liar in Grane. Typical of his tall tales was that he once carried a stone flag on his back and it was so heavy that his feet sank three inches into the solid rock!

At one of the Grane cotton mills there was a cutlooker who was severe with any weaver who brought in defective pieces. One day one of the men weavers brought in a piece that was full of flaws. The cutlooker gave him a good telling off and finished by saying that some of the weavers "wur a gormless lot".

"Happen we are, bud we'er mentioned in t' Bible", replied the weaver.

The cutlooker doubted that, but he was told, "Well, if tha'll look in t' fifth chapter of Matthew tha'll read' 'Blessed are the peace-makers (Piece-makers)', but id ses nowt abeawt cutlookers".

A story which indeed deserved the title: "Piece that passeth all understanding".

MORE ROSSENDALE ANECDOTES

On her first morning, an American teacher on an exchange visit went into the classroom at a local school, and the first thing she saw was dead flowers in a vase on the teacher's desk. So she asked the children where she should put them. "In the bin in the playground", they said. So she took them into the yard, and could not find the bin. A small boy was coming in through the gates, so she said to him: "Where's the bin?" He replied, "Aw've bin on an errand fer th' Headmaster".

Astounded to find his name on the second team list, a wicket-keeper in the Valley rushed to a member of the committee to ask why he had been dropped from the firsts. "Well, you hurt your hand last Saturday", said the committeeman. "Did aw?", replied the stumper. "Aw'll show thee whether aw hurt it or not", and he proceeded to put his fist through a pavilion window!

Owd Roddle had to go under a low railway bridge to get to his stable with his donkey and cart, and the donkey's ears got sore by rubbing against the low roof. After much thinking, Roddle hit on a solution. He borrowed a hammer and chisel and he was busy cutting grooves in the roof to accommodate the donkey's ears when a friend who was passing asked him what he was doing, and said: "Tha'd find it yezzier to get a spade and dig deawn wheer donkey's feet tread". "Nay, durn't toak so daft", said Roddle, "It's donkey's ears ut's sooar, noan its feet".

LONG GEORGE

(From "Lancashire Characters and Places" by Thomas Newbigging)

The power-loom breaking riots of 1826 are an exemplification of the bitter feelings that were evoked by the application of steam-power to the turning of machinery.

The rioters in Rossendale made havoc with the new-fangled looms, which they believed would ruin their trade as hand-loom weavers, and take the bread out of their mouths. Their mode of procedure on attacking a mill was to place a guard outside, then the ring-leaders entered; first they cut out the warps and destroyed the reeds and healds, and then with a few well-aimed blows they demolished the looms. On the cry being raised, "th' soldiers are coming!", one old fellow cried out: "Never mind, lads, we met as weel be shot by th' soldiers as clemmed by th' maisters".

I have mentioned this circumstance by way of introducing "Long George", the constable of Bacup during those disturbed times, an eccentric character whom I knew well. George stood six feet two inches in his stockings, hence the prefix "Long" to his name. It was but little that George and his myrmidons could do to prevent the mischief, and so with the instictive sagacity of the "watch", they wisely kept aloof from the scenes of outrage and spoilation.

Long George was a familiar figure in Bacup for many years after being superseded in his duties of constable by the police as we now have them. At the beginning of his time, when he was a village constable, he lived in Lane Head Lane. On one wintry night, cold and stormy, the snow drifting heavily, a night when folk could hardly keep their night-caps from being blown off, some young fellows determined to play a trick on George. So they waited until they knew he had got well into bed, and then they went up to his house in the Lane and thundered at the door. George got up, put his head out of the window, and saw two or three snow-covered figures down below.

"Whatever dun yo want, chaps, at this time o' neet?" he called out.

One of them shouted back in reply: "George, yo're wanted down at th' Dragon yonder, first thing!"

"What's th' matter theer!", asked George.

"Ther's about twenty of 'em yonder feighting a' of a rook, an' if thae doesn't look sharp and come down and sunder 'em, they'll be one half on 'em kilt!"

But George was not to be caught as easily as they imagined -- he saw through the trick that was attempted to be played on him, and ruminating for a moment, answered: "I'll tell yo what yo maun do, chaps".

"What maun we do, George?" they asked.

"Go yor ways back to th' Dragon", said George, "and lay 'em out on th' tables, as mony on 'em as gets kilt, an' i' th' morning I'll come down an' count 'em, and with that he crashed the window down again, leaving the discomfited jokers to find their way back to the bar-parlour at the Dragon as best they might.

Latterly, George did duty as a bailiff, attending auction sales, keeping the door, and handing the drink round to the thirsty bidders. He wore a blue coat with metal buttons, knee breeches and brown stockings, with a pair of clogs at least fourteen inches in length, and a sole an inch and a half thick. He was also adorned with a blue apron which was usually tucked round his waist, and he wore for years an old felt hat that had scarcely a vestige of brim left. George, when I knew him, lodged with two elderly maiden sisters, Ann o' th' Kiln and Judie, but he kept his own room in order, and did his own cooking.

One evening George's supper was on the fire, and some practical jokers, being on the look out, attracted his attention outside, whilst one of them slipped in and emptied a cupful of salt into the pot. George on sitting down to his evening meal found the porridge so over-seasoned that it was impossible to eat them. He tried again and again, muttering to himself: "thae'll ha' to come to 't, George!" but it was of no use, he had to give them up at last. Determined, however, that they should not be thrown away or otherwise wasted, he got a pudding cloth, and tying them up in this, hung them from the ceiling of his room, and instead, thereafter, of salting his porridge in the usual way, he cut a slice from the over-salted compound as long as it lasted and put it in the pot, so saving both salt and oatmeal. By frugality and self-denial George managed to save a considerable sum of money, and was in the habit of lending it out on security at good interest.

(*Footnote:* The Rossendale Free Press of October 13th, 1900, relating the same tale, concludes: "Many years elapsed before he heard the last about his patent for salting porridge".)

AGREEMENT MADE FEBY. 13. 1850

to clear out the River Bed,

We hereby agree to clean or get out of the river all the stones that have been thrown into it, or got in in any other way. That is, we agree to remove and take out of the water-course all stones of the size of a pint pot and larger. The place to commence at, opposite south gable-end of a house where a person of the name of Amos Hardman, a shoemaker, lives, and on the premises of R. Munn & Bros, bottom of Back Irwell street. From there to clean it wholly up under the arches as well as open spaces to the bridge leading over the Messrs. Aitken's new mill, Waterside; the water-course to be cleansed or opened up to the depth it was 13 years ago; or if that cannot be fully ascertained, to go as low as the spring of the arches; or where the arches are flagged or paved in the bottom, the said flagging or paving to be made and left clear, and the fall to be kept uniform from the bottom end, or commencing part, to the top end. The parties contracting to have the stones for their own benefit, except a few belonging to Mr. Lord, which are building stones, and opposite his own premises.

If it is necessary to lead or wheel any of the clay or dirt out, the said clay or dirt to be put on the side of the road as convenient as possible for the parties getting it out. This is mentioned, as it is fully understood that the river is to be well cleansed out.

The price for the whole job to be 25£, and to be paid so that there is always something on hand. The job to be completed by the latter end of June or sooner if the weather is favourable, to commence this day.

Bacup, February 13, 1850.

Richard Roberts,
James X Leach

Witness Moses Whitehead.

I agree to pay them the above mentioned sum in the way mentioned above.

R. Munn.

PAUPER FUNERALS

(culled from the Bacup Times, November 27th, 1877)

The paupers who die at Pike Law, (Workhouse) are buried at Rawtenstall Cemetery, and many are the comments made by onlookers as they witness the unseemly haste with which these poor creatures are hurried to their pauper's grave.

The hearse containing the corpse is often driven at such a speed as to keep the poor followers on the trot.

They are, generally, a few old inmates from the workhouse, male and female, and at times one may see them almost out of breath, wiping the perspitation from their faces with apron or coat-sleeve. This is an injustice to the living, and an insult to the dead, and it reminds one of the lines of Hood:-

Rattle his bones -- over the stones
He's only a pauper whom nobody owns.

To call the attention of the Guardians to this scandal we think will be sufficient.

MORE ROSSENDALE ANECDOTES

In the days when there were many hard drinkers, they would at times leave their work to go on the rant. The womenfolk had a hard time of it, but some could look after themselves, like old Matty. Her husband returned home after a bout, and fell asleep in the chair. When he awakened, he said he was hungry, and demanded his dinner.

"Tha's had it", she retorted, "and tha's nod gettin' another". When he said he hadn't, she said, "Well, lick thi lips on thi' chops and tha'll see". He did and could taste mutton fat, so concluded he must have had the meal.

-- Matty didn't tell him she had smeared his mouth with the fat while he was asleep.

The late Alderman Jerry Lord of Haslingden was an eloquent speaker, and he used the local vernacular with good effect. At the induction of a new minister to a local church, in a speech of welcome, Jerry gave the minister an insight into the Rossendale character. "Tha'll find t' fooak reaund here are like a gradely prata-pie. Ther's a lot o' hard crust on 'em, but iv tha delves deawn tha'll find plenty o' good meyt".

THE ST. ANNES LAND AND BUILDING COMPANY

In 1874, Mr. Elijah Hargreaves of Rossendale (a full-faced bustling Lancashire business-man) was walking along the sea-shore from Blackpool to Lytham whilst on his summer holidays, when he got the idea of building a new seaside resort between Blackpool and Lytham of a different character from either of them. At that time there was just a bleak foreshore between the two places.

He called at the Clifton Estate Office at Lytham to explore possibilities, got a sympathetic hearing, and later in the year the St. Annes Land and Building Company was formed, and got a lease on a square mile of land.

It consisted of eight Rossendale business men and was registered on October 14th. For the first twelve months or so the company held their meetings at the Queen's Hotel, Rawtenstall, but the company offices were transferred to St. Annes in 1876.

The very first rented house was a bungalow and it was taken by a Mr. and Mrs. Heap from Rossendale. They arrived by train and then had to tramp across sand dunes to their new home. They actually stayed in the district for fifty years and watched St. Annes grow up all around them.

Many other Rossendalians lived in St. Annes during its early development. These included Mr. Clement Rawstron who was the first postmaster and his son Mr. William Rawstron who was the first postman.

The whole story of the development of St. Annes, now incorporated with Lytham as Lytham-St. Annes can be read in "Sand Grown" by Kathleen Eyre, who is a local historian and broadcaster. Another recent book which covers similar ground is "Rage of Sand" by Gabriel Harrison, published by Ernest Benn in 1971.

MORE ROSSENDALE ANECDOTES

A tackler with a boil on the back of his neck was told by the doctor to keep his eye on it. He said to the doctor, "Aw cornd do thad. Aw'm noan a contortionist".

(In the early 1850s) the block of buildings between the George and Dragon Inn and the Mechanics' Institution were then used as a blacksmith's shop, at the Bridge-street end; and the end abutting Yorkshire-street was occupied by James Maden, better known as "Jim Sam", who sold greengroceries, sweets, etc.; afterwards Robert Crabtree ("Little Bob") took possession, and turned it into an earthenware shop mainly. A truly comical chap was "Little Bob", and no mistake; but his wife was just as gentle and quiet, and some head taller than her husband. Bob was altogether illiterate, but he managed to do tolerably well in business, though somewhat "hampe-red" by one or two of his family. The blacksmith's shop belonged to Joseph Moore, another decent fellow in his way, but he likewise was unfortunate through the shortcomings of his progeny. The shoeing-shed of this place was used on a Saturday as a hot-pea and penny-pie emporium, kept by "Skenning Joe". Many a "lark" was played on Joe by the rough boys and youths who frequented the booth; but after the frolicks were over they would generally make amends by additional purchases. Opposite to this "shanty of Joe's" was the shop of old Dick Baldwin. Richard was a wholesale dealer in potatoes, oranges, and greengrocery, and after his business extended he built the shop in Market-street, now occupied by Mr. Schofield, draper; the old buildings were pulled down by Mr. Salmon, and the present handsome structures erected.

* * * * * * * *

Todmorden Road was a veritable hive of industry from Tong Mills to Sharneyford; the coalpits of Slackgate, Hoyle Hey, Oaken Clough, Greave, Parrock Lumb, and Sharneyford were at their best, when none are now being worked but the latter; many of the mills long ago ceased to run, and the industries have been removed to other parts of the town, Burnley-road and Newchurch-road profiting thereby. Just after we removed to Green's Mill the first flood of my recollection occurred. It was in the summer of 1849. The thunder and lightning were very heavy, and water ran down the lane from the direction of Maden Lodges like a river. Great alarm spread among those parents who had children at school, so far away as Underbank,

I had three sisters then attending St. John's School, and as soon as my father and one or two neighbours could get from their houses they went in search of their several children. It was a difficult quarter to get into Burnley-road, but at last their task was accomplished and all the children were found in the upstairs room of a house at Waterside (next to the one occupied by Old James Whittaker, better known as James o' Dyers), the water having completely filled the kitchen and was within three steps of the bedroom. Bridge-street, St. James'-street, and the Club Houses were in an awful plight, much damage was done to property.

The flood which occurred two years afterwards I had personal cause to remember. We were then living at Lane End, and the farmer's son (Chaffer) and I had a capital "kitchen garden", made in the sandhole behind Fir Trees, in Rochdale-road, where various kinds of vegetables had grown and were ready for sale. One Saturday afternoon, however, a thunderstorm broke over the district, and everything was washed down the slopes into the pit bottom, and thus perished my hopes which had been "built upon the sand". Between this time and the great flood of 1870 many deluges and floods occurred at Bacup, for I have seen Yorkshire-street flooded twice in one week. The George and Dragon Inn was a great sufferer before the kitchen and the pavement round the building was raised. At the time named no sooner had they got the house tidied, but the other flood again filled the lower rooms to the depth of five feet and the clearing out of mud a foot deep had to be begun over again. On this occasion the omnibus to Rochdale (which then left the Green Man Hotel) was carried down to the Dragon door by the force of the water, neither horses nor bus being heavy enough to overcome the force of the water which ran down the street from Todmorden-road. A great improvement at times of floods was made shortly after the Old Local Board became established, as the bed of the river was partially cleaned out and some other improvements effected, though all has not yet been effected that might be; nor have the Town Council yet risen to their responsibilities in this matter either in regard to the state of the river bed or the contour of the streets.

* * * * * * * * * *

The most comical character of his day in Bacup was George Haworth, better known as "Old George Round th' World". George was a millhand, and worked in the twisting and winding-on room; but he left this occupation and afterwards kept a beer-house at the top of South-street, facing Providence Chapel, Tong-lane, and from thence removed to the then new Police Station in Todmorden-road, which was used only for a short time after the demolition of the old dungeon. George got a license to this place and called it the Red Lion Inn, re-named the Wellington by the late Coun. John Lord. In the prime of manhood George had the misfortune to lose his first wife, and some time after he again took to himself one older in years than himself, and she made him a very good helpmate. Both were of a very careful nature, and George was always on the look-out for bargains. At the time of the Russian War heads of families in Rossendale were hard pressed to make ends meet, as flour then was sold at over 60s. per sack, the same quality being sold today at about one-third that sum. One day, on going past Carter's warehouse, now occupied by Mr. Bentham, wholesale grocer, George saw a sack of flour at the door, and the price ticketted upon it. Calling out for "attention", Mr. Carter himself appeared, when George remarked that he wanted the flour, and put down the price. He began to tie up the sack to take it away, when the tradesman endeavoured to stop him, saying he had plenty inside; but George said he had bought that one, and he would have no other. After tying the sack, George told Mr. Carter to stand back if he did not want hurting; and without more ado he swung the sack across his shoulders and carried it home -- a wonderful feat certainly for one 60 years of age; but George was a powerfully-built man, and a true son of Anak, as many had cause to remember.

* * * * * * * * *

Another peculiar individual living at this time was John Kershaw -- "Old Gab" -- as he was generally called. He was a pig butcher, and lived in Boston, or on "th'owd Brig", going over Hempsteads, and two doors from the shop of Mr. Richard Ashworth, now occupied by Mr. Berry, auctioneer and valuer. I have often seen Kershaw go down the steps leading from the front of his door into the river, and there wash the entrails of the animals in the river in order to make them fit to use for black puddings and sausages. Fancy this kind of thing being done in these days of fine tastes and "pure" food! But at this time fish were caught alive in the river Irwell, higher up the stream at Broadclough. How pleasant would it be now were the river restored to its former purity; and if the River Commissioners were only to rigorously enforce the powers invested in them by Parliament, this much-to-be-desired consummation might very soon be realised, and without great expense either to manufacturer or to the community at large. Some other notables in their day were James and Betty Fielding, of the Bull's Head Inn, the former of whom got so abnormally corpulent that he would habitually go to sleep while conversing with customers; "Potato Tom", a greengrocer, got in a similar condition, and both died suddenly; William Forshaw, of the George and Dragon, who was formerly a printer; Old Piper, of the Bull's Head vaults; James Nuttall, of the Angel Inn, who removed to Marton, Blackpool; John Hartley, of the Green Man, (the two latter were indeed "models" in their business). Of Thomas Sharp (Old Sharp), Betty Pilling (Old Naughty's wife), James Maden, grocer, (Jim Sam) --- I must speak on another occasion.

* * * * * * * *

The first Parliamentary election one remembers in this neighbourhood was in 1859 -- that for South Lancashire. At that time Lancashire was divided into two great divisions only -- North and South. The Newchurch Township, or the northerly and westerly sides of Bacup were in the former division, and Spotland Township, extending from Cowpe to Sharneyford and as far as Facit were in the Bacup area of the Bacup southern and easterly division. Great interest was taken in this contest, and innumerable "squibs" appeared on the walls, for there were then no hoardings for posting purposes, and poetical effusions were circulated. One of these rhymes, headed "The Little Chap and Queer", ended with a shout of "Hurrah, for Johnny Cheetham", and a certain "Historian of Rossendale", who had just come into the town, was given credit for the witty and lively document, but he entirely repudiated authorship. Mr. James Greaves, Mr. Robert Smith, Mr. Charles Stewart, and Mr. Sam Hall, however, were responsible on their respective sides for the bulk of the other literature, and things were very lively from the nomination day up to the close of the poll, a full week or more elapsing between each event. Mr. Charles Turner, the Conservative candidate was returned.

The "sixties" were not only a very eventful period in Bacup, but the famous Bacup Old Band was in the zenith of its popularity throughout the musical world, as well it might be, for no other brass band within living memory had ever accomplished the fetes of "our boys" in prize winning. From the Belle Vue contest of September 1st, 1862, to the same date in 1871, they entered 48 competitions, and carried away a prize at each. In the last four years they brought away first honours on every occasion but seven, one of these being a tie for first prize. (During these ten years they won 32 1st Prizes, 8 2nds, 2 3rds, and 5 4ths, besides the tie). The members of the band during most of this period were the following: Solo cornet, John Lord, conductor; solo soprano, William Greenwood, 2nd soprano, John Sanderson; 1st cornet, Henry Brearley, 2nd cornet, Alexander Hamer, 3rd cornet, John Whittles; flugle horn, Joseph Lord (brother of conductor); 1st tenor, James Lord (brother of conductor), 2nd tenor, Edward Nuttall; baritone, Abraham Ashworth; solo euphonium, Richard Marsden, 2nd euphonium, John Stevenson, 3rd euphonium, James Lord (cousin of conductor); 1st trombone, Josiah Ratcliffe, 2nd trombone, James Lord (father of conductor), 3rd trombone, George Greenwood; 1st bombardon, John Smith, 2nd bombardon, James Lord (loom jobber), 3rd bombardon, Enoch Holt; side drum, Thomas Sutcliffe; bass drum, Thomas Ashworth.

* * * * * * * * *

The Troy Silver Mining Company will never be forgotten in Bacup and Rossendale. The latter part of 1868-9 and the "seventies" were great times in the mining world, and, unfortunately, the mania spread into the Rossendale Valley -- then often spoken of as the "Golden Valley". But since some artful dodgers from the other side of the Atlantic succeeded in draining it of about £120,000, that phrase has not been so often heard. When the prospectus was issued with such glowing colours, everyone who had a few pounds to spare, or likely to have from their earnings, gladly snapped up a few shares, and some ordinary workingmen weavers invested as much as £100 in the undertaking. The shares became inflated in value before a pick had been struck at the site of the mine, which was located in Ogden County, Nevada, in the new State of Colorado, and it was thought on all hands that a virtual new Eldorado had been discovered. In less than two years from the time of floatation the £1 shares easily fetched about three in the open market; and one influential and highly respected Bacup gentleman (who was not in at the first allotment of shares) purchased a large number at that figure -- three pounds each. One small tradesman at Smelt put in £500, and a friend of his, a poor weaver, £100, every farthing of which they lost. One doctor was reported to have held £10,000 of share capital, and a certain cotton manufacturer £15,000; while a woollen manufacturer down the Valley had also placed nearly the same amount in the undertaking. Many workingmen lost all their savings in the concern, and one or two shopkeepers became crippled for life by over-reaching themselves. And so the tale of this totally-speculative concern might be greatly extended; but I will spare the outraged feeling of readers, by simply remarking that on March 11th, 1876, the "White Pine News", an American paper, had in it an advertisement of the sale of the plant, etc. which never earned a tenth part of its cost.

* * * * * * *

A person called at the old surgery in Rochdale-road, which occupied a portion of the ground whereon the Maden Public Baths now stand, and wanted to settle up with the Doctor. He was only an ordinary working man, but circumstances had arisen which made him anxious as to his indebtedness to the Doctor. But he was met with the remark, "Well, you cannot well afford to pay much for doctor's stuff, give me ten shillings and I will give you a receipt in full settlement, so that you will be right if anything should happen". There are scores of instances where Dr. Worrall never received a single pennypiece for medical attendance.

For several years during the Doctor's earlier life, he kept a monkey called "Jack", and sometimes it would be in a cage in the surgery, and at other times he would have it in his sanctum sanctorum (the back room of the surgery), and few people indeed were privileged to get a peep in this "holy of holies". Here the Doctor at that time usually slept, and for several years after his beloved mother's death, he scarcely ever slept in the house. Jack was a great pet of the Doctor's, who used to experiment upon him, study his habits and idiosyncrases, "a la Darwin", and dose him with anaesthetics; and some marvellous antics would Jack go through while under this influence, and at times he would lie there as if dead. After a time, however, the Doctor got tired of his pet and became as other men to some extent -- that is, he began to live a more civilised life; took a greater interest in town's affairs by becoming a member of the Burial Board and Local Board, and was chairman of the latter body for several years. For a considerable length of time he fulfilled the duties of Medical Officer of Health without fee or reward, at a saving to the town of many hundreds of pounds. During all this time Dr. Worrall was also connected with the Mechanics' Institution, on which he had conferred great benefits in many ways. For the innumerable services to the town and the lasting improvements which had been effected to the community at large mainly through his instrumentality, the Doctor was presented with his portrait in oils.

So much, indeed, had Dr. Worrall won the affection and esteem of the public, that when the town became incorporated it was expected by everyone that he would be chosen as the first Mayor of Bacup, but some few individuals thought otherwise, and he was practically driven from public life. Dr. Worrall never married, and died 18th January, 1889, aged 64 years. A granite obelisk 18ft. 6in. in height is engraved to the memory of Joseph Hardman Worrall, Esquire, Member of the Royal College of Surgeons and a Justice of the Peace for this County.

* * * * * * * * * * *

I should be sorry not to make some reference to one, who, though not a native of Bacup, he was nevertheless esteemed and honoured by all who had any dealings with him. I refer to the late Councillor Simcock, who had quite a roving nomad life during his youth. He was a native of Staffordshire, and his parents were what are commonly called "gipsies", and Israel Simcock resided among them until he became a young man. Shortly after he came to Bacup, about 50 years ago, he lived in Temple Court, where he had a pot shop, and during the day he went about hawking from house to house with a large basket on his head. Coming under good influences, he had joined the Christian Church, and he very soon became a much respected tradesman and upright in character. When the Young Men's

Christian Association was in existence during the "sixties" Mr. Simcock was one of the leading members, and nothing pleased him better than to mix amongst those who had been better educated than himself. He delighted in the company of studious young men, and after he had gathered more knowledge himself, he was ever willing to help them forward in the battle of life. Israel Simcock was a keen observer of men and things, as becometh his tribe, and from his own experiences he knew the failings and weaknesses of human nature, consequently he had a great influence over the young with whom he came in regular contact. Many were the adventures by night and by day he used to relate to the few in whom he could confide the dark and unpleasant years of his early life. Sometimes he was weeks away from home and never slept in a bed, and the tent or perhaps an empty or disused building would be utilised as a bedroom; and at other times those with whom he was temporarily living pieces of wood did duty for chairs. But when Israel Simcock became "a changed man", he at once forsook his old associations, and continued to live an altogether different life ever after. Thirty years ago he was in a large way of business in the China and earthenware trade, and for a considerable period he was sole agent in the Rossendale and surrounding districts for some extensive potteries, from which he received commissions on all their trade turnover, and it was from this source that Israel made the greater portion of the money which he managed to scrape together. He earned this commission by being the first to sell and introduce into these districts the goods sent out by firms from whom he received commission. His business aptitude and the sound common sense which Israel Simcock brought to bear on public questions caused him to be placed on the Old Local Board and Burial Board, and later on the Town Council, for no one had the welfare of his adopted town at heart more than he. For several years Mr. Simcock was a teacher of the Men's Bible Class at Mount Pleasant, and a large portrait of him hangs upon the walls of that school, opposite to that of his one time co-teacher -- Thomas Disley. But years before he attended the school just named he was a teacher in the Old Union Street Ragged School -- now called Thorn School. along with Mr. James Heyworth, late Town Clerk, and some others, though only about two of these now survive. Israel Simcock was also a highly valued class leader -- an office on which he set the utmost store, and of which he felt the greatest responsibility. Amid all the activities herein set forth, he never lost his love for the old haunts of his childhood, where for many years he strove to do "some little good" by having a few dozen "Joyful News" distributed every week among the neglected pprtion of the community there. About a couple of years before his death Mr. Simcock left the Town Council and took a small farm at Broadclough, having retired altogether from the "pot" trade, to which some of his sons succeeded. After this he began to feel the ravages of time and the wear and tear of former years told upon his hitherto iron frame. At the end of April, 1893, he went on a visit to his native place in Staffordshire, from which he had to return hastily, as he felt much worse. The doctor was called in and everything possible was done for him, but he only lingered for a few days. Though his pain was acute he murmured not, for he said he put everything in the hands of "King Jesus", whom he had tried to serve so long, and whom he should soon see "eye to eye". In this frame of mind he passed away on the 9th of May. Such was the ending of Israel Simcock, the once strolling gipsy, who was not certain as to the year when he first saw the light; though he understood that he was born about 1825.

* * * * * * * * * *

Besides all these commercial and industrial changes, the social customs and manners of the people have greatly altered for the better; still there is probably room for improvement, for are we not enjoined "to go on to perfection". From 35 to 50 years ago nearly all working-class families lived in two-roomed houses, and the following is a fair sample of what they had to eat and drink: -- It is breakfast time and the mill close by is about to stop and release the workpeople to their morning meal. In the house are two or three young children, the mother is just about to pour the meal porridge from a large iron pan into a large brown earthenware dish. On the large round table, set in the middle of the floor are as many brown "mess pots" as there are members of the family over two years of age. In these utensils, which held about a pint, skimmed milk has been put, or perhaps "small drink", or ale, and there is a horn or iron spoon in each. In comes the father, and five or six boys and girls -- they were called lads and lasses in those days -- four or five sit down on chairs round the table, and the younger ones have to stand ("they grow while they are standing" it used to be said). The father dashes his spoon into the porridge dish and lifts as much as he can; the children put in their spoon and take out only a little at once, and then put it into the milk; and so they go on, dipping into the porridge dish and milk alternately until all is used up, and then off they "go to th' mill agen" until noon. For dinner, in the same house, there is flour porridge, poured on large dish plates, in the middle of which the good house wife has put a piece of butter and brown sugar. In go the spoons in turn until the whole is cleared up; after which is tabled bread and butter or treacle, or cheese and bread, and away again to the mill. To the evening repast there is meal porridge once more, with milk or treacle. Breakfast and what is now called "tea", formerly "baggin", were sometimes varied by substituting "churn milk" (buttermilk), but "new" milk was scarcely ever seen, and occasionally there would be tea and bread and butter on Saturdays and Sundays. The dinner, too, was varied in this way. On baking day, there would be a potato pie made in the large brown dish, about 7 lbs. or 8 lbs. in weight, mostly without beef or mutton, though a few "bones"; then a little currant and mint cake -- that is the currants and mint were placed between two layers of rolled out dough, and then baked. On another day the dinner would consist of "waff", a mixture of meal and treacle boiled like porridge, but often made stiffer, ending with a little bread and butter or cheese; or yet the dinner might be "stir-about", comprised of meal, bacon fat, salt and pepper, partly boiled like porridge, and partly baked. Another dish for dinner was "pan pie", made of similar ingredients as potato pie, put into the porridge pan and boiled; this was a readier way than heating the oven, and so "wasting" coal. The next baking day there might be to dinner a huge "collop mowfin", or cake, measuring some 15 or 18 inches across on which were placed rashers of bacon. The cake was cut in wedge-shaped pieces, but rarely was there a bit of bacon to each; no, the younger children and half-timers had to be satisfied with the fat which had run from the rasher. On Saturdays and Sundays there might possibly be a little fish, beef or veal, but very rarely. If tea was served it would generally be made from hyssop, pennyroyal, himeberry leaves, or other herbs, sweetened with treacle. No tea as we now know it, could then be procured under 4s. per lb., and lump sugar was about 7d. per lb., while brown cane sugar might be bought for 4½d. per lb. These meals were served on a round deal table without tablecloth or even as much as a newspaper as a substitute. What a contrast is all this very common fare, compared with delicacies and "bits of tastes" tabled to breakfast and tea at the present day. Some of the younger people can scarcely realise that their fathers and grandfathers were so limited in their eating and drinking . . . . .

* * * * * * * * * * *

MORE ROSSENDALE ANECDOTES

An old lady in an "Old Folks" Home not far from Rawtenstall was writing a letter and she stopped and said to her friend, "How do ye spell uzzle?" "Uzzl?", said her friend, "Aw durnd know. What are you writing about?"

"Well, Aw'm orderin' a vest out of this catalogue and Aw want one uzzl fit mi".

"Ay, tha doesn't mean uzzl", said her friend, "Put wod'l, Aw con spell that for thi".

The circus was coming to a small Lancashire town, and a man leading two elephants down the road was stopped by a small boy who asked him, "Will you give me one of your elephants?" to get the reply, "Aw'd like to do but Aw darnt. We counted 'em before we set off this morning".

A boy had been taken to the doctors by his mother to be examined. The doctor said to him, "Open your mouth and put your tongue out".

"Eh?" said the lad. Being asked a second time, he said: "Wod?".

So his mother gave him a clout, and said: "Oppen thi gob an' pop thi lollicker eawt".

A certain Rossendalian visited Niagara Falls. The guide was waxing eloquent, and enthusiastically. "Say, do you realise there are millions of gallons of water going over those falls every hour?"

"Ah well", replied the Valley man, "There's nowt to stop it".

A MEETING WITH CHARLES DICKENS

In 1838, Charles Dickens and John Forster, along with H.K. Browne (Phiz), visited Manchester. They had letters of introduction to James Crossley and others from W. Harrison Ainsworth.

One of the objects of Dickens' visit to Manchester on this occasion was to see the two brothers William and Daniel Grant who were calico printers at Ramsbottom, and had an office in Cannon Street, Manchester.

Ainsworth had often told Dickens about the Grants, their remarkable history, personal traits, and certain pecularities of manner and dress, believing that the two brothers would furnish excellent characters for Dickens to study. Ainsworth had known them from boyhood, when he often saw them in Cross Street Chapel and in the streets of Manchester.

Dickens determined on this visit to see and study from life these two quaint benevolent old merchants of his friends' native city of whom he had heard so much. One of the letters was to a friend Mr. Winter, and Ainsworth gave him the hint that Dickens wished to see the Grant brothers; and accordingly the latter were invited to attend a dinner at his home.

This was at "The Stocks", Cheetham Hill Road, and here it was that Dickens saw the Grants for the first time. Their humanity, simple-mindedness, and generosity were the attributes that struck Dickens about these two worthies, and thus he found the originals for the Cheeryble brothers in his novel "Nicholas Nickleby", thereby giving them enduring fame.

Canon Richard Parkinson was one of the party that met together, and there was a very lively time between the Canon and John Forster, whose wit was no match for the strong powers of repartee exhibited by his Lancashire friend. "Phiz", who had illustrated Pickwick, took notes and made rough sketches of the personal appearance of the two brothers for his Cheeryble characters.

MORE ROSSENDALE ANECDOTES

An election candidate was quite deflated when he called on an old lady to be told, "Ay, tha knows nowt, an' hardly that".

A CRICKETER LOOKS BACK

"Bliss was it then to be alive„
To be young was very heaven".

These words seem still to be a fair description of the summer of 1949 in Bacup. If they can be faulted, it is because those who were not so young found it very near to Heaven to watch Everton Weekes in all his dazzling brilliance on those wonderful sunny Saturdays. To play with him, to play in that Bacup side, was a privilege none of us will ever forget.

The memories that follow have not been checked. Maybe some incidents belong to later years, and possibly some errors have crept in. On the whole, I doubt it. Not many of my memories are so vivid and fresh.

It was the third match of the season when I joined the side. The previous week, Weekes had played an innings of tremendous skill on a difficult wicket at Church. The explosion of unprecedented brilliance was to come in the next two matches. They were against Lowerhouse and East Lancashire.

I had a unique hat-trick in that match against Lowerhouse. It was unique in this sense -- no other bowler has ever played such a minor part in his own hat-trick! I just sent the ball down and joined the spectators in watching the drama. The second ball popped up off the bat and dropped in the region of gully, yards away from the nearest fielder, Weekes at slip. He threw himself along the ground and just got his fingers under the ball.

Even he couldn't catch it but he lay there knocking it in the air until the wicket-keeper dived across and made the catch. The spectators needed time to digest such a spectacle but they (or we!) did not get it. I sent down another ball and, for a brief fraction of a second, felt critical of Weekes. He had changed position and had left a yawning gap between himself and the wicket-keeper. The last time I saw the ball, it had left the edge of the bat and was speeding down the gap for a four. It was not a four; suddenly, quite impossibly, the ball was in the hands of Weekes. It was only later in the pavilion that we realised that Weekes's miracles added up to my hat-trick.

Following those catches, Weekes scored over 90. I suppose it was a good innings but I doubt if many remember much of it. The week after, we saw pure magic which will never be forgotten. We went to

Blackburn, always keen to do well against East Lancashire. At the end of a superb match the points were shared. We were 10 short and our last pair were in. It was an exciting end to a glorious match.

The Australian all-rounder, Dooland, showed some great hitting for East Lancashire. I can still recall the ball I flighted to him. It never actually went out of sight until it landed in the school yard outside the ground but it went high enough to strain the neck muscles of the boundary fielder so far beneath it. More was to come, for, most tragically, Dooland ran out his partner at 49 . In disgust he began to throw the bat. Not one of the next three balls touched the grass after feeling the scourge of his bat.

When East Lancashire declared at 220, the task of getting the runs seemed impossible. I can still recall the skipper, Tom Graham, whose approach was so philosophical, telling Weekes to have a pleasant innings but not to bother about winning. The reply was simple: "We are going to win".

The real reply was not in words. Twenty-nine minutes from the start of our innings, Weekes reached 50. He was out after a little over the hour at the crease for 92. Only one shot was in the air; a four, miles away from any fielder, yet on that day it seemed a blemish. We talk of shots scorching the turf. Never did a batter pursue a scorched-earth policy as did Weekes that day. As we collected, spectators gave tributes as well as money. It was really one tribute: "We have never seen anything like it before".

I still feel that I have never seen anything like it before or since. There have been better batters no doubt. Has anyone had the ability to hit such severe fours from any kind of ball to any part of the field?

A week later the paper carried the headline question, "Can Freer stop Weekes?" The Rishton professional, Freer, was a bowler who had played once for Australia. In the league in 1948 he had had a marvellous season. The crowd was vast at Lanehead when the game began. We had not to wait for drama.

Freer bowled his first ball to Weekes, hit him on the pad and claimed. Slowly and reluctantly the umpire raised his finger. It was like a dramatist killing the star in the first scene. The crowd was stunned. Some latecomers turned back. In the pavilion, a horrified,, stupefied silence reigned. It was not broken by me -- a local preacher's vocabulary was hopelessly inadequate. Banham, bless him, spoke out. Never have three simple but strong words been spoken with such awe!

Meanwhile Dunham had the unenviable task of going to the

wicket. I doubt if he imagined the glory that he was going to find there. Freer had to toil long before he had any other success. Dunham with 81, Banham with another 50 and other useful scores enabled us to declare and later to win. The match that began so desperately ended in triumph.

All this was in three matches. The rest of the season was anti-climax. It must have been. So long afterwards, I can feel the strength of this logic and yet know that it was not so. It was not so for the players and it was not so for the spectators. Saturday followed Saturday -- each one we were tempted to describe as "the best yet".

Against Colne at home we declared with plenty of runs on the board. I came on to bowl when the opening batters were still together. I sent down a pitifully poor delivery, a slow offbreak drifting down the leg side. The batter missed his pull and was hit on the pads. Why the wicket-keeper claimed or half-claimed, I could not and cannot imagine. I stood in the middle of the pitch shaking my head. The batter looked beyond me in horrified astonishment for the umpire's finger was raised. I was aghast and sent apologies to him through his partner. The partner was sensible and sportsmanlike; 10 minutes later he was given out to an equally doubtful decision, and departed with his calm somewhat disturbed!

Meanwhile the real drama was at the other end. Alley had come to the wicket. Only a couple of years ago, he was a veteran still feared in county games. We faced him in his prime in 1949. There was no grace in his batting. He was as strong and as cruel as a bull.

The opposing bowling wasn't hit, it was mauled. We had to get him and get him quickly. I had my instructions and, the very first ball, I managed to do as instructed; to the left-hander, a ball pitching middle and leg and turning away. There was a snick and Banham, behind the wicket, caught the ball. Half singing, half claiming, he went on what an Australian aborigine would call a "walk-about". He was half way to the boundary when he realised that things were awry. The umpire had said "not out!". The problem, Alley was still there. His bat looked as light as a feather in his hands.

Shortly afterwards he was back in the pavilion. I reasoned that he would never expect me to send him a slower ball. I risked one and he plopped up a catch to mid-off. That Dick Dunham, after catching the ball, should take off his new cap (we were wearing them for the first time on that day), throw it on to the ground and stamp on it seems inexplicable now. In the tension of the moment it seemed natural and, in any case, we should not have minded if he had eaten it.

The game at Rawtenstall was never to be forgotten, perhaps more for the mass of spectators and the colour of the summer dresses in the sunshine than for the excitement of the game itself. There was lots of good cricket and, at one stage, we had hopes of victory, but the amateur batter, Incles, saved the day for Rawtenstall. I remember trying to "buy" his wicket. I paid enough in easy boundaries but never looked like getting him out. It was Lancashire League as the rest of the country never imagines it. The two professionals, Weekes and Hazare, were surely in the class of the world's best six batsmen but the game finished with an amateur in complete control. As he was an opponent, I took no pleasure in the fact at the time. After all, we had no illusions that cricket was only a game!

To think of the magic of Weekes is natural. He was supreme and superb. Those who would write off the teams as "one-man-affairs" had plenty of reminders that this was not true. One innings stands out in this respect. At Bacup, we were overwhelmed by the spin of Dooland and were all out for a little over 70. Of this total, Entwistle scored over 50.

We were no one-man side but we had in it the most exciting cricketer with whom one could be privileged to play. Runs poured from his bat all season, astounding catches were made and his bowling was a tribute to his determination to be all that he could be for his side. His bowling was to be recognised, inadequately and belatedly, by the West Indies later.

Twenty-one summers ago. Ours was a feast that will provide for our nostalgia for another 21 years. To Weekes himself, to every colleague in that team, to every spectator and supporter and to the committee that one so easily takes for granted, I feel indebted for life. However, even Weekes could not have made magic of some of the wet summers of recent years. 1949 was a summer of sunny Saturdays -- a fitting and necessary background to the glory of the cricket.

* * * * * * * * * * *

EVERTON WEEKES' RECORDS FOR BACUP

In 7 seasons from 1949 to 1958 he scored 9019 in 150 innings, averaging 97.7. In the same period he took 453 wickets for 6938 runs -- 15.31 runs per wicket. He scored 1000 runs in every season as Bacup's professional, the highest aggregate 1518 in 1951, in which year he reached his 1000 runs by the end of June.

Run aggregates:	1949:	1470 runs in 26 innings, average 70.
	1951:	1518 runs in 24 innings, average 89.2.
	1952:	1292 runs in 23 innings, average 80.7.
	1953:	1322 runs in 22 innings, average 94.4.
	1954:	1226 runs in 17 innings, average 158.25.
	1956:	1158 runs in 20 innings, average 97.33.
	1958:	1033 runs in 18 innings, average 93.9.

His highest league innings was his 195 against Enfield in 1954, and in his 7 seasons at Bacup he scored 32 centuries and 50 half-centuries. His average scores against Lancashire League clubs were as follows: v. Accrington 71.93; v. Burnley 77.9; v. Church 54.2; v. Colne 68; v. East Lancashire 90.28; v. Enfield 82.57; v. Haslingden 127.42; v. Lowerhouse 94.12; v. Nelson 164; v. Ramsbottom 95.5; v. Rawtenstall 90.11; v. Rishton 79; and v. Todmorden 171.8. – And during his career with Bacup, Weekes hit a century against every club in the Lancashire League.

* * * * * * * * * *

MORE ROSSENDALE ANECDOTES

What a woman doesn't know about newspapers isn't worth knowing. One woman was talking to her husband -- "I notice by the paper that Mr. Jones died on Sunday". "It is a mistake, my dear", said the husband, "he died on Monday". "But the paper said Sunday". "I know, but it was an error in the print".

-- "I thought so too, at first, but I got half a dozen copies of the paper, and it was the same in all of them. They couldn't have made the mistake over and over again".

Servant (to mistress): "I don't care to have you go out in this weather in that dress". Mistress: "What business is it of yours which dress I wear when I go out?" Servant: "I beg pardon, but you promised to give me that dress when you had done with it, so I consider I've got something to say about it ..." (Culled from the Bacup Times about 1880).

BRAVO, SPRINGS ! BRAVO !

Bravo ! well done Springs ! England's champion band !
   On Fame's high pedestal now you take your stand;
Won fair and square, you're foremost in the race,
   Merit alone has put you in that place.

Three times you've done it, thrice this trophy won,
   No other band this honour boasts, not one;
To this high point all others cast their eyes,
   And own you winners of this premier prize.

Accept our greetings, all throughout this vale,
   From lofty hills, o'er which the clouds oft sail;
Down its deep valleys, rolling right along,
   Is heard this gladsome, welcome, greeting song.

All greet you, the aged with hoary hair,
   Mingle their welcomes with the young and fair;
Schoolboys and girls know what great things you've done,
   And prattling infants lisp -- "Our band has won".

"Labour and Love" -- so was this music named,
   That brought together bands renowned and famed;
You've worked and won, and now you stand above,
   You had the Labour first -- now take the Love.

Oft have we read upon our history's page,
   Of conquests won by war's fierce lust and rage;
But this is nobler, better far are these
   Grand triumphs in this victory of peace.

Music, most sacred of all Heavenly gifts,
   Angels know well thy art, their voices lift
In praises to that Being throned afar,
   Who called a chorus from the morning stars.

Often when lofty eloquence has failed,
   With strong and weighty words the foe assailed:
Thundering around, and filling men with fear,
   It is thee -- Music -- that can draw the tear.

Once more then greeting, strangers may have shown
   Their wealth of welcome, and you may have grown
Used to their praises, as you journeyed through,
   But here's a welcome, honest, homely, true.

Your welcome here is best; raised is each voice,
   In loud hurrahs ! both friend and foe rejoice:
From every corner of this hill-bound land,
   We proudly greet you -- England's Premier Band.

A MOORLAND CHARACTER

Whenever Ah feel like trav'lin back i' Time to see mi lusty forebears, Ah allus visit Tupper. To me, he's a grand owd Briton -- a livin'' ' embodiment o' t' warrior breed 'at made England what it used to be...

Last week Ah dropped in on him to witness one of his daily problems an' achievements -- to weysh off his pit-dirt wi' a single keetleful o' hot watter. Nobbut havin' a weyshin-up bowl fer t' job, his system has to werk on th' easy instalment plan:- Hands an' arms, one pint-pot-ful, yed, face an' neck, two pint-pot-fuls, trunk an' legs, as monny damp sponge-fuls as thers watter left for. Apart fro' leavin' him a bit on t' grey side, t' system seems to pan eawt o' reet an' wi' o' t' watter in t' world he could never weysh his back, bicose bein' muscle-bound he connot reych it.

* * * * * * * * *

"Ay, but it feels grand havin' a bit o' comp'ny", said Tupper, droin' a crumpled shirt o'er his yed. "Ah con toak a lot better when Ah've som'dy to speik to!"

"What's that tha's getten' i' thi shirt neck-hoile?" Ah axed him.

"Studs are no good, thers nowt licks a good nut an' bowt".

"Floor booards are gettin' worn wi' thi havin' no carpets deawn", Aw said.

"Well, thads wod Aw pay part o' mi rent for", said Tupper.

* * * * * * * * *

MORE ROSSENDALE ANECDOTES

When "Have a Go" visited the Valley, Wilfred Pickles told a story about two married women. They worked as weavers together, but their husbands had quite good jobs and they both agreed that it was too much both weaving and running a home. One of them hit on an idea to get rid of the weaving and when she got home told her husband "Yon tackler keeps winkin' at me". "Does he?" said her husband, --"'tha mon gie thi notice". So the day after she told her friend of the success of the story, and her friend decided to try the same one. On getting home she said to her husband: "Yon tackler keeps winkin' at me". "Does he?" said her husband, -- "tha wants to wink back -- tha'll ged two mooar looms".

BACUP POLICE INSTRUCTIONS : 1887

(Extracts from the Instruction book printed in 1887 by Tyne & Shepherd at Rossendale Printing Works, and sealed with the Common Seal of the Borough).

"You are appointed under the Municipal Corporations Act, 45 and 46 Vic., c. 60, by the Watch Committee of the Borough of Bacup, as a Constable for the Borough, and have jurisdiction in the County of Lancaster, and within every County being within seven miles of this Borough".

He shall at all times appear in his complete uniform when on duty, unless permission is given him to wear plain clothes. When off duty plain clothes may be worn. When in uniform he must not wear plain clothes over his uniform, and when in plain clothes he must not wear any portion of his uniform.

If absent from duty through sickness, 1/- per day shall be deducted from his pay for the first four weeks, and 1/6 per day for the second and third four weeks; and at the expiration of those periods, his wage to be dealt with as the Watch Committee under the circumstances shall see fit.

He shall not leave the Borough, except on duty, without permission of the Chief Constable.

"Your character as a Police Officer as well as in private life should be above reproach, you must therefore be particular in the choice of your companions, and avoid the practice of taking intoxicating drink when on duty; if you resolutely decline it when offered, you will become respected for your sobriety and decision of character. Experience has proved that coffee or cocoa is better adapted for keeping the body warm and comfortable in cold and wet weather than spirits or beer".

Calling or knocking people up in the morning is strictly forbidden.

You are to observe the streets on your beat; as to their cleanliness, and make a report of all such as you may find in a filthy condition, also all such ash-pits as may be so full as to require emptying.

You must consider it a part of your duty to remove orange peel, etc. from the footways, wherever seen, as by so doing you will render good service, and may be the means of preventing serious accidents to pedestrians. Any person wilfully and continuously throwing orange peel, etc. on the footway, with the evident design of causing annoyance, and exposing the public to danger, is liable to a penalty of forty shillings over and above the amount of any damages caused.

The following are some of the offences you are required to suppress, viz.:- Selling, opening, keeping open, or exposing for sale any intoxicating liquor therein, during the time his premises are directed by law to be closed. The hours of opening and closing are:-

	Opening	Closing
On Weekdays	6–00 a.m.	11–00 p.m.
On Sundays, Christmas	12–30 p.m.	2–30 p.m.
Day and Good Friday	6–00 p.m.	10–00 p.m.

Constables on whose beats Firemen or Turncocks reside, on receiving notice of a fire, or discovering the reflection of a fire in the air, are immediately to inform them of the same.

You should arrest any person whom you have just cause to suspect of having committed, or being about to commit, any of the following offences. In such cases you must judge of the intention of the person from his situation and behaviour:-

"Abduction, Abortion, Accessories to Crime, Accusation of Crime to obtain money, Aggravated Assaults, Attempted Murder or other attempted felonies, Bestiality, Bigamy, Burglary, Coining, Corrosive Fluid Throwing, Counterfeit Coin Uttering, Damaging Bridges, Demanding Money with menaces, Embezzlement, Escaping from Custody, Extortion, Forgery, Gunpowder Placing to endanger life or property, Housebreaking, Horsestealing, Larceny by any means, trick or otherwise; Manslaughter, Murder, Rape, Receiving Stolen Goods, Rescue from Custody, Robbery, Sacrilege, Sodomy, Stealing, Threatening-Letter Writing"

"Constables will not be permitted to burn gas in their rooms while in bed, except in cases of sickness; and all lights must be turned off by the Constable last leaving the room for duty, or other purposes. Gas being abundantly provided, lamps or candles will not be allowed to be taken into the men's bedrooms on any pretext whatever". (Station House Regulation No.6)

"Constables must not leave water running in the basins nor in the bath, nor dirty water in them". (Station House Regulation No.9)

SCALE OF PAY, ADOPTED ON 1st APRIL, 1891.

INSPECTOR:	On appointment -- £97.10.0d per annum	
	After 3 Years Service: £102.14s. per annum	
	After 6 Years Service: £107.18s. per annum	
	After 10 Years Service: £113.2s. per annum	
SERGEANTS:	3rd Class --	On appointment: £1.12.0d per week
	2nd Class --	After 2 Years: £1.13.0d per week
	1st Class --	After 4 Years: £1.14.0d per week
		After 7 Years: £1.15.0d per week
		After 10 Years: £1.16.0d per week
CONSTABLES:	5th Class --	On appointment: £1.4.0d per week
	4th Class --	After 6 months: £1.5.0d per week
	3rd Class --	After 1 Year: £1.6.0d per week
	2nd Class --	After 2 Years: £1.7.0d per week
	1st Class --	After 3 Years: £1.8.0d per week
		After 6 Years: £1.9.0d per week
		After 10 Years: £1.10.0d per week
		After 14 Years: £1.11.0d per week

Merit Pay, at the rate of 1s. per week, may be granted to Sergeants and Constables in addition to the above.

Footnote: The Bacup Borough Police Force, of which a photograph taken at the time of the 1937 Jubilee appears elsewhere, effectively policed Bacup from 1st August 1887 to 31st March 1947, when, along with the police forces of Accrington, Ashton-under-Lyne, Clitheroe and Lancaster, they were merged with the Lancashire Constabulary. Bacup's Chief Constables were: James Cummings (1887 to 1891), John Harland (1891 to 1914), John Niven Campbell (1914 to 1920), Ernest William Sturt (1920 to 1938), Robert William Priest (1938 to his death in 1946).

A BIT OF OLD BACUP

During the latter part of the 19th century when the river Irwell was open -- and slaughter-houses then occupied the site where the Cenotaph now stands, a portion of the road nearby was known to all and sundry as "th' bostins". This particular area is situated towards the rear of Woolworth's, and more recently it was known as Boston Place.

Following the covering of the river approximately in 1900, the name Boston Road appeared, which had been repeatedly corrupted from the original "boose-stang" or beast-stang (most local farmers still refer to their cattle as beasts). Here it was that the drovers used to tether the cattle while they refreshed themselves at the nearby "Bull's Head" alehouse. The word "boose"is equivalent to the more modern "stall" whilst the connecting pole was always referred to as "stang" by northerners of my generation.

A correspondent of the Bacup Times during the 1930's stated that during the period in question, his father strongly objected to the Town Clerk of Bacup about the term "Boston Road". Which in fact, it never was, the etymology having no basis in actual fact. Nevertheless, the offending title Boston Road was allowed to remain.

* * * * * * * * *

(Footnote: The Bacup Times dated February 16th, 1895, includes the following extract:

> "Last week, one of the oldest -- if not the oldest -- pieces of architecture in Bacup borough was demolished. We refer to the old Boston Bridge in Burnley Road, which, owing to its dilapidated condition, has been closed for some time, and a temporary wooden bridge erected close by. The original bridge is believed to date from 1632, but whether it has been replaced is not known. Anyhow, the proverbial "oldest inhabitant" says it was an old bridge 70 years ago".)

BACUP CRICKET CLUB, winners of the Lancashire League Championship and Worsley Cup, 1923. Team: Back row: F. Hartley, T. Dickenson, J. Midgley (senior), capt., A. G. Slater (professional), R. Ratcliffe. Centre row: J. Musk, J. Midgley (junior), C. Roberts, H. Holt, Front row: F. Jackson, J. Lord, F. Hargreaves.

BURNLEY ROAD leading into the centre of Bacup about 1890, showing the uncovered river Irwell up to the Bull's Head Hotel and bridge, with Boston on the left.

OLD KENNELS, BOSTON, Burnley Road – the site of the present war memorial. Note the open river Irwell and the pre-"Regal" building, which was a skating rink. (Compare with the other photo of Boston and the Bull's Head.)

IRWELL SPRINGS PRIZE BAND, taken when they won the Belle Vue Championship in 1905. Conductor at the time -- William Rimmer.

The GEORGE AND DRAGON INN and Gibson's Tripe Shop about 1910, with the Mechanics' Institute just visible on the right. The roundabout in the centre of Bacup now occupies this site, the buildings being demolished about 1925.

BACUP.

Taken from the Report to the General Board of Health, 1849, by the Superintending Inspector of Bacup, William Lee, showing the area covered by the Report.

ROOLEY MOOR ROAD climbs from Rakehead up to 1520 feet near Top o' Leach, then meanders down past the old Moorcock Inn towards Rochdale. Parts of it were paved during the "cotton famine" about 1862. The Old Bone House, sometimes called Intack or Intake, was last owned by "Dicky" Plumb who served refreshments to workers in the quarries above Cowpe.

BACUP BOROUGH POLICE FORCE Jubilee Photograph, 1937. Back row: P.C. William J. Pauling; P.C. John Kay; P.C. Ernest Langton, P.C. Richard Calland; P.C. Benjamin Burton. Centre row: Inspector John Barrow (retired); P.C. Richard Holden; P.C. Joseph Walsh; P.C. Norman Scott; P.C. Abraham M. Jones; P.C. Harvey Lord; P.C. Fred Jenkinson, P.C. Cornelius Coward; P.C. William G. Wales; P.C. Henry Gribble; Station Sergeant Frank Jackson; P.C. Robert Wild; P.C. Henry G. Marsh; P.C. Charles W. Windle (retired). Front row: P.C. Thomas Bennington; Sergeant William Martin; Detective Sergeant Percy Bayley; Dr. J.D. McVean; Chief Constable Ernest W. Sturt; Inspector John D. Thomlinson; Sergeant John Spencer; Sergeant Richard E. Russell; P.C. John Askew. P.C. Fred Lye was absent at the time.

HARRY TOWNSEND – the Boy Wonder Walker.
See page 187.

BACUP CRICKET CLUB, 1951 – Back row: Jack Dunham, Tom Graham, J. Ashwort Stanley Hall, B. Dawson, S. Banham, H. Larter, (scorer). Front row: D. Howart E. D. Weekes (professional), J. Roberts (captain), P. Barcroft, J. Ratcliffe.

MAY SUNDAY ON ROOLEY MOOR

Before the war I always went
   Up Rooley on May Sunday,
For at the Moorcock Inn that day
   You'd meet with all and sundry.
There were hundreds there from Rochdale,
   From the Whitworth Valley too,
From Rossendale and Heywood,
   It was called the "Sermons" do;
The moor was "wick" with shouting crowds
   Till the first stars came out, pale,
And there never was a Sermons Day
   When they didn't sell out of ale.
Many and many a year ago --
   I've heard my father tell --
There were gypsies, quacks and card-sharpers
   And wrestling booths as well.
I wonder how it started --
   This old-time moorland fair --
It must have been the Chartists
   Who first assembled there.
In the eighteen-thirties
   When times were hard and grim,
They had their moorland meetings
   And sang the Chartists' Hymn.
But now the Moorcock Inn has gone,
   The Sermons Day as well,
There's nothing now but a heap of stones
   Where the lonely curlews dwell.
But though long years may come and go,
   My thoughts will ever stray
To a lonely road and a windswept moor
   On Rooley Sermons Day.

* * * * * * *

UT SCHOO' AFORE T' FIRST WAR

Ring worms an' jacket sleeves shiny wi snot
   An yed-lice an' scabs as like as not,
An' clooas ut stunk an' favvered rags
   Wi' wrostlin' an feightin' o' t' dusty flags.

Inside t' schoo' ther' wur neer no noise
   Or schoo'-maister ud soon bi caning t' boys,
Bud onny on us ut t' others thowt mard
   Wur punced an oined eawt i' t' schoo'-yard.

When marble-time coom reawnd i' spring
   We laiked at "poddle-oile" an "ring",
We used glass-allys, we co'd em "pops"
   Eawt o' mineral-watter bockle tops.

Aw geet mi "spence" on a Fridi neet
   Id wur nobbut tuppence bud it seemed oreet,
Aw could ged a pennoth o' peys an' chips
   Or a hawpoth o' everlastin' strips.

Or a penny-bockle if t' day wur hot
   An Aw ne'er missed wod Aw ne'er got.
Fer a fuutbo' wi med a bo' wi rags
   An t' goils wur jackets put deawn o' t' flgas.

Bud Aw luk back o' th' owd schoo' wi' pride,
   Wi did t' Three Rs, but mooar beside
Wod Aw larnt theer ut wark an' play
   Has geet mi through mi life's long way.

A BOY WONDER WALKER

A damaged monument in Bacup cemetery, a short obituary in the columns of the Bacup Times for October 24th, 1903. and a photograph reproduced elsewhere in Bacup Miscellany are all that is known of a little boy who became renowned for walking.

His name was Harry Townsend, the son of Mr. George Townsend, born in Bacup, and at the time of his death lived in Oldham Road, Rochdale.

He was born in 1895, and little is known of him until the year 1903, except that his health was somewhat delicate, necessitating an absence from school in 1901 which lasted for six months. However, with plenty of exercise and vegetarian diet, he gradually became stronger, and, says the Bacup Times, he "has since undertaken some remarkable walks for one so young".

This was in 1903, the year in which he commenced walking in public. The Bacup Times records that "a short time ago he walked from Ilford to Romford, a distance of 21 miles, in 4¾ hours. Next he managed a circular walk from Rochdale to Bacup, Walsden, and Littleborough (21 miles), which was accomplished in 5 hours 10 minutes, though the boy had a strong head wind against him for ten miles".

Harry Townsend also walked from Rochdale to Halifax, and on Saturday October 14th, 1903, he covered the 19 miles from Chorley to Southport on foot. The following Saturday he was due to walk from Bury to Manchester. But he died that morning.

The obituary report informs us that the doctor was called to see him on the Thursday, and found him to be suffering from a "little inflammation of the tonsils -- an ailment he frequently had", but was otherwise perfectly well, and had some football practice afterwards. Later he became ill again, and when the doctor called on Friday, he diagnosed broncho-pneumonia, and "despite all that could be done for him, death took place about 1.30 a.m. on Saturday".

The well-known boy walker was only eight years of age.

Hasledene was a typical example of any Lancashire town. Its stone pavements were worn and polished smooth by the clogs of past generations. Its streets in the centre of the town consisted of houses of the back-to-back type. The streets' only illumination came from a gas lamp placed about the middle of each street. The door steps and window sills of the houses were kept clean and bright by the weekly application of the rubbing stone, coloured brown or white, as preferred by the housewife.

It was a regular sight on a Friday night to see the women and young girls down on their knees, a steaming bucket of hot water and floor cloth in front of them, busily scrubbing the stone flags in front of the house, then finishing off by applying the rubbing stone to the front edge of the doorstep and window sill.

Anyone foolish enough to walk on the flags when this washing down process had been completed would naturally expect a clout round the ear-hole with the mop rag, and receive a good telling off into the bargain; this was indeed something to be avoided.

The rubbing stones were lumps of sandstone; they were in exchange for rags and woollens from the barrow of the "Rag and Bone" man. Empty jars and bottles were also exchanged for sand; this was sprinkled on the stone floor of the house -- this came into contact with the clog irons, and the crushing action helped to keep the floor reasonably clean.

In these humble dwellings, the only covering of the stone flagged floor was by a "pegged rug" which was made out of well worn jackets and coats, cut into strips and felted into a canvas backing. This produced a thick warm rug of many colours. It had pride of place in front of the fire-grate gleaming with black-leaded brightness, its steel top-bar and steel fender polished to perfection by much sweat and elbow grease on Friday night.

Above the fire-grate was the mantelshelf, this was draped with a red plush cover fringed with red bobs. Occupying the centre of this shelf was a large photograph of Dad in his army uniform, his waxed moustache added to his military bearing. Two large brass candlesticks looking like sentinels, stood one at each end of the shelf. The hearth stone was in a rich cream colour.

Two wooden rockers in antimacassars stood one on each side of a deal extension table. This was covered by a square of American cloth, its pattern faded and its surface worn and peeling, caused by the constant washing down it received by the damp dish-cloth after every meal.

Attached to the wall nearest the slop-stone was the "pot-shelf" stacked with plates of all sizes, pots and jugs hanging from brass hooks. Draped in front of the window were a pair of long lace curtains hanging from a thick wooden pole, also a green roller blind for use when necessary. Adorning the window bottom was a fully grown Aspidistra plant in a dark green bowl.

One of Hasledene's characters was nick-named "Owd Peg-leg". He was the Lamp-lighter and Knocker-up. These were jobs that his infirmity allowed him to do, they did provide his bare necessities. At five-thirty sharp each morning, "owd Peg-leg" would be on his rounds. The tap-tapping of his wooden leg could be heard as he wended his way round the darkened streets. He carried on his shoulder a long wooden pole with wires attached, these he rattled against the window panes and never failed to waken the sleeping occupants, who quickly dressed, and, rubbing the sleep from their eyes, hurried down the stone steps to snatch a butty and a pot of tea.

Then, all too soon, the morning stillness would be shattered by the blasts of the factory sirens, sounding their persistent warning that it was time they were on their way to the factory. They knew only too well that late comers were fined, or the factory gates would be closed against them for that day.

Now above the dying wail of the sirens would be heard the sound of doors opening and slamming, coupled with the sound of the clogs of men, boys, women and girls hurrying through the dimly lit streets to the cotton factories. Through the pale light of dawn, the women were hardly discernible from the men, dressed in their clogs, thick home knitted wool stockings and shawls, chattering together as they joined the main stream converging on the factory gates.

After being confined for twelve hours in the hot weaving-shed or spinning-room, the hard and tedious nature of their work was at an end for twelve hours. The operatives rushed through the factory gates and out on to the stone pavements, laughing and jostling one another, glad to be released from their tiresome tasks.

At the "Fish and Chip" shop down the street they were ready for the hungry workers. The aroma from the chip pans meets them at the shop entrance, where they are unable to resist the temptation and walk up to the counter for threepennyworth in a newspaper, with salt and lashings of vinegar, these are eaten as they walk home arm in arm. This daily pattern of the cotton worker's life was for 5½ days per week, 51 weeks per year, with only one week's holiday, and this without holiday pay. That was the difficult part of holidays, no wages at the end of the week! So somebody had to be missed that week.

Another necessary evil of those times was the weekly visit to the "Pawnshop". Here articles of clothing were pledged to get a few shillings to buy food for the large families. When the next pay-day came along, these pledged articles were redeemed so that the children could wear them for Sunday School.

On Friday, pay-day, the streets were alive with "Clothing Club" and Insurance collectors busy on their collecting rounds. The doctor's man too would also be on his round, collecting whatever he could for medical services rendered, as little as threepence was acceptable. The older women helped the doctor in cases of child-birth, for in those days there was no registered Midwife, or District Nurse, or Maternity Hospital.

Friday night was bath night, a large iron cauldron normally used on washing day was filled with water and placed on the hob to heat. The zinc bath tub was brought out from under the stairs in readiness for Operation Bath-Tub.

It will be readily noted that bathing a large family was really something, heating all the water required on the fire, emptying the tub by bucket each time the water required changing. At the slop-stone, this was a back-breaking job for the parents.

Gone are those days and no regrets; gone too are those badly-lit streets of unsanitary dwellings and the old zinc bath-tub; the "knocker-up" and the early morning blasts of the factory sirens; the six o'clock start.

Thanks to the planners and developers, the old properties of the cotton towns have been demolished, and replaced by blocks of modern flats, landscaped housing developments set among trees, lawns and flower beds . . . Modern heating methods help to reduce the risk of air pollution to a minimum.

These are some of the memories relating to any Lancashire Cotton Town during the reign of King Cotton.

ALEX A. HOLT (1889 - 1965)

"Alec" Holt was born at Shawclough, near Scoutbottom.

He did not go to school until he was eight years of age, and at eleven he commenced working half time, assisting his father, Grimshaw Holt, in his business of Property Repairer, Stonemason, and Chimney Sweep, finally going to work full-time at thirteen.

In 1909, at the age of twenty, he started in business on his own account in the same line as his father, which he continued for about seven years.

Being a very enterprising man, he embarked in various other businesses, including Soot Merchant, Manufacturer of footwear, Bags and Bale sheets, waste merchant, etc., but he says, "I was never really happy as a dressed-up man. I had been brought up to work and liked it and was always the happiest with my working tools and could sleep better and sing more. The Waste trade was all right, but there was nothing to be seen for your labour, whereas with the hammer and trowel the results can be seen -- they are monuments for all time, you can construct and produce something that is worth looking at. You are proud of your efforts and it spurs you on for more and better results. To try and do your little part in this world to make it nicer and better, and if possible to try and be an example for others, then the result of your labour has been worth while".

In his early years, he had a great love for horses, and later turned to motor-cars.

Alec moved from Stacksteads to Cleveleys in 1920 as a master builder, and built hundreds of houses there. He became so well known there that he was known as "Mr. Cleveleys". He lived there until his death in 1965.

Alec was a great entertainer and conversationalist. He could always quote appropriately -- off the cuff -- from his tremendous repertoire of humorous verses. He loved to portray the shrewd witticisms, drolleries and whimsicalities of Lancashire life and character.

His philosophy of life is epitomised in the following lines which he composed himself:

"Howd up yer yed,
Cock eawt yer chin,
Stick a FEVVER in yer 'at,
An' mek t' best ov everything"
– Alex o' Cleveleys.

JACK'S CHRISTMAS LEAVE

By One of them!

Wasn't I glad to find the train getting near and nearer to good old Bacup. What a thrill it was to come through the Thrutch once again, and then to pass Lee Mill, and then under the bridge, and then oh! boy! here we were at Bacup. Blessed sound! Dear old home! I wondered if it would be changed at all. I hadn't long been away, but places have such a disconcerting way of changing at times.

It was all just as I had expected it to be. Just as I had pictured it so often. There were the dear old red buses passing up Market Street coming like bananas, just as usual and I thought of the long wait some poor souls must have had, and here the 'buses were coming in bunches as so often they had done before. My kit was heavy so I decided to have a penn'orth up to the centre. Getting off at the Bank, the first person I saw was a good old Mountite. "Hello", she said, "Are you here for Christmas? Well and I am glad to see you. Clifford was over last week but he's just gone back. How are you getting on? I hope you go to chapel, or church parade or whatever yo' lads call it".

I assured her that I regularly attended Church Parade and had made good use of the Methodist canteen. "Well, we'll be seein' you on Sunday I hope" she said as I left her, to go down Tower Street. Travelling along St. James' Street, I ran into Mr. Little who as usual was very cordial and anxiously enquired as to whether we were well catered for, etc. "Hello, hello" said a familiar voice, and turning round, I saw our dear old friend Edwin (I should say Mr. Barnes) rounding on us. Dear old Edwin. It wouldn't be Bacup if we didn't see him ambling around with his stick in his hand. How we shall miss him one of these days. He began to tell me what a wonderful treat the Messiah had been. "Didn't I wish I could have been there". Anyhow I explained that I had heard the "Messiah" where I am stationed, but of course I had to admit it wasn't a patch on the "do" up at Mount.

Wending my way homewards up South Street I had a glimpse of Daisy on her way to her dinner and I made a mental note that I must see her to thank her and the Committee for what they are doing for us lads who are away. Incidentally I hope she doesn't get a young man until the War is over, for if she did she wouldn't have the time to work for us.

Did I say it was Christmas Eve? Before I went to bed that night I had consumed enough mincepies to last a lifetime to say nothing of innumerable sausage rolls, meat pies, lobster patties etc. You see I went round to show myself to my friends and relatives and wherever I went I was made to eat. I think it was the lobster patties which caused most trouble, because when I finally turned in for the night, I had a most disturbed rest. For one thing I had thought of this lovely bed for weeks, but now that I was in it, I couldn't get used to the comfort of it. How I tossed and turned until I finally dozed off.

Then the fun began. First of all I found I was sailing over a very stormy sea, over mountainous waves which billowed around us at every turn. Suddenly I found myself on a raft which was comfortably fitted up with a three piece suite and a couple of typewriters. But what surprised me more than anything was the mermaids sitting on top of the waves. No matter how the wave lurched there was the mermaid comfortably seated on the top. It was the mermaids I think, who stopped me from being sea-sick. One couldn't -- well no, it was better to think of something else.

What did one say to a mermaid? What was the correct way of approach? I was pondering this, when suddenly I noticed one of them had a harp and was attempting to play it. It was the weirdest sound I have ever heard. I had already felt sick enough, but the music ? made me far worse. Suddenly, for some inscrutable reason I found myself in bed in a hospital ward and the kindly doctor was drilling into my head a pneumatic drill. It was an awful sensation. How I wished he'd get the operation over. It was like nothing on earth. I tried to get away from his grip, but I found that whatever they had given me to render me unconscious had locked my limbs and I was helpless. Move as I would I couldn't get away from that drill. Then I realised that the noise it was making was just like the noise from the mermaid's harp, piercing and insistent. Nearer and nearer came the drilling until I felt I could bear it no longer. I tore the thing from his hand, before I realised that I was able to move, and through the window it went. By this time I realised I was in bed, I turned and buried my head in the pillow. If only they would stop that noise -- if only they would go in the next street! Yes, that was it, right under my window -- what was it, cats? "O Come, All Ye Faithful, joyful and triumphant!" It was -- the Mount Carol Singers doing their worst!

BACUP'S MAYORAL ROBE AND CHAIN

The first Mayor of Bacup had no insignia of office, and this led to a lament in print by a Bacupian using the name "Bunthorne" entitled "Wanted, a Golden Chain!", sung to the tune of "Over the Garden Wall". This was partly responsible for the gift of the Mayoral chain by Mr. James Smith Sutcliffe, which was handed over on the 18th February 1885. The gift resulted in another outburst of song in print by "Bunthorne", sung to the same tune, this time entitled, "Found, a Golden Chain!".

The Mayoress's chain was given to Bacup in September 1922 by Mr. J. T. Hoyle, and worn for the first time when the Mayoress was a guest of the Mayoress of Preston at the Preston Guild of 1922.

Councillor Albert Howarth, speaking to a Bacup school, referred to the town of which he was the 61st Mayor.

"The country is divided into districts, and each year, each district elects a chairman, who also becomes the chief citizen of that particular district. If this is so, you may be asking yourself why I am called the Mayor and not Chairman, as are Whitworth's and Ramsbottom's chief citizens. This is because Bacup was granted a Charter 89 years ago, and became a Borough; this entitled the chairman to use the title of His Worship the Mayor and wear the appropriate regalia. Of course there was much more to it than that.

"My robe is red, which is the most favoured colour, but Rawtenstall and Haslingden, which are both Boroughs, have Mayoral robes of blue and purple respectively. The one I am wearing today is of course not the original one -- that was replaced a few years ago by the descendants of the original donors.

"I think the Mayoral chains are more interesting, because though many mayoral robes may be alike, no two chains are, each have their own characteristics. I am very proud to wear it, not only for the honour, of which I *am* justly proud, but also because it is much admired. On each of the links are the initials of all the previous mayors, except for the last few; it was felt that to add any more links would make it too cumbersome, it already weighs 3 lbs.

"On the medallion is the coat of arms, for which permission was granted one year after the Charter. On the top stands the figure of a deer which depicts that Bacup was once a dense forest, so dense in fact that it is said that a squirrel could travel all the way down the Valley without once touching the ground. Then farmers came in, and cleared some of the trees, and began sheep farming -- which led to the woollen industry. Then came the introduction of cotton to the Valley, and people began to pour in from afar to work in the cotton mills, which had begun to mushroom; these people required houses, and as there was stone in the hills above, suitable for building, quarrying soon found jobs for a large number of men.

"170 years ago, the population of Bacup was a mere 1400, and did not include Stacksteads. By 1881 this had risen to 25,000 and Stacksteads was now part of Bacup, which had now become a thriving, busy industrial town, with wool, cotton, and stone quarrying as their main indsutries. So when they came to choose their coat of arms, they chose to have on their crest a lamb's fleece or sheep skin, two bales of cotton and a block of stone, to represent the main industries. Whilst a squirrel and two bees were also chosen, to represent the characteristics of the inhabitants as being thrifty and hard working.

"It's very sad to think that only two more Mayors will have the privilege of wearing this chain; owing to local government change, Bacup, along with the other Valley towns will cease to be Boroughs. We do not yet know what our fate will be, but we are hoping we can stay together as Rossendale. Owing to this reorganisation, we will not now be able to reach our centenary, so instead we will celebrate our 90th year as a Borough during 1972".

(The official description of the Coat of Arms of the Borough of Bacup is as follows: Azure on a Fesse between two Bales of Cotton in Chief Or, and a Block of Stone with Lewis attached in Base proper, a Fleece Sable between two Bees volant of the third, in the centre Chief point a Squirrel sejent of the second, And for the Crest on a Wreath of the Colours in front of a Bale of Cotton Or, a Stag proper gorged with a Collar Vair resting the dexter fore-foot on a Trefoil slipped Gold). The coat of arms appears by permission on the cover of Bacup Miscellany.

* * * * * * * *

MAYORS OF THE BOROUGH OF BACUP

1882 to 1884	Alderman John Hargreaves.
1884 to 1886	Alderman William James Clegg.
1886 to 1887	Councillor James Smith Sutcliffe.
1887 to 1888	Alderman Joseph Lees.
1888 to 1889	Alderman George Shepherd (of Holmes Villa)
1889 to 1890	Alderman Daniel Greenwood.
1890 to 1891	Alderman George Shepherd (of Holmes Villa) for 2nd time
1891 to 1892	Councillor Henry Salmon.
1892 to 1893	Alderman William James Clegg for 2nd time (died Apr. 1893)
April to November 1893	Councillor Henry Salmon.
1893 to 1894	Alderman Thomas Disley.
1894 to 1895	Alderman George Shepherd (of Holmes Villa) for 3rd time.
1895 to 1896	Alderman Edwin Hardman.

1896 to 1897	Councillor John Henry Maden, M.P.
1897 to 1898	Alderman George Shepherd (of Holmes Villa) for 4th time
1898 to 1900	Councillor Ben Smith
1900 to 1911	Alderman John Hnery Maden (for 2nd period)
1911 to 1913	Alderman Joshua Craven Hoyle
1913 to 1914	Councillor Edmund Lord
1914 to 1916	Councillor James Henry Lord
1916 to 1917	Alderman Sir John Henry Maden (for 3rd period)
1917 to 1919	Councillor Samuel McLerie
1919 to 1921	Councillor Thomas Thompson
1921 to 1924	Joshua Thomas Hoyle, Esq. (the only instance of a Mayor of Bacup who was not a member of the Council. He was elected a Councillor in 1924).
1924 to 1926	Alderman Heyworth Whitehead
1926 to 1928	Councillor William Rhodes (died September 1928)
October 1928	Alderman Heyworth Whitehead
1928 to 1930	Alderman Walter Nuttall
1930 to 1932	Alderman John Brierley
1932 to 1933	Councillor Samuel Crabtree Smith
1933 to 1935	Councillor William Marshall
1935 to 1937	Alderman Eli Gledhill
1937 to 1940	Councillor William James Hartley
1940 to 1942	Alderman Thomas Coates
1942 to 1944	Alderman James Ireland
1944 to 1946	Councillor Ernest Barcroft
1946 to 1947	Councillor John Myerscough
1947 to 1949 (May)	Councillor James Henry Hargreaves
1949 to 1950	Alderman Arthur Rhodes
1950 to 1951	Alderman Frank Haworth
1951 to 1952	Alderman Thomas Ashworth
1952 to 1953	Councillor Jesse Crabtree
1953 to 1954	Alderman Herbert Lord
1954 to 1955	Councillor Firth Needham Rimmer
1955 to 1956	Councillor Ashworth Lord
1956 to 1957	Councillor Mrs. Ada Rhodes (the first woman Mayor)
1957 to 1958	Councillor John Edge
1958 to 1959	Councillor Jack Bradley Walley
1959 to 1960	Councillor Matthew Connolly
1960 to 1961	Councillor Roy Taylor
1961 to 1962	Councillor Albert Prescote Beaumont
1962 to 1963	Councillor Thomas Clifford Law
1963 to 1964	Councillor Mrs. Annie Stocks
1964 to 1965	Councillor Harold Rawson
1965 to 1966	Alderman John Crabtree
1966 to 1967	Councillor John Kershaw
1967 to 1968	Alderman Horace Brassington
1968 to 1969	Councillor Thomas Parker
1969 to 1970	Councillor Frank Banham
1970 to 1971	Alderman George Eastwood Mills
1971 to 1972	Councillor Albert Howarth
1972 to 1973	Alderman John Ingham Holt

ON THE USE OF MUSICAL INSTRUMENTS IN ROSSENDALE

The use of fiddles, flutes, clarinets, and occasionally brass instruments came to Accrington from the Rossendale district, where they were used at the charity sermons. One of the features was the singing of old hymns and choruses to old-fashioned music such as "Happy Simeon", composed by John Nuttall, of Lumb-in-Rossendale ; "Spanking Roger" and "Bocking Warp", composed by his father, James.

In the 18th and early 19th centuries, the form of singing was debated freely, and, sometimes, heatedly. The Baptists of Accrington introduced Watts' hymns into their church worship for the first time in June, 1829, but there is no mention of a choir until January, 1844. The first organ came in 1832, at Machpelah.

Then, as now, the anthem was a great institution at charity sermons. On these occasions the old musicians came forth from obscure corners to renew the glory of their early manhood. And how deeply in earnest the vocalists were! They positively perspired through their great exertions, and when they sat down there was a general mopping of heads and faces. In old psalmody there was very often repetition of lines, and in anthems the fugue was always to the fore. One remembers how the words were sacrificed to the music, and what ludicrous results sometimes followed. Many musicians will remember the piece where the treble led off with "My own sal", repeated it three times, was followed by other parts, and then unitedly came the complete sentence, "My own salvation's rock to praise", There was another, "We'll wash our hands", with its final "in innocence"; also "And in the pie" which ended "In the pious He delights". A modern congregation would be startled if some of its choir burst off with "Stir up this stew", but when they united they would find it ending with "Stir up this stupid heart of mine"; or to hear the command, "Take thy pill", which in the long run resolves itself into "Take thy pilgrim home". And what, too, of the pathetic plaints of the shrill soprano, "O, for a man", oft repeated, and then taken up by the more youthful seconds, next chirped by aesthetic tenors, and finally rolled off by the stentorian basses. Grotesqueness reached its meridian, the music quietened down, and in unison was breathed the inoffensive orison, "O, for a mansion in the skies".

TH' DEIGHN LAYROCKS bi one o' th' breed E.M.

Tune -- "Bocking Warp"

NAAH, all yo foak uts fond o' lore,
List to mi tale o' days uv yore;
When th' Layrocks true, began to sing,
Thoor fiddlers fairly touched ther string.

Aw think just naah aw see um stand
Wi' candle lifted, book i' hand;
While others on th' owd table spread
Ther book, un pept o'er th' fiddler's yed.

Then one, two, three, they all began,
Un th' crotchets, quavers, heaw they ran!
Th' owd singers sang, un th' fiddlers bow'd,
Th'effect ut th' song con neer be towd.

Ther singing wur so true un grand,
Id made fooaks yure on end to stand.
Un th' fiddlin' wur so brisk un sweet
Id fairly brought fooak to ther feet.

Ther hearts i' tune, ther lips i' song
Wi th' rising sun, un all day long
They sang ther tunes fro leet to dark
Un up i' th' morn just like a lark.

Un when ther work wur done ut neet
They met together, dark or leet,
Ther sowls wur full o' music rife,
True harmony ther aim o' life.

Eh! could yo but a yerd 'em sing
Yo wud to th' bats your music fling,
You'd neer try th' music trade no fur,
But pitch your singing aght o' th' dur.

It wur a taste o' heaven itsell,
To yer haah th' fiddles rose an' fell,
Un th' singing wur so grand un clear,
Yo' couldn't a helped but shed a tear.

Such singing neer wur yerd befooar,
All th' nabors stood aghtside ther door,
To listen to thooar songs o' praise,
That thrill'd all th' Deighn wi' heavenly lays.

May we like them so spend awr days,
Wi' music's charms i' all id ways;
Like them i' this employ so blest
Sink deawn like th' setting stars to rest.

So making life a cheerful song,
Do wod wi' con to thus prolong
The good o' thooar who nature blest
Wi music's charms i' heavenly dress.

A STORY ABOUT THE DEAN LAYROCKS

In his lectures on the Dean Layrocks, the late Alderman Compston of Crawshawbooth was very fond of telling the following story:

A young man had tramped one evening to Dean over two ranges of hills from Haslingden Grane in order to attend a rehearsal of the "Layrocks". When the practice had gone on until turned midnight he felt he should be going and some time later he said so, because he had "to be up middlin' soon i' th' mornin'...whereupon an enthusiastic old stager exclaimed, "Dost yer what Aw'm sayin' to tha? Tha'll never mek a musicianer as long as tha lives, tha't i' too big a hurry!"

THE WELCOME SONG

Aw'm a leet-hearted chap an' durnt care a rap, aw allus feel happy
an gay,
An o' through this life aw keep joggin along, aw never meet trouble
awf way;
Aw've a dear little wife to poo mi through life, two childer as breet
as t' day, ,
If a chap comes to see t'wife, childer and me, aw ax him in an then
say

CHORUS:
Th'art welcome lad, th'art welcome, gie us thi hond, owd chum;
Sit thi deawn an' draw up to t' fire, an mek thisel awhom;
Here's jolly good health, here's luck an' here's wealth, an'
whenever th'art passin' this way
Aw'll ollus bi glad, to si thi owd lad, th'art as welcome as
t'fleawrs i' May.

Some folk may freawn on a chap when he's deawn, if thi see him
thi'll turn t'other way;
Thi'll treat him wi' scorn if his coat's a bit torn, an' leave him to do
as he may;
Such folk as these arn't worth knowin', mon, ther conduct is greatly
to blame,
Tho' a chap may be rough, if he's med o' t' reyt stuff, its when a
chap's deawn he'll exclaim . . .

CHORUS:

So let us endeavour where'er we may be, to do a good turn if we con;
An' help one another wi' hearty goodwill, an' ollus act up like a mon;
Tho' fortune may smile on him more nor on you, its his luck an' a
little to spare
If his load is too heavy, then give him a lift, an' to him wi' pleasure
declare - -

CHORUS:

AW'M A LEET-HEARTED CHAP

LYNTON L.M GEORGE FIRTH

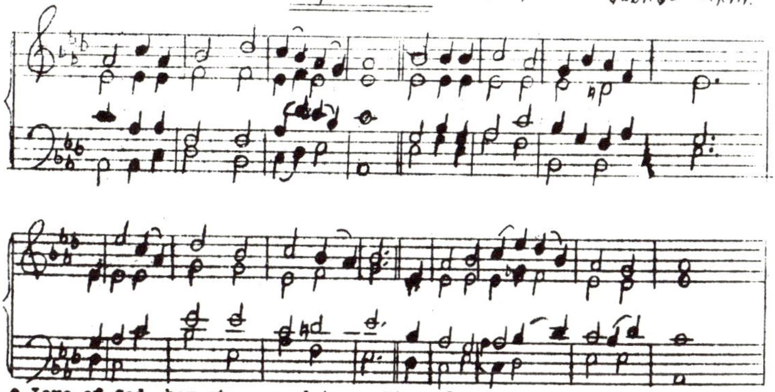

O Love of God, how strong and true. Eternal, and yet ever new
Uncomprehended and unbought,
Beyond all knowledge and all thought.

JACOB FROM BACUP

Words and Music by E. MOSTER-MERRITT

now he has mills of his own He acts as a kind of a
lev-er To mount me on For-tune's great throne I'll
cresc
cresc.
soon be in Par-lia-ment straight For Ba-cup I'm THE candi-date
Refrain
mf
I'm Ja-cob from Ba-cup: I'll make the world wake up. Oh what a shake-up there'll
mf
be! For Ja-cob from Ba-cup your wrongs he will take up
1.
f
2.
when he's a full-blown M. P. I'm
f

Song of the

"ROSSENDALE CHARITY CUP"

(Tune: "A Starry night for a Ramble")

1. We sing in praise of football,
   The various cups as well,
Our medals too, we'll wear them,
   And shan't we all be swells.
For we have fought through every game,--
   With courage and good will --
We never have been daunted yet,
   And we love our opponents still.

CHORUS: For its Whittaker, Hunt, and Taylor,
   Captain, Mitchell, Dan;
Albert, Eli, Charles, and Joe,
   And John the little man.

2. First we played with Rawtenstall,
   Then Loveclough the next;
We beat them both in a canter,
   And weren't they awfully vexed.
Now Rawtenstall was four to nought,
   Loveclough was three to one,
They both went home wi' thur' hearts in thur' clogs,
   And their money all was gone.

CHORUS:

3. We then did play with Rossendale,
   On Stacksteads' ground so grand;
And when the game was over,
   The teams did equal stand.
Jim Preston was the Referee,
   But did not suit at all --
For he changed his own decision
   In reference to a goal.

CHORUS:

4. The Tie was played at Dark Lane,
    On the 23rd of June;
Each side worked hard and sternly,
    To exactly the same tune;
But worst of all for Irwell Springs
    When half the game was o'er;
John Catlow he got crippled
    And didn't play any more.
CHORUS;

5. Again they played on the same ground,
    For Catlow's benefit:
For in the last match he had got
    His shin bone badly split;
This time the game was finished out
    Poor Rossendale they did ought,
To quit the field as best they could --
    For the game was three to nought.
CHORUS:

6. Such deaf'ning shouts you ne'er did hear,
    On a football field before,
For they brought the Cup and held it up,
    Which is made of Silver-ore.
It was then presented to our boys,
    As a trophy fairly won;
And may they hold it firmly
    Through many a summer's sun.
CHORUS:

7. Then shout hurrah for Irwell Springs,
    For Stacksteads, Rawtenstall too;
Loveclough, and Scout, and Rossendale --
    We have them all pulled through.
Then give three cheers for the Springs Brass Band,
    Who met and played them up;
From the George Inn to the Wellington,
    With the Rossendale Charity Cup.

CHORUS: For its Whittaker, Hunt, and Taylor,
Captain, Mitchell, Dan;
Albert, Eli, Charles, and Joe,
And John the little man.

The results of the final ties of the Rossendale Charity Cup were as follows :

1884	Irwell Springs 3, Rossendale 0
1885	Irwell Springs 7, Scoutbottom 4
1886	Rawtenstall 5, Haslingden Church Institute 0
1887	Irwell Springs 2, Church Institute 1
1888	Irwell Springs 4, Rawtenstall 1
1889	Rawtenstall 2, Rossendale 0 (after a draw 1–1)

MORE ROSSENDALE ANECDOTES

The following coal bill "emphasises its astronomical rise in prices in these modern times" (Harry Craven) :

GREAVE COLLIERY, BACUP, April 15th, 1885.

Delivered to O. Mitchell
By Townsend & Barlow

		£	s	d
Gross	14 cwt.			
Tare	4 cwt.			
Nett @ 3½d cwt =			2	11

(Note: The "tare" was the weight of the coal cart.)

MUSIC IN BACUP

Irwell Springs Band was formed in the Weir district in 1864. They won the Belle Vue contest in 1901 and 1905, and the Championship of Great Britain at the Crystal Palace in 1905, 1908 and 1913 -- their third success leading to the writing of the poem by "Shepster" which appears elsewhere. In addition, they were also runners-up at Crystal Palace in 1901, 1910, 1912, and 1925, and appeared at the Third Command Performance before King George V in March 1927.

Stacksteads Band, better known as the Prize Band, were Belle Vue winners in 1934 and 1935.

The Bacup Male Voice Choir and the Choral Society amalgamated in March 1936 to form the Bacup Choral Union. They have given concerts in the town and have brought to Bacup many of the country's leading artistes, encouraging competitive work in choral singing. On another page is reproduced the programme for the Male Voice Choir's First concert of the 1932-33 season, when the guest artistes included Kathleen Ferrier at the pianoforte. She did not take up singing for another eight years. The Choral Union broadcast on North Regional Service in January 1937 and again a year later.

Bacup Orchestral Society was formed in 1882 - five years earlier than some sources suggest, and gave their first Concert in November 1882, with vocalists Miss Bessie Holt, R.A.M. (soprano), and Mr. Henry Green (bass). The Society has provided splendid entertainment and introduced many notable soloists to Bacup, not least the Italian double-bass soloist Signor Giovanni Bottesini. The name of Rowland Hill will always be associated with the Orchestral Society first as a playing member, and later for 28 years as Secretary; when he died in 1962 he was the oldest surviving member.

Bacup Amateur Operatic & Dramatic Society dates from 1935, and has presented many successful shows which have raised large sums of money for local charities. They presented the British Amateur Premiere of "Camelot" in 1967, three weeks after a disastrous fire which threatened to ruin all their plans. The Amateurs' dearest wish is to make the Empire Theatre, which they have owned since 1968, a centre of culture for the area, not just a place where musicals are produced twice a year. Fred Simpson, Charles Baxter, John W. Lord and the Brearley brothers are among many whose efforts have led to the success of the B.A.O. & D.S.

THE ROSSENDALE DIALECT

(A lecture given by Richard Ashworth to the Lancashire Authors' Association on the occasion of their visit to Rawtenstall on June 10th, 1916).

The common impression of the ordinary individual who has not given much thought to the subject is that the dialect is intensely rude and vulgar, and the sooner it is done away with the better. I venture to say that a short study of the subject would alter that opinion. No lover of history or poetry would ever set up such a claim. To the historian it is simply invaluable as showing at what period certain words were prevalent in certain districts, and what races of men inhabited these districts.

Our language is constantly changing, and it is incorrect to say that dialect represents degradations of the standard language. Modern English is derived from Middle English, a language spoken originally in the Midlands, with additions from the Norman, French, literary, scientific, classical and other sources.

Lancashire itself has many different dialects, and it is a mistake to speak of the Lancashire dialect; it should be the Lancashire dialects. I certainly caught the latter edge of the dialect as it was spoken sixty years since. Since then, there has been a considerable deterioration. The dialect may be described roughly as real dialectical words, which have been derived from our invaders chiefly on the east coast. These, of course, are Scandinavians, Danish and Dutch. Then again come the corruptions of ordinary words, and lastly what might be described as a bastard dialect.

I may give you a few examples of what I consider real dialectical words.

Take the word *agate,* meaning to commence, to begin; *aghendole,* which was known in Rossendale as *"neckleton",* and was a measure of meal; *awce,* to prepare, to begin (used in another sense as to attempt to court). *Addle,* with two meanings -- (a) to earn, (b) of an egg which is bad. *Attercrop,* a Scandinavian word for spider. *Brackle,* broken weather. *Braids of,* like unto; *clammed,* starved for food. *Cleek,* to snatch; *creathes,* measles, *fayberry,* gooseberry.

Our old friend *gradely* is quoted by every one who knows the dialect, and so also is *jannock;* the first means -- properly, honestly, squarely; and *jannock* is very much the same. *Kist* of course for chest; *laik* for play; *nesh,* delicate; *lither,* for lazy; *neyve,* for fist; *oind,* to be put upon; *quarrel,* a pane of glass; *roos,* to praise; *shive,* a slice. *Swad,* outer covering of green peas; *stolled,* sick of, loathing; *slatter,* to spill, *snod,* smooth; *threap,* to disagree; *thronce,* a long walk; *wote,* to tumble over; *tent,* to mind; *wisket,* basket; *weeshion,* cushion; *wicks,* all small insects; *wut,* for hot; *yet,* for heat.

These are only a few examples out of 200 others.

In the corruptions, one might mention *een* for eyes; *kuss* for kiss; *neeld* for needle; *ooslum* for Wolstenholme; *peeurk* for perch; *reek* for smoke; *pooak,* for bag; *oon,* for oven; *leet,* for light; *breet,* for bright, etc.; and of course many others.

Another feature of the Rossendale dialect is the German or Hoch sounds which we always have in the Scotch. In the Scotch the words *nicht* and *licht* and *loch* have this sound, and the old Rossendalians used it in *heegher* and *lougher* -- for higher and lower; in *drooghan* for drunk; *faughen* for fought; *shough* for shoe; *soughen* for sunken; and a great many others.

There were also the Rossendale proverbs, and I will give you only one or two, as there is not time for more. "Keep thick wi thad at's nought, an' thad at's good ull do thee noa harm". "Eatten meyt's sooin forgetten". "Tha hangs t' fiddle ut der sneck". Etc., etc.

Rossendale similes are also interesting, and there is a large collection of them. "Swears like a trooper". "As drunk as a lord". Etc., etc.

There are also historical phrases and oaths, of which I only give one -- "By Him ud made little apples". This was said to evade using the name of God, and, strange to say, is a common expression in the Welsh language.

The great hallmark of the Rossendale dialect is the way in which *ou* and *ow* are pronounced. It is simply impossible to write them down phonetically.

There are also a lot of local sayings, of which I will give you two or three only. "They'll ha' to have een all reawn to watch some fooak". "Mony a pratty nought". "Ower kep an' under wrought un doesn't care a curse for nought". Etc., etc.

Another point is the way the *al* and *ol* are written and pronounced. *Sote* for salt, *Howt* for Holt, *gowd* for gold, *Cown* for Colne, *mote* for malt, *bowt* for bolt, *sowdger* for soldier, *cowd* for cold, *fowd* for fold.

Another peculiarity of the dialect is as follows: -- *Shorn'd,* for shall not, *darn'd* for dare not, *arn'd* for have not, *morn'd* for must not, *durn'd* for do not, *kurn'd* for care not, *corn'd* for cannot, *weern'd* for will not.

In conclusion let me tell you a distich which an old gentleman told me, probably dating back 100 years. "Fro witches un wizzards un long tailed buzzards, un creeping things i' t' dyke bottoms, Good Lord deliver us".

(Note: Richard Ashworth, known locally as Dick o' Deborah's, was a very successful business magnate and felt manufacturer. He had many interests. He was an expert orchid-grower, a member of the Lancashire Authors' Association, and a keen student of the Rossendale dialect. He was also interested in local history, and when some of the houses in Old Street, Newchurch, (Old Gate), were being demolished many years ago, he removed two datestones to save them from destruction. One dated 1745 bears the figure of a human head; another dated 1769 is square like a small font. These datestones are in the rockery of the garden at "Ashlands" -- the house being built by Sam Ashworth Lord in 1863. The stones are mentioned by Richard Heape of Healey Hall in "Date Stones and Sundials in Rochdale and District", published 1927.)

MORE ROSSENDALE ANECDOTES

Quarry men in Bacup a hundred years ago were strong, tough, and hard-bitten, and had a rough sense of humour. One rough morning a quarry master went up to his quarry, and saw one of his men who had to walk across a plank to the other side of the quarry. The wind was blowing, and he hesitated in crossing. The master looked up at him and said, "What's to do, Joe, art thi freetened o' walking on that plank? He replied, "Naw, Boss, I'm freetened o' walking off".

ROSSENDALE DIALECT IN MY TIME

Before the First World War, most people spoke the dialect, but it has declined since, for three reasons -- mass-communication, the raising of the school-leaving age, and a mistaken idea that it is the speech of the ignorant and is therefore vulgar.

Actually it is of absorbing interest to linguists and philologists. Jacob Grimm (1785-1836), better known as the author of Grimm's Fairy Tales, studied the Teutonic languages and enunciated "Grimm's Law" to describe the regular sound-shifting or consonantal interchange between Sanskrit, Greek and Latin, Low German and High German. To give one example -- d, th, and t are interchangeable. This throws light on many of our local pronunciations -- id (it), nod (not), wod (what), three trunk (tree trunk), and the Irish pronunciation murther (murder). Another example, the interchangeability of K and ch throws light on Kirk (Church), kist (Chest), Kesmas (Christmas), and Kessenin (Christening).

A consideration of metathesis, the transposition of sounds or letters in words, is also helpful. Brid (bird); brast (burst); brunt (burnt); aks or ax (ask); lantron (lantern) are obvious examples. The pasture by the river Brun would get the name Brunley, but this has changed now to Burnley by this process of metathesis.

Many dialect words can be traced to the Norse, Swedish or Icelandic, and some have come down nearly as they were in Old English.

Een	for	eyes	is Old English
Mun	for	must	is Icelandic *muna*

Many of our words can be found in English literature:

Neaf	for	hand	in Midsummer Night's Dream;
Shoon	for	shoes	in Milton's "Comus";
Kitlin	for	kitten	in Robert Herrick's "Hesperides".

Some of the dialect words are strong preterites, e.g. *scrat,* for scratched.

Cowd, gowd, naakt for cold, gold and naked are close to the Dutch *koud, goud, naakt; brat, boggart, brock* and *gob* are Celtic; *brig, war, drukken, addle, deg, gate* are Scandinavian. There are many more examples of the relationship between foreign languages and our dialect.

A deck of cards, theayter, and advertisement are now regarded as Americanisms, but were used commonly fifty years ago in Rossendale. Clerks were *pronounced* Clerks (not clarks) and sergeants were not *sa*rgeants. The coroner was the crowner (why use Latin, corona = a crown), and it was always five and twenty past five (*never* "twenty-five past").

It seems to be general that the further south we go the longer are the *a* vowels, and it is to be hoped that Rossendalians will stick to the short ones and not be bullied into changing path, bath, master and plaster into p*aw*th, b*aw*th, m*aw*ster and pl*aw*ster, and I hope Rossendale United will have a good centre-forrud for many years to come, and that Rawtenstall and other Valley cricketers will "ged 'em i' t' block-oile".

MORE ROSSENDALE ANECDOTES

A farmer's lad who lived o't' tops went into the jewellers in the Valley town to purchase a gold engagement ring.

"Aw want a gowd ring", he said.

"Eighteen carat?", asked the jeweller.

"Naw, Aw'm nod", he said, "Ah'm eighten tawfee".

A mechanic who was very religious used to spend his dinner hour exhorting his fellow workers to forsake the primrose path and follow his example.

"When t' Day o' Judgment comms", he thundered forth one day, "an t' Angel Gabriel blows on t' trumpet . . ."

" "Th' owd mon wouldna get t' chance i' this department", one of the listeners interrupted sadly. "'E'd get 'is trumpet pinched".

AMUSING PECULARITIES OF LOCAL FOLK SPEECH

Ordinary and every-day conversation in Lancashire's less cosmopolitan towns and villages yields many amusing expressions which cannot be heard elsewhere. Speech in the Rossendale Valley is still predominantly dialectical, and one often hears the frequent and natural repetition of one or more words which lend to the whole a strong alliterative flavour. Often a speaker's inability to express himself adequately fizzles out in a faltering fiasco of this nature -- "Well, like . . . ah'm a bit inclined to agree like. He is like that like . . ."

A man of my acquaintance had a dog which ran off during a blitz. Tearfully he told me, "Id hasn't bin sin sin".

I heard two factory lasses making an appointment for Sunday afternoon: "O, alreight, ah'll be up abeawt four!" Her friend retorted, "Bi up before four, bi up bi hofe past three, wi ha' tay bi four!"

A somewhat different and rather quaint example concerns two young men in a local slipper works. A: "Ah say, dost ti mind lendin' thi long brush?" B: "Ah don't mind if ah do, ah don't", A (with mock sarcasm): "What's ti mean, tha doesn't mind if tha does, tha doesn't!"

A local guillotine operator, asked how he could always set his knife to perfection, confided: "Ah just adjust it".

Two friends of mine were discussing which route they should take for their homeward journey to a neighbouring valley. They could either take a short cut over the "hill-tops" or proceed by the main road.

A: "Are wi gooin' t' top rooad or t'rooad rooad?"

B: "T'rooad rooad".

A: "Na then, then!" (English equivalent: Very well, then!')

To introduce a topical touch -- here is the question and answer: "Hasti a cig?" "Nod an odd un!"

I overheard the following scrap of conversation between two middle aged women who obviously had not met for some considerable time: -- "Next time ah'm i' Bacup, ah'll co'll an' ha' tay wi' thi". With great enthusiasm her friend exclaimed: "Aye do, an' we'll have a reight good do if yo do do!"

The vocabulary of a certain Bacup miner is noteworthy for the word *shuzheaw* (as how). "What meks thi keep sayin' shuzheaw?" " objected an exasperated listener, "Ah dunno, shuzheaw!" he replied.

In an old record book at the Bacup Natural History Society is an example which phonetically fits the local dialect perfectly. I am inclined to think however, that it is not of local origin, but rather that it is an elaboration of an English theme, comprising a play on words with the same sound as *onion,* -- One of a group of manual labourers produces a clay pipe, and lacking the necessary match, appeals to his pals -- "Han onny on yo onny on yo?" They shake their heads. "What! Hasn't onny on yo onny on yo?" "Nowe, noan on us has noan on us!"

Some time ago at Rochdale, I heard Mr. T. Thompson give a similar example when illustrating the Bury dialect. Two housewives were standing in their respective backyards awaiting the municipal dustman:--

Q. : "Hast t'bin men bin?"
A; : "Dost me'n t'dust men?"

MORE ROSSENDALE ANECDOTES

On a crowded bus, two women stood next to each other, one of whom had so many parcels that she couldn't get at her purse to pay her fare. So she asked her neighbour to pay her fare. She never got sat down, and when the bus reached her stop, got off without ever having squared up. Her indignant companion said to the conductor: "Don't let her go, I haven't got my money back off her". He replied: "Oh, she's always doing that on this run".

However, when she tackled the parcel-laden woman about not having given her money back, the latter swore she had never set eyes on her before, and wasn't going to give her any money -- and went off, dropping one of her parcels. The conductor had been watching the proceedings, and remarked to the defrauded fare-payer: "You want to keep that".

She did. – It turned out to be a load of tripe.

A MON'S BEST FRIEND

Com on neaw, "Bruce", un set thi deawn,
On th' hearthrug ut mi feet,
Tha'd beawn t' catch thi dee'uth o' cowd,
Thi coytes o' soppin' weet.
Tha shouldna roam areawnd in t' storm
When tha's a whom like this,
Fer, if tha wor t' dee, owd mon,
Thi company aw would miss.

Tha's bin a gradely pal t' me
Sin' tha wor bud a whelp,
Un when aw've felt deawnhearted, lad,
Tha's allus bin a help.
Noa matter wod aw say t' thi,
Tha looks t' understand,
Tha seems to soothe mi achin' heart,
Wi' just a lick on t' th' hand.

It's grand t' tak thi eawt a walk
A wand'ring o'er yon hills.
It's fun t' see thi romp abeawt,
Un splash thi'sell in t' rills;
Then sit un watch thi shake abeawt
Un rub thi face on t' greawnd:
T' listen to th' owd Layrock's song
Un see fer miles areawnd.

A better friend could ne'er bi fon,
Soa faithful an' soa true;
Aw'm fain t' have thi love, owd lad,
Fer real friends are bud few.
Com here and let mi wipe thi deawn,
Tha'rt shiverin' wi' cowd,
Aw wouldna like t' part wi thee
Fer all thi weight i' gowd.

Tha hasn't ony pedigree,
Tha'rt noan a special breed,
Tha'd just a little mongrel dog
Bud tha knows wod Aw need.
An, if Aw've ever hurt thi, lad,
Aw know as tha'll forgive,
Aw hope aw'll awlus have thi, pal,
As long as aw sholl live.

NEWLY BORN

God bless thee, little bonny face,
An' bless thi pulsin' heart,
To own thee, well it's no disgrace,
We'n loved thee reight fro' t' start.

Tha's sich a chubby turned-up nose,
An' gradely breet blue een,
As sure as tha's ten twiddlin' toes,
Thi name is "Sweet Kathleen".

Thi mother is a gradely lass,
Noan better could ta want,
Fer thee, hoo's let all pleasure pass,
An' warked just like an ant.

Her fingers fair like leet'nin' moved,
To mak' thee babby things,
In her, a mother's love is proved --
Whene'er hoo beighs and sings.

Ah've bin away -- but neaw Ah'm here,
Reight preawd Ah' feel o' thee,
It's heaven to sit in th' owd arm chear,
Wi' thee laid o'er mi knee.

This place, we've often called eawr heawse,
Tha's made into a wom!
An' tho', noan allus like a meawse,
To thee Ah'm fain to com'.

When first Ah held thee in mi arms,
Wi'in eawr humble fowd,
Thi face wer' wreathed in babby charms,
O' one a fortneet owd.

OPENING SEASON.

First Concert

PROMOTED BY THE

Bacup Male Voice Choir

IN THE

MECHANICS' INSTITUTE,

BACUP.

SATURDAY, NOVEMBER 5th, 1932.

Chairman: REV. J. E. ROSCOE, President.

Artistes:

The Sunnyhurst Instrumental Trio,

BLACKBURN.

Violin - - I. COBOFSKI.
Violoncello - M. PRESTON.
Pianoforte - KATHLEEN FERRIER.

Soprano - Madame ANNIE STOCKS.

Bass - - JAMES HARGREAVES.

Tenor - - - ERNEST LAW.

Tenor - - GEORGE LENNEY.

Accompanist - - HERBERT MILLS.

BACUP MALE VOICE CHOIR.

(Conductor: Coun. J. H. Hargreaves.)

Artistes for the first concert promoted by the Bacup Male Voice Choir, formed in 1932.

BACUP MALE VOICE CHOIR, 1932-36. Front row: Jack Butterworth; William Hirst; Ernest Law; Arthur Lawton; Herbert Horsfall; James H. Howarth; Robert Wynne; Barker Holden; Jesse Crabtree. Second row: William Thompson; Arnold Hargreaves; George Cowell; Richard Stansfield; Richard Hargreaves; James Henry Hargreaves; Richard Percy Law; James Hargreaves; Albany Schofield; Harold Pilling; Edward Rourke; John Higgins. Third row: John Spencer; Duke Seville; Joshua Wadsworth; Fred Collinge; Robert Rigby; James Collinge; Harry Schofield; Alec Southern; Edward Gannon; William Walker; Clifford Stansfield; John Cropper; Herbert Warburton. Fourth row: Fred Lloyd; Fred Hey; John Crabtree; Edwin Ashworth; John Loney; Edgar Shepherd; Fred Beardsworth; Albert Buckley; Clifford Walton; George Lenney; Thomas Wadsworth; Ewart Beardsworth. Dick Stansfield (?) Back row: Fred Simpson; Alfred Wilson.

MURIEL ROSCOE

Born in Chester on June 20th, 1909, educated at St. Peter's Collegiate School, Wolverhampton, and Bacup and Rawtenstall Grammar School (moved to Bacup in 1918). Attained her Associateship of the Royal Manchester College of Music in 1929, and her L.R.A.M. in 1931. Daughter of the Rev. J. E. Roscoe, Vicar for 31 years (1918-1949) of Christ Church Bacup. Music mistress at Stockport Municipal Secondary School, Elocution Mistress at Bury Convent High School. Broadcasts from North Regional, Singing and Dramatic Department of the B.B.C. Became one of the youngest ever adjudicators at Music Festivals. Died November 7th, 1935, aged 26, after six months' illness. Sir Hugh Robertson described her as "a girl in whom the nightingale sang."

DAVID BILLINGTON, Bacup's champion swimmer.
See pages 232–233.

BACUP AMATEUR SWIMMING CLUB about 1924. Standing: John Allen, Martin Tattersall; sitting: Jimmy Tucker, Billy Foster (he won 98 medals in all); Joshua Chatburn; lying down: Walter Savage. This photograph was taken at the bottom of the "little bath".

EBENEZER BAPTIST CHAPEL AND SCHOOL, Lanehead Lane, Bacup. The parent of all the Baptist churches in the area (see notes on Churches and Chapels). Demolished about 1964.

MOUNT PLEASANT WESLEYAN CHAPEL, Bacup. The earliest Wesleyan Methodist church in Bacup (see notes on Churches and Chapels). Demolished about 1953.

Bacup Market, Temple Court. The open market was moved here from a site near the Police Station and the market hall in May 1956.

TWO OF THE VALLEY'S BEST FOOTBALL TEAMS

BACUP BOROUGH F.C., Lancashire Combination champions 1946-47 with 61 points. Team: Standing: Harry Noy (trainer), Frank Edwards, Harold (?) Hurst, Billy Vaughan, Tommy Nuttall, Harry Spencer, Jack Hughes, Jimmy Howarth, Jack Ashworth. Front row: George Wilson, George Golden, Ken Upton, Joe Deakin (captain), Jack Isherwood, Charlie Howes, Gwyn Jones. (On the right of the photograph can be seen Blackthorn School).

ROSSENDALE UNITED F.C., Cheshire League champions 1970-71 in their first season in that League, with 67 points from 42 matches. Team: Standing: Alan Kirkman, Tony Unsworth, John Pearson, Glyn Barker, Jack Kershaw (training assistant), Dennis Crompton, John Wood, Eddie Birchall, David Wild, Roy Wilkinson, Charlie Wroth, Les. Rigby (manager). Front row: Doug. Welsh, Tommy Nuttall (trainer), Peter Bourne, Billy Greenan, Bob Woods (captain), David Crompton, Ken Fletcher, Jimmy Hammell, Walter Roberts.

Open–Air service in Moorlands Park, Bacup, to Commemmorate the signing of the 1918 Armistice. Note members of the Council on the front row.

But com' cherub, it's time fer bed,
   Na then chilt! owd thi din!
Dear, dear, don't let it neaw be said --
   Thi Dad cornt tuck thee in.

That's better love, neaw off to sleep,
   Another day is done,
May God o'er thee his watchin' keep,
   'Til t' risin o' the sun.

BETSY JANE

Ah allus liked to sit i' t' Sparra' Park
When t'sun were shinin' warm an' breet;
For t' birds were singin', even in t' dark.
An' fleawrs wer' bloomin', left an' reet.

Us owdfooak liked to toke, an' sumtimes larn
Fro' others, wod they 'ad to tell;
An' Betsy Jane could allus spin a yarn
Thad often made us laugh as well.

One day, a smart young fella sat on t' seat
Next door to eawr's, an' Betsy Jane
Jus' winked at us -- then turned to t' lad to greet
Him, wi' a face 'at sed i' pain,

"I know tha'll understand lad, if Ah tell
Thi, durn'd sit theer or bad luck might
Be thine. For look what chanced to Peter Bell.
He's buried neaw; dee'd o' Monday night.

He'd only wed a week or two ago.
(He allus used to use thad seat)
Ah feel ill-awf for 'er, his widow Flo';
Who looked so 'appy, on 'er weddin' neet.

Bud neaw he's gone, an' hoo left on 'er own;
His birthday would a bin, let's see,
Aye! Friday next, but future's never known
-- So t' Party's off: he wer' only ninety-three . . ."

ORSE EGGS (An old Bacup tale)

Fer helpin wi a flittin, Joe'd addled hawf a creawn,
So he whistled as he mooched abeawt i' t' streets o' Bacup teawn --
"Ah'll buy mi a bit of summat", sed Joe, "as eaw it be"
-- An' he'd hardly spoke when a bladder o' lard i't' butcher's caught his 'ee.

T' butcher's lad wur stood at t' dur, so Joe axed him "What's yon? --
Id favvers a egg o' some sooart, bud its too big fer a pon";
Neaw butcher's lad wur full o' gam an' liked a bit of spree,
So he said to Joe, "It's a 'orse egg" -- wi a twinkle in his ee.

"Heaw would yo hatch it then?" said Joe, "would you keep it warm an still?"
"Oh no", said t' lad, "thi hatch eawt best wi' rowlin 'em deawn a hill--
Tha could tek it aboon t' market, an' rowl id deawn yon broo,
Ther' nobbut a bob apiece, tha knows, why doesn't ti hev a doo?"

When Joe set off wi' t' bladder o' lard, t' lad laffed till he wur rockin',
Bud Joe didn't keer, he sheawted back, "Ged back i' t' coit tha't clockin'";
He rowled his egg deawn t' market broo, bud lost it among t' fooak,
Ah think some lads ud picked it up an' ta'en it fur a joke.

Bud as he geet near t' Trade Oile, kep bi Mesther Collinge then
A rabbit scuttered eawt through t' dur, it'd getten eawt t't' pen,
Joe's een popped eawt an' he sheawted, "Aw've hatched mi egg, by heck!"
-- An' he chased it up through t' market broo, as far as Bacup Rec.

He lost it then i' t' moorland mist, but he said, "Ah'll noan give up"
So he traycled back to t' butchers an' said to t' lad, "Tha tupp,
Tha knew yon wur a race-orse egg, that's why tha brast eawt laffin'
This time Aw'll hev a cart-orse egg, bi quick, an' no mooar faffin'".

TH' MARKET DAY UT BACUP

Han yo' ever bin i' Bacup
On a Wednesday afternoon,
If yo' had, yo'n sin things lively,
That's if th' weather's bin i' tune;
Yo' may ston o' th' front o' th' Market,
Where eawr "lectrics" mak' a stand,
Then yo'll see eawr Valley ladies
Step off th' car boath large an' grand.

Then they'll wap reawnd th' music corner,
Mak' ther way up Market-broo,
Come i' touch wi' Joe fro' Owdham,
Un he mak's a fine to do;
Starts un treats um to a banquet,
Hands eawt fruit to o' o'reawnd,
Then he sings a fruitful solo,
Title: "Everything is good and seawnd".

Un then they'll look to th' other side,
Where everything us sweet,
Where th' childer stan' wi' longing een:
To see um -- it's a treat.
It's where th' mothers buys ther toffy,
Pear drops, un Peppermint;
Ther'se sweetness o' o'er th' market greawnd
Oather soft, or hard us flint.

Neaw further on moor fruit yo'll see,
Un it's o' th' vary best,
Un should yo' feel inclined for tripe
Yo' con get it wol yo' rest.
If yo' want a taste fro' th' briney
Yo' con have it vary nice,
"All fresh un good", says the fishy men,
"Aw'll cut yo' piece or slice".

Neaw as yo' turn to th' tother side,
Yo' come across a friend

'Uts noted for good celery,
Un whose flewers yo connot mend.
Yo' leave this friend un turn aside,
Un there! a waggonett,
Inside a chep John Jeweller,
Ut's selling gowd un silverette.

My word! he has a tale to tell,
He's th' moast generous chap on th' greawnd,
"Givin' away", yes "givinn' away",
That's if yo'll ston yere greawnd.
Bud th' wimmen moastley sidles reawnd,
Past Fortune-telling chap
If they con get to th' bargain stall,
They dunnott care a rap.

Neaw this us th' stall -- they getten reawnd,
Where th' wimmen knocks stuff deawn,
They throw't abeawt ut leetning speed,
Price fro' thruppence to a hawf-a-creawn;
Some on um ston's an hewer or two,
Watchin' thur wimmen sell,
This they find us to ther tooth,
So reawnd that stall they dwell.

Till o' ut once it comes to th' mind
Ther'se lots o' things they wantin',
So off they pop, reawnd th' other side
For lace un drapery rantin.
They flit abeawt fro' stall to stall,
Mixed wi' a friendly greetin',
"A, Mary, heaw ta goin' on",
Then they howd a little meetin'.

Thad meetin' doesn't howd so long,
For they find ut time us goin',
So off they goa, inside this time,
Ther bargain hunt pursuin'
Th' stall howders ready to oblige
Wi' owt, boath big or small,
They do ther best to suit the purse
Ov oather gret or small

Ther'se no mistake ut th' wimmen's day
Us proved a reight big draw,
Un a lot o' th' hubby's follers on
Yo'll see, if yo're nod slow.
"If aw'd to choose wi' Blackpool",
Aw yerd a woman say one day,
"Aw'se choose th' owd Bacup Market,
It's true neaw, wot aw say".

NOBBUT A THOUGHT
Heart o' Rossendale

I've spent a week in Rossendale,
   By gum! it has bin grand,
For every time I walked in t' street,
   Some friend would grip mi hand.
It didn't matter wheer I went,
   Deawn t' Vale or Cribden Hill,
I seemed to meet all kinds o' folk,
   Who axed -- "Heaw arta, Bill?"
So much concern they showed for me,
   Mi hat felt like a creawn,
Which allus proved, time an' again,
   It's folk ut makes a teawn:
Some think it grand to rest awhile
   An' live beside the sea . . .
But *I* find on the promenade
   There's *thousands* -- an *just me.*
To say t' next field has greener grass
   Is nobbut just a tale,
For it's hard wark to match the heart
   -- That beats in Rossendale.

(*Note:* One resident in Stacksteads told the author that after reading the above poem, he had decided *not* to remove from Bacup. It was the sixteenth line that did it.)

BLACKPOO'

Thi con goo ut likes to t' Sleepy South an' frizzle an' fry i' t' sun,
Aw'd raything goo to Blackpoo' wheer ther's summat gooin' on;
It's lively, th' airs as good as wine an t' shows are t' best on Earth,
An' t' fooak yon are waarm an' wick an' fond o' gam an' mirth.
Aw've bin gooin' nigh on fifty year, thad's best part o' mi life
-- Aw went theer when Aw'r cooartin', an' Aw goo theer yet wi' t' wife,
Aw used to goo in t' good owd days when Blackpoo hed t' Big Wheel
An' a toathri bob ud pay fer a show an' a gradely slap-up meal.

Just eawtside t' Central Station when t' train wur gooin' slow,
Aw' like to luk through t' winda at t' backs of a lodgin' heawse row,
Fer t' names ov o' th' landladies wur white-weshed up o' t' wo's.
An' t' places wheer thi coom fro, here's a toathri Aw reco'.
Ther wur Mrs. Coop fro' Wigan ut number Thirty-Three,
An' Mrs. Mobbs fro' Halifax "two minutes from the sea",
A Mrs. Howt fro' Rattenstull, hoo lived ut "Home from Home",
An' Mrs. Clegg fro' Rochdi, an' Miss Pinch fro' Hipperholme.

Aw once hed digs near t' Foxhall, wi'd uz dinner i' relays,
An wi'd sit eawtside i' t' garden 'til t' first sittin went away;
Bud wod bi thad wi loiked it, fer t' buskers coom i' t' street
Wi' banjoes an' black physogs -- Aw thowt id wur a treat,
Aw used to like to walk o' t' cliffs as fer as Uncle Tom's,
Or goo eawt afore brekfast fer a coffee an' rum o' t' prom.
Wi'd buy o' t' latest copies ut wur wrote bi Lawrence Wright,
Then sing 'em reawnd t' piano, i' t' digs till late at night.

Wi read o' t' comic pooast cards -- fat ladies, drunks an' duffers,
A favourite then wur a Blackpoo Trip wi folk astride o' t' buffers:
Heaw grand id wur to sing in t' creawd in a Feldman's song arcade,
Or heark to t' talkin' dolls o' t' sands, an' quacks o' every grade:
A mornin' dance o' t' Central Pier ud pass a pleasant hour,
An we loiked to yer Reg Dixon on his organ i' th' owd Tower;
Aw'm noan much ov a sailor un id ollus med mi queer --
But Aw neer missed gooin' t' t' Queen o' t' North to Douglas fro' t' North Pier.

Neaw Blackpoo's gooin' classy, soon ther'll be no Golden Mile,
Teawn Ceawncillors are "with it" an' ther' gooin' mad on "style";
Ther mekkin drastic changes i' yon owd familiar scene,
Aw's miss yon Central Station an' yon Talbot bowlin' green --
Th' owd stashun wur so handy, when yo got there yo wur theer
A minute's walk fro t' promenade, near t' Tower an' near t' North Pier.
When links wi' t' past are brokken, it hurst owd folk like me,
Bud happen thi'll mek it better, we's just have to wait an' see.

FIRST O' MAY

Ah geet mi up on th' first o' May,
Afore th' owd cock had crowed.
Ah knew ut wife had bought a hat
In th' Easter springtime mode.

There'd be no peace o' mind fer me,
If ah laid there in th' bed,
Wi th' sun as breet as yon new hat,
Wi th' bloom, sun never bred.

"But did ah like id", does ti say?
Ah doubt if monny would;
Except, perhaps, our billie-goat --
To him, id tasted good!

If ah could be as true to taste,
An' tell th' wife wad ah thought,
Ah'd be as smart as th' billie-goat,
But dunnot think ah ought;

Fer thad could be the end o' me,
As weel as th' wife's new hat.
Ah'll leave th' owd goat to prove his point,
An' let id stop at that.

T' MOORS

Hast e'er bin reight up on t' moors
Weer t' skylark rises, sings and soars
An' t' magpie chatters on t' stone wall
An' trees just winna grow at all?
Hast sin all t' snow turn pink in t' sun
When t' winter's day is nearly done?
An' t' new-born lambs all clean an' white
Run under t' ewe when they'n ta'en fright?
Hast felt th' east wind fair freeze thi marrow
An sin th' hares' footprints up in t' meadow
Or sin a 'awk reight up in t' sky
Looking deawn wi' 'ungry eye?
Tha'll see a crow or two up yon
But they waint gie thee ony fun --
They're far too busy findin' food
An' makin' noises summat rude
It's best in t' Summer – Bit wi get.
When tha con walk baht gettin' wet
An' sit awhile an' look at t' view
Tha allus sees there's summat new
An' summat else it's 'ard to get
It's quiet theer, tha con bet
Tha thinks things eawt an' plans thi life
An' fer a time gets rid o' strife.
It does thi good, an' costs thi nowt
An' makes life better than tha thowt
Tha gooas back whoam wi' ruddy cheek
An' a appetite that winna keep
Tha sleeps reight weel an' keeps thi 'ealth
It's summat tha cornt buy wi' wealth
So what abeawt a walk on t' moors
An' get thi feet off t' flags and t' floors --
Feel t' soft grass spring under t' foot.
Come on an' get reight eawt o' t' rut
There's mony folk 'ud pay a lot
To ' ave what we reawnd 'ere 'ave got
Tha'rt lucky if th' nobbat knew
Tha's getten things like moors to view.

MI CLOGS

I used to catch t' tram
And go to mi wark,
Set off in t' dayleet
And come back in t' dark.

I went clatterin' deawn t' rooad
An' folk knew to shift,
When they yerd these gret clogs
They acted so swift.

There were good pals to me
In all sorts o' weather,
Not these fancy stilettos,
In all sorts o' leather.

One day I'd a brainwave,
I geet a fresh job,
A grand pair o' shoes
At just thirty bob.

I'd to put these owd clogs
Once more owt o' seet,
Mi boss were allus
Interested in t' feet.

I give him a black look
When he turned his back,
If he'd a just catched me
I'd a sure getten t' sack.

This new job Ah geet
Were in a grand heawse
They had a gret cat
Ut wouldn't catch a meawse.

Wherever I went,
I were allus in t' news,
All they could talk about
Were these mi new shoes.

An' so that's th' end,
O' mi faithful owd clogs,
If it weren't for t' new shoes
They'd a sent mi to t' dogs.

A DIALECT GLOSSARY

Aboon	Above
Addle some brass	Earn some money
Ah	Oneself
Aliker	Vinegar
Ar-jarrin	Arguing
Band	String
Beigh	Rock a baby
Boggart	Apparition
Boose	Cow-stall
Brast-off	Begin
Brat	Apron
Camp	Entertain with your company
Ceawr	Squat
Chunner	Mutter
Clatter	Clout, or hit
Cleak	Snatch
Clip-up	Embrace
Coaken	Strain before vomiting
Cove-licked	With a left-handed squiff
Coyle	Coal
Cram'd	Bad-tempered
Crowner	Coroner
Cruckle	Collapse in a heap
Crudded	Curdled
Deesh-cleawt	Dish-cloth
Deggin-can	Watering can
Delph-chap	Quarryman
Donned-up	Dressed in best clothes

Eawl-leet	Twilight
Favour, or Favver	Resemble
Fleck	Flea
Flit	Remove
Fotch	Fetch
Fratch	Argue
Galluses	Braces
Gawby	Dunce
Gaum	Understand
Gawp	Stare open-mouthed
Ginnell	Narrow passage between buildings
Harmin-after	Teasing with imitative remarks
Hippins	Nappies
Hoo	She
Howd on	Pause
Ill-off for somebody	Sorry for them
Joe Soap	Oneself (strictly slang rather than dialect)
Kayther	Cradle
Kayther-corner	Cradle nook; warmest place reserved for the baby
Keep company	Court

Keigh-paw	Left-handed
Keyk	Lean drunkenly
Kitlin	Kitten
Lant	Urine
Latchin	Catching, infectious
Leawk	Rough coarse grass
Let	Alight (of a kite)
Long Keks	Long trousers
Mad hig	Bad temper
Mar'd	Soft and pampered
Meawt	Moult
Meight	Meat
Mizzle	Drizzle
Moo'd eawt	Full up, crowded
Moppet	Mischievous child
Mop-steel	Mop-handle
Mornt	Must not
Mousand	Mildewed
Nesh	Tender
Onny	Any
Oon	Oven
Pouce	Naughty child
Pow	Hair-cut
Powfagged	Puzzled and irritated
Proven	Provender for animals
Punce	Kick
Ratch	Stretch
Reek	Smoke
Reight	Right
Rive	Tear
Sharn-clap	A dollop of cow-dung
Shepster	Starling
Shippon	Cow-shed
Shive	Slice
Sinnabun	Sinew-bound
Sken	Look obliquely
Skew-whift	Awry
Slopstone	Sink
Smook	Smoke
Sneck	Door-latch
Sny	Lift the nose superciliously
Sunday–jump	Sunday coat
Sweal	Burn off dead grass
Tay	Tea
Tent	Mind (a dog is spoken of as a good tenter)
Thisel	Thyself
Traunce	Tedious walk
Wick'thing	Insect
Winteredge	Clothes-maiden
Witchered	Wet-shod
Woat	Overturn
Yezzy	Easy

HOTELS, INNS, TAVERNS AND PUBLIC HOUSES
in the Borough of Bacup about 1882.

Do you fancy a pub crawl round Bacup . . . ?
How many pubs do you remember . . . ?
How did they get their names . . . ?

The following is a list of 59 hotels and public houses within the borough about ninety years ago. Various other clubs, beer-houses and off-licences have not been included. Today 20 of the following list are still in active service. Others not listed include the "King George V Hotel" (the "Bull's Head" replacement), the "George and Dragon Hotel" (replaced the "Carriers Arms"), the "Park Hotel" (now demolished, but replaced the "George Inn") and "Forest House Hotel".

An asterisk (*) means the building has been demolished. A dagger (†) means the building is now used for some purpose other than a public house, e.g. works, museum, private house, warehouse, shop or chip-shop, -- or is simply derelict. Owing to the uncertainty of the position of any apostrophe "s", these have been omitted entirely.

Bacup to Sharneyford

* Bulls Head Hotel, Yorkshire Street. (Site of the King George V Hotel).
* Angel Inn, Yorkshire Street. (Site of Woolworths).
Queens Hotel, Yorkshire Street. (" ... only the Angel came between the King and Queen")
* Buck Inn, Lanehead Lane. (Site behind the Queens Hotel).
* Cricketers Arms, Lane Head. (Site opposite Stanley Mount).
† White Horse Inn, Yorkshire Street. (Now a chip shop).
† Hare and Hounds, Yorkshire Street. (Now Bacup Natural History Society Museum)
† Green Man Inn, Yorkshire Street. (Now the Labour Rooms)
* Bay Horse, Yorkshire Street. (Site near the end of Tong Lane).
Wellington Hotel, Todmorden Road. (Former police station and the Red Lion Inn).
† Green End Tavern, Green End Street. (Now a private house).
Crown Inn, Greave.
Flowers Inn, Todmorden Road.
† Barley Mow, Todmorden Road. (Now a private house).
† Hit or Miss, Todmorden Road. (Now a private house).
* Bull and Dog, Todmorden Road. (Site near Height Side farm lane).
* Blue Ball, Todmorden Road. (Site near Height Side farm lane).

Bacup to Deerplay

Irwell Inn, Burnley Road. (Built over the River Irwell).
* Roe Buck Inn, Higher Broadclough.
Weir Hotel, Weir.
† Half Way House, Weir. (Now a private house).

Bacup to Britannia

* George and Dragon, Bridge St. (Site of roundabout over River Irwell).
† Golden Lion, Bridge Street. (Now a butcher's shop).
* Spread Eagle, Temple Court. (Site of the open market).
† Mason's Arms, St. James' Street. (Now a shoe shop).
† Thorn Inn, South Street. (Now a food shop and cafe).
Joiners Arms, South Street.
Waterloo Hotel, Union Street. (Built over the River Irwell).
British Queen, Union Street.
* Moulders Arms, Irwell Street.
* Butchers Arms, Irwell Street.
New Inn, Rochdale Road.
* Loom Jobbers Inn, Rochdale Rd.(Site almost opposite the Empire Theatre).
* Carriers Arms, Rochdale Road. (Site of the George and Dragon Hotel).
* Victoria Inn, Rochdale Rd.(Site almost opposite Greenhill Garage).
Wellington Hotel, Rochdale Road, Britannia.
† Britannia Inn, Rochdale Road, Britannia. (Now a private house with 1821 date stone).
Travellers Rest, Rochdale Road, Britannia.

Bacup to Stacksteads

Market Hotel, Market Street.
† Commercial Inn, Market Street. (Near Union Street).
Waterworks Inn, Market Street.
* Glen Inn, Market Street. (Site opposite Plantation Mill).
Swan Hotel, Market Street.
* Railway Inn, Market Street. (Site opposite Manor Street).
* George Inn, Newchurch Road. (Site of the later Park Hotel, demolished 1967).
* Fullers Arms, Newchurch Road. (Site on Pippin Bank).
† Holt Arms, Newchurch Road. (Now a shoe warehouse).
Royal Oak, Newchurch Road.
† Odd Fellows Arms, Newchurch Rd.(Now a house, with 1836 datestone).
† Cemetery Hotel, Newchurch Road. (Now a pigeon clock works).
Farholme Tavern Newchurch Road.
Commercial Hotel, Newchurch Road.
* Loyal Arms, Blackwood.
Railway Inn, Newchurch Road.
† Atherton Holme, Siding Street. (Now a private house).
Hare and Hounds, Newchurch Road.
Bee Hive Inn, Newchurch Road.
* Grocers Arms, Newchurch Road. (Site opposite and west of the Bee Hive Inn).
† Glen Inn, Glen Bottom. (Now sewing machine works. Note "Glen Inn bait stables").

Two public houses may seem obvious omissions from the above list – the "Deerplay Inn" and the "Dog and Partridge", but neither are within the official boundaries of the borough of Bacup!

RAINFALL IN BACUP

The rainfall in Bacup was for many years given a very full summary in the Bacup Times, indeed the first issues of that paper compare the first quarter of 1864 with that for the previous year. In 1864, 3.20 inches of rain fell in Bacup during January, 4.34 inches during February, and 3.10 inches during March. In 1865 the figures are: January – 5.25 inches, February – 4.20 inches, March – 1.78 inches.

Rainfall statistics have been maintained at Cowpe Reservoir since 1915, at Sheephouse Filter Station since 1922, and also at Cragg. Annual summaries appeared in the Bacup Times, and from 1942 to 1965 merited a couple of pages in the Bacup Corporation Year Book.

The average annual rainfall at Cowpe and Sheephouse is as follows:

Average at Cowpe, 1915 to 1971	56,75 inches per annum
Average at Sheephouse, 1922 to 1971	55.85 inches per annum

The driest year on record was 1933 when a mere 34.22 inches of rain were recorded at Cowpe, whilst at Sheephouse the figure was even lower – 31.85 inches. The wettest year on record locally was 1954, when Cowpe recorded 77.36 inches of rain, and Sheephouse 75.07 inches.

The driest month on record was June 1925, when Cowpe recorded 0.13 of an inch of rain, whilst the wettest month was October 1938, when 14.64 inches of rain fell, 4.62 inches on the 2nd and 3rd of that month. The Sheephouse figure for October 1938 is 13.45 inches.

The wettest single day, however, was July 12th, 1941, when 2.90 inches of rain fell. The wettest day since then was September 20th, 1968, when Sheephouse recorded 2.87 inches of rain -- almost as much. And on August 29th, 1945, Sheephouse recorded 2.88 inches of rain.

The Cowpe figure is usually regarded as "the" rainfall figure for Bacup, but the Sheephouse figures are included to give an accurate assessment of the weather situation as read on both flanks of Bacup.

Year	Total rainfall in inches		Highest (month)	Lowest (month)
	Cowpe	Sheephouse		
1915	49.17	(from 1930)	10.00 (December)	0.89 (September)
1916	51.67		9.87 (October)	2.79 (July)
1917	46.51		10.33 (October)	1.34 (February)
1918	59.47		13.33 (September)	1.12 (April)
1919	45.53		8.79 (December)	1.30 (February)
1920	55.26		9.06 (July)	1.60 (October)
1921	47.19		8.76 (January)	0.41 (June)
1922	52.67		6.10 (December)	1.04 (October)
1923	63.65		7.97 (November)	1.43 (June)
1924	59.84		9.47 (August)	1.44 (February)
1925	50.14		8.42 (February)	0.13 (June)
1926	52.00		8.70 (November)	1.78 (December)
1927	59.02		9.34 (August)	2.31 (December)
1928	64.86		11.88 (January)	0.82 (September)
1929	49.93		9.26 (November)	1.53 (February)
1930	57.45	48.98	8.39 (August)	0.93 (February)
1931	59.26	53.82	10.76 (November)	0.75 (March)
1932	45.80	43.23	8.34 (October)	0.29 (February)
1933	34.25	31.85	11.04 (October)	0.91 (December)
1934	54.09	49.77	9.08 (December)	0.44 (February)
1935	63.84	59.77	11.04 (December)	1.60 (May)
1936	59.99	56.81	7.30 (December)	0.88 (May)

Year	Total rainfall in inches Cowpe	Sheephouse	Highest (month)	Lowest (month)
1937	47.21	42.79	7.81 (February)	2.33 (November)
1938	69.46	66.22	14.64 (October)	1.01 (April)
1939	61.84	59.72	9.36 (July)	1.86 (September)
1940	53.88	51.93	10.52 (November)	1.03 (June)
1941	51.35	44.63	9.02 (August)	0.64 (June)
1942	57.59	52.17	9.46 (January)	1.12 (June)
1943	57.46	52.56	8.80 (August)	1.76 (March)
1944	62.22	58.41	9.95 (November)	0.91 (March)
1945	53.00	54.51	7.57 (October)	0.68 (November)
1946	64.56	69.97	10.29 (November)	1.58 (May)
1947	51.81	56.19	9.23 (March)	0.27 (August)
1948	57.23	60.84	13.07 (January)	2.35 (March)
				2.35 (May)
1949	54.60	58.09	9.13 (December)	0.69 (June)
1950	65.27	66.66	10.30 (September)	2.54 (May)
1951	63.65	65.50	11.14 (November)	1.11 (October)
1952	55.35	52.39	6.84 (January)	1.96 (February)
1953	51.73	48.78	7.18 (July)	2.36 (January)
1954	77.36	75.07	11.83 (October)	0.98 (April)
1955	45.93	47.52	7.52 (December)	1.23 (August)
1956	59.98	56.92	13.09 (August)	1.44 (February)
1957	60.16	59.51	8.67 (October)	0.59 (April)
1958	62.34	64.15	9.33 (February)	2.02 (April)
1959	49.64	50.77	11.08 (December)	0.51 (September)
1960	69.43	65.04	9.68 (November)	1.79 (June)
1961	64.45	59.25	8.89 (January)	2.01 (March)
1962	58.97	55.35	9.15 (August)	1.63 (June)
1963	54.75	51.32	8.30 (November)	1.96 (December)
1964	55.14	55.86	9.60 (December)	2.12 (February)
1965	66.41	64.81	14.22 (December)	0.80 (February)
1966	70.31	69.26	9.75 (February)	3.01 (January)
1967	69.92	69.23	12.18 (October)	2.24 (April)
1968	63.90	60.04	13.07 (September)	2.00 (December)
1969	48.56	48.59	9.05 (November)	1.46 (October)
1970	55.45	59.62	9.23 (November)	0.42 (May)
1971	42.25	44.76	5.75 (October)	1.51 (September)

* * * * * * * * * *

From which tables it will be seen that every month of the year has at some time featured as the driest month of a year. So far, April, May, and June, have avoided being the wettest months in any year. There are however, several other rainfall figures in excess of 10 inches in a month, and apart from the figures cited in the above tables, these are as follows:

1918 – 10.31 inches in December; 1935 – 10.47 inches in September; 1951 – 10.95 inches in December (Cowpe figures).

"Dry" months, with under 1 inch of rain during the month, not cited above, are as follows:

1921 – 0.64 inches in February; 1959 – 0.93 inches in February, and 0.83 inches in August (Cowpe figures).

DAVID BILLINGTON (1886 – 1955)

David Billington was born in 1886 in Bacup, the son of Bacup Baths Superintendent Edward Billington, and achieved early distinction as a swimmer, bring designated as "Boy Champion of England" at the age of 12 years in 1898. He won his first Championship of the Northern Counties in 1900, over a distance of 1000 yards, and repeated this success in the following five years, making six consecutive wins. He also won the Northern Counties 440 yards in 1903. When he won the 1000 yards in 1905, this race was in Sefton Park Lake, Liverpool, and was the last occasion on which this was used for swimming events.

He won ten National Championships as follows:

440 yards Salt Water	1901, 1903 and 1904
500 yards Freestyle	1902, 1903
880 yards Freestyle	1903
One mile	1903, 1904 and 1905
Long Distance (5 miles, 60 yards)	1905 (His time - 68 mins. 55 secs.)

This last race was held annually in the River Thames, and was originally called the "Lords and Commons Race", because the first trophy was presented by Members of Parliament, from 1877 to 1879.

In 1905 he competed in one of the greatest Continental races of that period – the 7½ mile swim in the River Seine through Paris. The organisers of this race accepted both professional and amateur entries for the race, started them together, but counted the events as a separate race for each class. When David returned home after swimming in the race, he was declared a professional, and was suspended by the Northern Counties Amateur Swimming Association for a breach (however unwittingly) of the amateur law. He appealed to the A.S.A. Committee in November 1905, and after long consideration, the appeal was dismissed. At the following Annual General Meeting of the A.S.A. it was stated that a new agreement had been reached between the A.S.A. and the Union des Societies Francais de Sports Athletiques on the question of the Amateur Law. The question of Billington's suspension was again raised in these new circumstances, but the original decision remained.

So after winning over 300 prizes as an amateur, David Billington was forced to turn professional in 1906. However, he was still as good as - if not better than - the professionals, and in fact at one period held every world professional swimming championship from 100 yards to 13½ miles distance.

He won the Seine race several times. And in 1913 he retained the one mile world championship, finishing over a hundred yards in front of the famous Australian swimmer Dickman. As an amateur he had several times opposed the Australian swimmers Percy Cavill and Barney Kieran, both of whom in due course won A.S.A. championships. David Billington later visited Australia, and as a result called two of his children after the names of the towns he visited – Sydney and Adelaide.

He won the King Edward VII Cup, which was awarded for a combination of speed swimming and life saving. Later, he gave a swimming exhibition in London before royalty. His photograph in Bacup Miscellany is taken from a book he wrote entitled "How to become a good swimmer" (Hutchinson, 1926, 114pp.).

In 1929 he went to Canada as coach, instructor, and manager of the civic baths at Hamilton, Ontario, and it was not long before his protegees there were winning swim after swim – proving his ability to coach as well as perform himself.

It is reported that for many years he used to dive from one of the piers at Blackpool, where he used to set fire to an asbestos suit he was wearing before take-off. In later years he lived in Radcliffe, and died there on February 4th, 1955. His grave is in Radcliffe Churchyard.

(Footnote: At the time of the Olympic Games in London in 1908, the F.I.N.A. (International Swimming Federation) was formed, and it was not until that time that Amateur Champions of the World (as Olympic winners) were officially recognised. From the time of the formation of the A.S.A. in 1869, and in fact before, many persons claimed to be Champions of the World, and by certain performances were unofficially recognised as such.)

* * * * * * * * * *

CARDINAL ERROR

A gret clatter o' clogs an' a lot o' noisy -- but good natured banter, disturbed th' early mornin' peace as t' "black sowjers" fro' th' Hill Top pit coom marchin' away off t' neet shift.

Their subject matter, generally speikin', would hardly have impressed Oxford don chaps, but then, what good would Oxford dons be at Hill Top?.

Ale, dogs, pigeons, horses an' wimmen, i' that order, wer' t' main topics o' ev'ryday conversation. An' this bein' Derby day they wer' exchangin' ther' fancies fer t' big race.

"Th' Agha Khan has a good un runnin' today", said Joe Jenkins to Billy Banks.

"Ah raythar fancy it misel", replied Billy. "It's as fine a filly as Jack Hampson's dowter -- a real thoroughbred!"

"A chap 'at compares racehorses wi' beauty queens should never get wed", said Joe. "Ah wouldn't like to think 'at onny o' my sisters . . ."

"No fear o' that", grinned Billy sheepishly, "They favvour thee too much!"

Just then, they coom abreast wi' Owd Jacksy, who wer' strugglin' breathlessly up t' broo to join t' mornin' shift miners.

"What's ta fancy fer t' big race?" axed Joe.

"A sure winner, that's what!" panted Jacksy. "An' a reight romper o' one it is, too! Ah seed it oal i' mi dreeom soon on this mornin'. Plain as a pikestaff it wer'. Ah could even yer th' horses snortin' an' thumpin' an peawndin' on behind. It wer' better nor sittin' wi' t' top hats i' Tattersall's".

Joe grinned

"What's th' horse?" he axed impatiently.

"That's mi trubble!" snapped Jacksy irritably, "tha doesn't allus get direct names i' them sooart o' dreams. Tha gets it mooar jumbled like -- i' what they co'll symbolic form".

"Ah see", said Billy drily, "th' horse's name-plate wer' a bit on t' dim side, eh?"

Owd Jacksy bristled, an' lukked daggers at Billy.

"Show mi t' list o' runners an' Ah'd pick it eawt in a flash", he snorted. "It name links up wi' religious matters. Summat to do wi' church affairs. If only Ah could ha' sin a mornin' paper on t' way up . . ."

"Why didn't ta get one?" challenged Billy.

"Bicose they hadn't com' thru, an' Ah couldn't wait no longer", snapped Jacksy.

"Let's bi gooin' Joe, we're gettin' nowheer fast!" said Billy scornfully.

"Howd on a minute", said Joe thoughtfully, "He's had sich dreeoms bifore. Tell mi Jacksy, when tha werked in t' Deep Level, didn't they used to co'll thi Mother Shipton?"

Owd Jacksy's eyes went as narrow as t' slits in a venetian blind.

"Ah'll ha' noan o' thi danged impudence", he warned. "Here, tek this ten bob note. Go an' get a paper an' read thru t' probable starters 'til tha coms to t' name 'at reminds thi o' church matters. An make mi bet read ten bob win".

"Fair enuff", exclaimed Joe, "an Ah think Ah'll ha' t' same on fer misel".

"Ah'll make mine read thrippence each way", sniggered Billy.

"Ah'm gooin' neaw", said Jacksy urgently. "Remember what Ah've towd thi, Joe . . ."

Reychin' th' eawtskirts o' t' teawn, Joe wer' soon scannin' t' listed runners.

"It's here! It's here!" he gabbled excitedly. "Parson's Nose, that's it!"

"Parson's Nose is a ronk eawtsider", objected Billy.

"Not so leawd", warned Joe, "if this gets eawt it'll breyk oal t' bookies, an' we shorn't get paid. By Gum! but just imagine Jacksy pickin' this in a dreeom, an' not even knowin' what wer' runnin'".

"Just a minute, Joe", said Billy deawtfully, "doesn't it strike thi 'at Parson's Nose seawnds mooar like a back-ender nor a winner?"

"Tha gret fool, tha corn't mix th' eitin' of a fowl's back end wi' religious matters", observed Joe respectfully.

Billy wer' suitably impressed.

"Ah think ah'll risk ten bob", he said.

Ther' wer' a lot o' noise in th' Alecan Arms that neet, an' snuff reek to meawnt a naval smook-screen. Significantly -- a tantalisin' aroma o' rich Havana cigars suggested t' bookies had done very weel for thersels. True, ther' wer' notable exceptions. Little irritatin' pockets o' resistance, to be smooked eawt some other time . . .

"Well, Billy, Ah wonder what's keepin' Owd Jacksy?" ventured Joe, liftin' his third pint.

"He's standin' just eawtside yon", said t'waiter, "Luks reight deawn in t' dumps, he does. Happen had a bad day tha knows".

A minute later Billy coom back pushin' a reluctant an' nervous lukkin Jacksy.

"Ah'd a job to get him in", panted Billy. "He's mooar like a chap 'at's had a neetmare nor a twenty-five to one winnin' dreeom".

"Get him a pint quick", ordered Joe anxiously. "He luks like he needs it!"

"Tell mi what happened", faltered Jacksy faintly.

"Ev'rything went just like tha said owd mon", grinned Joe. "As soon as we seed it name we knew straight away, didn't we Billy? Parson's Nose -- church matters, tha knows. Here's thi winnins' owd sport, so sit up, breeten up, an' sup up!"

Jacksy's meauth twitched into a nervous smile, an' beads o' swet stood eawt on his brow as he picked up a crumpled Sports Special.

"Toakin' abeaut these Derby horses", he confided craftily. "Ah wonder if yo' could tell mi t' meanin' o' *this* horse's name?"

"What's it co'lled?" axed Joe.

"Ecclesiastical", stammered Jacksy flushin' guiltily.

"Nowe!" said Billy dumbly.

"Ah've never yerd that word befoore", sniggered Joe.

"Thank God!" said Owd Jacksy fervently.

A QUESTION OF DEGREE

Ellen Newton looked round the gleaming room, fluffed-up a cushion, patted her new hair-do into place again, and said it was about time they were here. From the depths of his armchair, Walter Newton remarked that she'd overdone things a bit. "When you took me home for t' first time, your mother eyed me over, laughed her head off, and said we could have our tea in t' kitchen".

"Well, I'm not our Phyllis, and you're not Colin, are you? He's a university student, and I'm not asking a hintellectual to eat in our poky back hole. He'll be used to something better than that.

"When's he's been wed as long as me he'll be used to owt", said Walter. "He'll be glad to take things as they're thrown at him".

"You look put on, I must say", Ellen retorted. "In a couple o' years it'll be our silver wedding and you can do nowt yet except melt butter for me to spread".

"Every craftsman needs a labourer", said Walter. "Besides, our Phyllis doesn't look so bad off bread and butter, does she?"

"That's beside the point", replied Ellen. "I want her to have a better chance than I had, and that's why I want to make Colin feel at home when he gets here. Phyllis says he got nine "O" levels when he were only fifteen, and four advanced levels at seventeen. He must have a marvellous headpiece on him".

"If he were all that clever he wouldn't be thinking o' getting wed", Walter reasoned. "That'll soon bring him back to ground level".

"You've never had any time for heducation, had you? When I asked you to go to night school to enrol for machine-drawing, you came home as assistant caretaker. And you didn't stick that job for more than a month."

"It were only because I couldn't reckon my wage up", said Walter. "They paid me two-an-eleven an' five-sixteenths of a penny an hour, for forty-two-and-a-half hours a week, plus time-and-a-quarter for t' first seven hours overtime, and double-time at weekends, less insurance and superann', plus an overall allowance -- I used to spend my day off sorting it all out".

"You've always given up too soon, that's your trouble. I wish I'd had the chance of a university student -- I'd have jumped at it".

"I'm glad to meet you, Mrs. Newton, and most flattered, if I may say so", broke in Colin's pleasant voice.

She blushed to the roots of her home perm. "Oo, you did startle me; I never heard you come in".

"They say listeners never hear any good of themselves", laughed Phyllis, "but judging by what we've just heard, mother, it's quite evident I shall have to watch you when Colin's around -- dad, this is Colin".

Walter shook his hand heartily. "Glad to know you".

"I'm pleased to meet you, Mr. Newton. Phyllis has told me a lot about you".

"Did she tell you that I have some letters behind my name?" asked Walter, "KTGH, to be precise".

"She didn't. What do they stand for?"

"Keeping Th'owd Girl Happy", replied Walter. "And I don't mind admitting it's a divil of a job at times".

Th'owd Girl bustled back into the room with the teapot and quickly organised things to her liking. During tea-time, Colin answered their many questions on university life, and Ellen was spellbound. It was another world to her and she lapped-up every spicy anecdote with great relish. She stirred her jelly and slopped custard in her tea, to Walter's great delight.

"You've got her in a band, Colin. She's never been so far gone since we went on our honeymoon".

"Take no notice of him", counselled Ellen regally. "This 'igher Heducation's above his head altogether. What are you going to do when you leave school?"

Colin explained that he hoped to qualify as a scientist, but that he had a lot of hard work to do before then -- B.Sc., M.Sc., and his doctorate. "My thesis will be on coconuts, and then I shall probably join the brain-drain and go out to the Philippines for further research on the world coconut problem".

"I never knew there were one", said Walter, "excepting how milk gets inside 'em. There's always plenty about when t' fair comes".

"You'd be surprised", said Colin. "Production has to be increased to satisfy the expanding market in a great variety of articles with a base of coconut oil -- synthetic detergents, synthetic rubber, plasticizers, germicides, insecticides . . ."

"If there's any homicides, Perry Mason's your man", Walter broke in.

"Who'd have thought of coconuts being used for all them things?" mused Ellen. "You'll have to give a talk to the Townswomen's Guild next time you're on leave".

“My plans on those occasions don’t include sharing him with any other women, mother”, laughed Phyllis.

“See what I mean, Colin?” said Walter. “She’s boss already, and she’s only known you a month”.

“I like it that way, Mr. Newton. I think your daughter’s wonderful”.

“You never said anything like that about me when we were courting”, said Ellen, after the lovelorn pair had retired to the kitchen, to wash up behind closed doors. “In fact, you never spoke at all on Saturday night until you’d read your ‘Last Sports’ from cover to cover”.

“I should think not, either”, replied Walter. “My father always said that I wouldn’t go far wrong in life if I got my priorities right”.

Later that night, Walter was dozing off when Ellen’s elbow jarred his spinal column. “Are you asleep yet?”

“I were”, said Walter, “but I’m paralysed now. What’s up?”

“How do you like him ? You’ve never said”.

“He’ll do”, Walter replied. “I think he’s on my side, and he’s not greedy with his cigs”.

“He’s smashing”, said Ellen. “And did you notice his lovely white collar? Somebody takes a pride in seeing him turned out spick-an’-span. He’s from a good home, that’s plain to see. And what about the way he gazed at our Phyllis all through tea-time? It fair made me long to be young again”.

Walter laughed till the bed shook.

“What’s biting you now?” asked Ellen.

“I were just thinking”, chuckled Walter. “If they do get wed and move to t’ Philippines and we go there for a holiday, you’ll look a bonny object in a grass skirt an’ a few beads, flogging coconuts for ’em down in t’ bazaars”.

“You’re no James Bond, yourself”, replied Ellen, acidly. “Especially when you’ve left your teeth on t’ sink for t’ night -- And have you put the cat out?”

“Aye, I have”, said Walter, “an’ if you’d listen a bit instead o’ yapping so much you’d hear it courting behind t’ shed. And I’ll bet it hasn’t stopped to worry how milk gets in coconuts. Pipe down now, and try going to sleep by degrees”.

CLOGDALE WAKES -- or, POINTS OF VIEW

For a great many successive years, Joe Darwin had contributed to the modest fortunes of the good landlady at "Seaview". This sisterly soul had not only rewarded such fidelity with extra-special privileges, she had bestowed upon Mrs. Darwin the affectionate appellation -- "Our Lizbuthan".

And once again, Clogdale wakes week had brought the Darwins. Joe deposited the suitcases, acknowledged the profuse welcome, and firmly declined an incoming cup of tea.

"Not just now, lass", he said, mopping his brow, "Ah sizzle like a factory boiler wi' a full head o' steam".

"It's th' reight colour but th' wrong flavour", observed Lizbuthan sharply.

"Ah wer thinkin' o' summat a bit cooler", said Joe, mopping his brow. "Ah'll not be long" . . .

Having administered to the tracts of his tropical interior, he proceeded to the promenade, inhaling the fresh sea-breezes to his full capacity. The weighty hand of Luke Longstaffe, descending heavily upon his back, contributed largely to a somewhat premature deflation.

"Nay, dammit mon", said Joe, "tha comes like a ton o' coal down a cellar grate-hole".

"Put it theer, owd lad", boomed Luke joyfully. "Ay, but Ah've fairly missed thee sin Ah coom to live retired. Ah do miss th' owd faces at Clogdale mill. How's things back yonder? When didta land in? How long arta stoppin? How's th' missis?"

"Tha talks like a machine gun", said Joe, "Let's have 'em one at once, as Jack Newkin said after their third set o' twins".

"As Ah wer sayin', how's th' missis?" axed Luke.

"Reight as rain after haytime", said Joe, "Ah left her unpackin'. We're here for th' week. Complete rest an' change tha knows. To forget ev'rything . . . "

"Just what tha needs", said Luke, "to forget for a time. To get away fro' th' rattle an' clatter o' Clogdale mill".

"Aye," said Joe, "to get away fro' natter, bother, an' blizzards o' cotton fluff".

"An yet", said Luke,"thers summat about a cotton mill . . ."

"Cotton mills are nowt nobbut foundries 'at have bin whiteweshed", said Joe, derisively.

Luke's eyes dimmed slightly, and his "yonderly" expression

bespoke the sentimentality of his feelings. "Thers times when Ah wish Ah wer back again", he said sheepishly. "Seems to me th' owd life Ah knew, wer better nor th' new life Ah didn't know".

"Soft'nin' o' th' brain", said Joe sadly. "Thy uncle Ben's brass has gone wheer thers most room for it. These new Rockefeller friends o' thine'll cry shame on thee".

"Tha doesn't understand", said Luke. "Here tha con make fabulous acquaintances -- but few real friends. Here tha'rt never accepted, nobbut tolerated. Th' local poet put it this way --

'Ay, yo' folk, who vain aspire
To grab some brass, an' then retire,
To leave owd friends an' scenes behind,
Is th' next o' kin to livin' blind."

"That proves nowt", said Joe.

"It proves ev'rything", said Luke. "Give a little lad th' choice o' two guns, an' he'll choose that 'at meks most noise".

"So does an empty barrel, tha damn fool", said Joe.

"Tha doesn't alter a bit", said Luke grinning broadly, "tha'll oather win or draw, tha'll noan be licked".

"When Lizbuthan relinquishes th' title, Ah'll be th' new champion at our house", conceded Joe.

"What class o' goods are yo' weavin' these days?" axed Luke eagerly.

"First class", said Joe, "but then Ah wer never one for carryin' me work about. Ah'm here to forget it. Ah con throw off it just like throwin' off an owd coat".

"If only Ah could do th' same", said Luke wistfully, -- "If only Ah could get me mind to retire. Ah'm sleepin' bad . . ."

"Buy thiself a mallet an' use it", said Joe. "It'll guarantee sleep beside knockin' some sense into thy head".

"An' when Ah do drop off", said Luke dismally, "Ah start weavin', an' Ah weave til Ah wakken. Monny a mornin' Ah'm fit for nowt til dinnertime".

"What a wicked waste o' skilled labour", said Joe. "Tha'rt workin' for nowt mon. Swop me bank books an' tha'll be fain to get back an' be paid for it . . "

"Is owd yon slave-drivin' Slattery th' manager yet?" axed Luke.

"He is", said Joe.

"Ah'll stop wheer Ah am a bit", said Luke.

"So will Ah", said Joe, "but just now me system needs summat a bit more soothin'. Sand an' silence. Nowt noisier nor th' song o' th' sea".

"When tha's rested thy mind a bit tha'll think diff'rent", said Luke. "Just now tha feels tha's bin through a big bombardment complete wi' flyin' shuttles. It's drummin' in thy brain. Tha can't shift it -- it's theer. Tha doesn't need remindin' . . ."

Joe looked out to sea, muttering to himself -- "It's a funny world. One comes here to forget; another, to remember".

"What's that?" axed Luke.

"Ah wer just sayin'," said Joe drily, "Ah think we're in for a grand week".

"Ah wish it wer a month", said Luke. "Still, a week's better nor nowt. Tha'll be a bit o' comp'ny for me".

"Tell our Lizbuthan that", said Joe, "an' hoo'll go nap wi' both fists. Hoo wer never one for playin' solo".

"Ah wer thinkin' tha could bring me up-to-date wi' all the news", said Luke hastily.

"Doesn't your William Henry send thee th' Saturday paper?" axed Joe.

"Aye, after he's had his weekend meals on it", said Luke; "he fairly likes his jampot. Last week Ah got a lovely sunset . . . Ah've had it framed, an' th' Art Club connosuir is ravin' o'er it. 'Aurora Borealis', he purred, 'a genuine Rabini executed in the Italian stucco style".

"What did tha say?" axed Joe.

"A 'ell of a mess executed by William Henry", said Luke.

Joe shuffled restlessly. "Well, Luke owd pall', he said, "happen we'll meet again afore th' next week-end".

"Next week-end?" echoed Luke incredulously. "Ah've arranged a full programme . . . Monday, we could nip up to th' club for a few pints. Tuesday, th' Agricultural Show, then back to th' club. Wednesday, th' club bowlin' tournament . . ."

"Ah'm practically a life member", said Joe. "Arta sure tha'rt free for Thursday?"

"Aye", said Luke. "An' Friday we could have a private session on th' bowlin' green. It tastes better outside".

"An' Saturday", said Joe, tha con go an' help Lizbuthan wi' th' funeral arrangements".

"Tha'll do thy best", said Luke. "Onnyway, Ah'm tekkin' my holiday soon". "Arta doin' foreign parts?" axed Joe. "Nowe, a little beauty spot called Clogdale". said Luke. "Tha'll be stoppin", said Joe, "book single".

A ROSSENDALE IDYLL

"If tha' doesn't put th' fiddle deawn, Millie, and stop thi' skriking, I'll drive mi clog through it, neaw then". And so saying the woman seized the child's ear and dragged her away from the table whereon her music score was reared.

This littel martyr to music was a pale, pinched-face girl of fourteen, with a pair of large lustrous eyes that grandly redeemed her features from the type of the operative class. The little ear, too, still smarting and bleeding, was exceedingly delicate in its convolutions, and a mass of rich, black hair, combed up in factory fashion, sat like a crown upon her head.

It was the old story, already too often told, yet alas! to be often told again. Years ago Millie's father left the village to seek his luck as warehouse clerk with a firm of famous Manchester merchants, whose mills stood in the valley below. In their employ he soon rose to a position of trust, marrying the only daughter of the poor French professor with whom he lodged. Twelve months afterwards, when little Millie was born, his already happy life perfected itself into an ideal of household joy; and for eight brief years husband, wife and child were snug in their mest of love. Then fate, cruelly jealous of their undisturbed peacefulness, thrust out its hand and snatched away the mother bird; not, however, before she had bequeathed to her little one a passionate fondness for music and a rare old violin upon which she had taught her to play. Within two years the father succumbed to an epidemic, and then the fledgling was alone. It was now that her aunt's rude hand was stretched out to cage and carry her off to the village of her fathers, where she found, instead of the sheltering wing and brooding care she so much needed, the dangers and sufferings and exposures of child-labour in factory life.

To one so finely organised and delicately reared this change was at first almost fatal, and sorely did Millie suffer from the lack of the shelter, the sunshine, and the song surrounding her early days. There was one inspiration, however, that never failed her -- the divine inspiration of music. She heard it everywhere. As she lay at night upon her hard bed its strange melodies swept through her brain, and even during the tedious hours of her taxing toil the whirr of the machinery and the vibrations of the floor, despite their discordant sounds, beat out the old tunes to which she had listened and which she had learned to love in the happy Manchester home. In her spare moments she would steal away to the cloughs for which the valley was so famous, where the waters fell in liquid sounds and the winds played their symphonies amid the tops of the umbrageous trees. She loved most, however, her mother's legacy, the dear old violin; and with it carefully held under her arm (for the utilitarian aunt had pounced upon its silk-lined case for the purpose of a work-box) she would climb the heights where the moors stretched out in heathery glory, and sitting down, so touch its trembling strings as to make them echo the swish of the wind amid the herbage and the plaintive cry of the plover wheeling overhead. When opportunity offered, and her aunt was mellowed by a passing mood of tolerance, she ventured upon a practice "indoors", bringing out some old piece learnt long ago, or some new selection she was only too eager to learn.

Unfortunately, however, this violin was a source of continual annoyance to the aunt, who hated the sight and sound of it because once the property of "the French hussy" whom her brother had so offended her in taking as his wife. Moreover she was a member of a cold Puritanical sect worshipping in a cheerless barn-like structure on the hills, known as Mount Zion, and who started aside at every evidence of aestheticism and joyfulness as baits laid by the devil for the decoy of souls. But the most weighty objection of all to Millie's persistent pursuit of her favourite occupation was that it took up the moments the exacting woman determined her niece should give to household work. Thus it came to pass that every sound from the violin roused the slumbering bitterness in the woman's nature, edging her tongue with cruel words and prompting her hands to brutal deeds.

As Millie sat in the corner of the darkening room, her ear still smarting, her heart, big with disappointment and grief, now and again unburdening itself with hysterical sobs, the woman once more rounded on her, and with raised voice cried out:

"'owd thi din, wilt ta, or i'll poo thi other yer for thee. Be off to bed wi thi, and smor up thi babbie cries in th' blankets".

Millie slowly climbed the stone stairway to her desolate chamber, with its whitewashed walls and underdrawn rafters. In this room three beds were ranged, into the smallest of which the sobbing child soon crept. No sooner had she lain down, however, than she forgot her trouble, for a melody came stealing in upon her which the machinery of the mill had rattled out to her during the long hours of that day's toil. She had never heard it anywhere before. It was only one of many that came and went, leaving behind them memories in which she found a solace. With this melody in her mind, and occasionally finding utterance in her voice as she hid her head under the bed-clothes to escape the quick ear of the woman below, she fell asleep, awakening early in the morning to find the sun streaming in through the chamber window, and even glorifying the leaden faces of the surrounding sleepers.

Stealthily rising and taking up her clothes, she stole downstairs and dressed in the kitchen, to lessen the risks of awakening the household, and then, quietly taking the violin from the hook whereon it hung, slipped it under her arm, and bounded off to Raven's Clough to play to her heart's content until the shrill whistle of the factory summoned her to the day's toil.

Once seated under her favourite tree, she drew the bow across the strings, and soon there went forth on the still air of the summer morning the strange, sweet melody the factory wheels had played to her on the previous day, and the haunting sweetness of which had soothed her to sleep in her last night's sorrow. On and on she played, lost in her harmonies. The six o'clock alarums from the surrounding mills shrieked and rent the air with their discordant sounds in vain. She was without ear for their cries: other voices were speaking in her soul. She had a sense for other sounds.

At last she came back to earth again and tremblingly realised her sin. The breakfast hour was lost, her aunt was outraged, while upon herself she had entailed more suffering at the hands of the heartless woman under whom a cruel fate had thrown her.

But Millie was not a girl to cry over spilt milk; so bracing herself together she hurried in the direction of the house in which she lived. The news of her delinquency, however, had already reached the ears of the aunt; for the girls who lodged at the same house, and who had just arrived for their hurried breakfast had broken the news of Millie's absence, the hawk-eye of the woman missing the violin from its accustomed hook.

Before Millie could explain or express her sorrow, she was received by a cuff on the ear, and the violin was snatched from under her arm and re-hung upon the hook in the wall.

"I'll teach thee to be fiddlin' when tha ought to be working", cried the vengeful woman. "Naw, mind, tha dosn't come whoam to thi dinner today, and if tha does tha'll geet nowt. Be off wi thi, and when tha's goan, I'll talk to thi fiddle a bit, that I will".

" "Don't hurt the violin, Auntie", wailed the child.

"Be off wi' tha, and leave thi fiddle to me, tha' brat of a French hussy".

How long that day was to Millie none will ever know. Wearily, oh! so wearily, the hours dragged. A blazing sun burned down upon the weaving sheds. The men were stripped to their waists and many of the girls worked in their bodices. Millie's little hands were moist, and her ends got down so that the shuttles were continually being stopped. All her deftness seemed to forsake her. Her temples throbbed and she was weak for want of food. At the dinner hour some of the girls offered her their scraps on condition she would sing to them some of the old songs taught her by her mother in the happy past. But she could not. Even her never-failing angel had forsaken her, and the words burnt like fire on her lips.

Half-past five, and there was a stampede for the open. But outside was sultry and dark clouds shut in the valley. There was thunder in the air; indeed, its sound might then be heard coming from the distant hills. The operatives hurried home to escape the storm, and Millie with them, to find upon her arrival that two things were missing -- her aunt and her loved violin. The one had gone to a tea meeting at Mount Zion, and the violin no longer hung in its accustomed place upon the wall.

"Uncle, where is my violin?" convulsively cried the child.

"Nay, lass, I doan't know. I've none meedled wi' it".

"Oh, dear! oh, dear! I cannot live without it. And it was my mother's, too. Wherever can auntie have put it?"

A little urchin standing by the open door, and hearing the cause of Millie's excitement, now thrust in his dirty face and cried: "Thi aunt's throwed it in th' delph-watter. I seed her do it mysel this afternoon as she were beawn to Mount Zion".

* * * * * * * * * * *

By this time an Egyptian darkness had spread over the whole valley. Rain fell in torrents, and the lightnings, like arrows, were abroad. Strong men trembled, and hysterical girls shrieked and wrapped their faced up in shawls. For some hours the elements fought as though they would batter into destruction the world around which they raged. Then the thunder retreated to distant hills and the skies cleared. In the cold blue the stars glimmered and the summer moon rode majestically in the heavens. The people in twos and threes, came and stood by their cottage doors and sniffed with pleasure the now no longer surcharged air.

Millie's aunt came back from Mount Zion, talking about "the heavens being rent as a scrowl", pausing at last in her unctuous quotations to ask if Millie was in bed.

Millie! Millie! Where could Millie be? No one had seen her. No one knew anything of her.

"Mebbe goan to luk for th' fiddle", suggested the uncle, at which the aunt's face blanched with fear.

* * * * * * * * * *

The following morning at half past five, as a gang of quarrymen were going to work, they espied a child floating in the water lodged at the bottom of a disused delph, and when the police were fetched to drag out the little corpse it was found to be Millie, and by her side there was a broken violin.

They buried her in the bleak graveyard on the bleak hillside; and foolish folk say that at midnight, when the moon is high, the sound of music is heard around her grave. If this be so, it is the music the shepherds heard in the Bethlehem field, for surely the angels can scarce forbear to sing a welcome to that little angel-soul who while on earth found her heaven in song.

TRAVELLING HOPEFULLY (By A. Nonnimus)

You chaps coming on leave will have realised that journeying by train nowadays is not the simple matter it used to be. That you reach 'ome at all reflects credit on your native intelligence, although we fear many precious hours of leave are lost through mistakes due to the black-out, and the removal of so many of the station names. It must be double difficult now that, in this part of the world, for the utter confusion of possible invaders, the Railway Authorities have given new names to all their stations; names which do not appear in any map or time-table. Whether this idea emanated from our revered old friend Mr. Fred Lloyd cannot be definitely ascertained, but we wouldn't put it past him.

The purpose therefore, of this little effort is to attempt to pilot you along the home stretch, that is from Manchester to Bacup, and the writer 'umbly 'opes that you may find it useful in negotiating this seemingly interminable last lap of your journey home.

Taking the journey stage by stage, we will give first the new name of each place, as announced by the station staffs, and, in brackets, the name by which you knew it in the old days.

We will now assume that you have already taken your seat in the electric train at Victoria; arranged your traps, made yourself comfortable, and lit a cigarette. You are promptly made aware, by sundry glances and an outbreak of racking coughs, that you are in a non-smoker. You gather your belongings, move to the rear, and go through the business of settling yourself once more.

You amuse yourself by watching your fellow passengers embark, listening with pleasure to snatches of gradely talk, and wondering where you will first encounter clogs.

Just as the train is due to start, the inevitable last-minute ladies bustle in, smiling. (Why ladies always smile after successfully boarding a train or 'bus will ever be a mystery).

The ladies choose a seat, forsake it for another, preen themselves a little, and prepare to sit down gracefully. The train starts with its characteristic lurch and they flop down suddenly, their hats over one eye. This is one of the Company's little jokes, known as "Skittle 'em", or, "Down Bobs your Auntie".

And now we are off; to dispose in more or less swift succession, of all those unncessary intermediate stations in the following order:–

1.	Zrow	(formerly Woodlands Road)
2.	Saul	(Crumpsall) -- (an easy one)
3.	Howki	(Bowker Vale)
4.	Haw	(Heaton Park) (See No.15)
5.	Sweets	(Prestwich)
6.	Besses	(Besses o' th' Barn) (also easy)
7.	Why me?	(Whitefield)
8.	Cleep	(Radcliffe)
9.	Ole change	(Bury)

Here you tumble out and squander quite a slice of your young life, stamping your feet and wondering how far you are from the North Pole.

In (over-) due course, around the corner, comes our Train; coughing and gasping as it manfully tackles the stiff gradient.

Thankfully you pile into the Compartment that feels snug and warm after the Charity-like temperature of the station. When the guard is satisfied that he has said 'Howdo' to every one of the station officials, we proceed.

Now our lion-hearted engine begins to swank a little and we bowl on joyously to

10.	Some say	(Summerseat) and thence to
11.	-------	(Ramsbottom)

Many reasons have been advanced for the secrecy observed regarding this station. Most of them are fantastic and all of them disrespectful. Porters of the call-out-or-bust variety content themselves with "BacuptraieenstoppingtraintoBacupBacuptraieeeen".

And so to

12.	Tubbee	(Stubbins) -- (Town Station)

Here the lady who got in at Ole Change asks is she 'Alright for Accrington'. You tell her she is all wrong and add to her mortification by explaining that had she spoken at the last stop she could have rectified her error. Assuming that all we have heard about soldiers is true, you will, if she is young and charming, advise her to get out and take the next train back. Should she be of the grim old battle-axe type you will suggest that she goes on with you as far as Rawtenstall, whence she can take a bus to Haslingden. This little business settled, we now have

13.	A or B	(Ewood Bridge)
14.	Ronsole	(Rawtenstall)
15.	How	(Cloughfold)

Do not confuse this with Haw (No.4). If in doubt open the window and take a deep breath.

16. Wadd (Waterfoot) (Or Waddy according to the more loquacious porters.)

17. Taxis (Stacksteads)

No further directions will now be required. There is no mistaking the next station.

Is Robert about to carry your kit-bag? Is he hen-meat. Never is when he is wanted.

You proceed via the Western exit to avoid those two awkward steps. You have arrived.

MORE ROSSENDALE ANECDOTES

J.H. Brearley tells of a gentleman who arrived at Bacup Station one morning, and when he got out of the station it was raining hard. He asked a little boy, "Does it always rain in Bacup?" The lad replied, "Oh no, it snows sometimes".

The story is also told of a little girl who went to school, not too clean. The teacher sent her mother a note saying that the girl was dirty, she smelled. The mother was very indignant. She sent a note to the teacher saying that she sent her child to the school to be educated, not to be smelled at.

Poor old Harriet Waite,
Has gone to meet her fate,
Doomed by her husband's
Cruel hand to die.

(All that can be remembered from a Broadsheet sold on Bacup Market.)

A ROOM WITH A VIEW

Mrs. Midwinter led the way up the steep uncarpeted stairs to the third landing.

"This is your room", she said, "It's nice and compact. I hope you like it".

Billy Cookson put down his portmanteau and took a newspaper clipping from his wallet. -- "Board residence, h. and c., two mins. sea and station, four good meals daily, all mod. con. -- Midwinter, Sunset View".

"Here, Maggie, read that an' tell me if tha thinks we'n getten to th' wrong address", he said to his wife.

"What do you mean?" Mrs. Midwinter asked sharply.

"When ah wrote for digs", he replied, "ah axed for a double-room on th' first floor. This isn't first floor. Ah were in some assault courses in th' army as didn't knock me up as much as them stairs".

"Everybody writes for that room", said Mrs. Midwinter, "so somebody has to be disappointed".

"Why pick on us?" asked Maggie.

"Law of averages", was the impressive reply. "You were the last to arrive".

"Tha might find that law workin' t'other road round when tha wants thi brass", hinted Billy. "An' what law had ti in mind when tha said as this place were nobbut two minutes fro' th' station?"

"Tha could nobbut do it in a jet bomber", said Maggie. "It teks nearly ten minutes to get to this 'ere crow's nest fro' th' front foor, never mind th' station".

"An what about this 'h. & c.' touch?" asked Billy. "Ah corn't even see a slopstone i' theer, let alone hot an' cowd watter".

"Mr. Midwinter brings up two jugs of water every morning at half-past six", replied the landlady. "If you're up at the right time one will be hot; of you're not, they'll both be cold".

"Ah suppose thi husband comes under th' general headin' 'all mod. con', does he?" asked Billy. "Same as me when ah'm a'whoam".

"Don't be daft", said Maggie. "Tha's just been telled as he's all part o' t'hot watter system".

"Wait till he comes in!" exclaimed the incensed landlady. "You'll hear something, then!"

"We'n seen plenty onyroad", said Billy. "Ah've never had a room afore where th' beams con get into bed wi' me. Nor one where ah have to get down on mi knees to look through th' winda. Sunset View's a good name for this shop. Th' only time we'll see ony sun is when it goes down under the' floorboards".

Maggie stuck an oar in before Mrs. Midwinter could reply.

"Heigh! Did ta say thi husband brings th' watter up at half-past six?"

"That's the rule here. Any objections?"

"Plenty", replied Maggie. "Half-past six is middle o' th' neet for fooak on holiday".

"That's the rule", repeated Mrs. Midwinter firmly.

"Let's hear a few more", said Billy, "then we'll know where we stand".

"There's a list pinned on the door of the toilet, which is on the first landing", she replied, "but there's one you might as well know now -- tea's ready in five minutes, so don't be late. We work to a system here. Your table is in the corner between the sideboard and the serving-hatch".

"Ah suppose that's th' law of averages again, is it?" Billy shouted as she went downstairs.

"If hoo geet a green quilt on here, it'd mek a good billiard-table", was his verdict of the bed's possibilities.

"An it's th' same owd do o'er th' clooas", said Maggie. "Not even a picture rail to hook 'em on".

"Ah've tekken good care o' that", said Billy. "We're not havin' th' same carry-on as we had at Bispham last yur. Ah packed mi hommer an' a few nails this time".

"Where did ti pack th' nails?" asked Maggie. "Tha'll ha' th' clooas torn to bits".

"They're inside thi pumps", he replied. "They'll do no damage theer unless tha forgets to tek 'em out afore tha shoves thi bunions in".

"We could ha' done wi' some cement as weel", said Maggie. "This basin's cracked to glory".

"Same wi' that dooment '; she added, looking under the bed. "An tha should see th' fluff. Looks as if there's been a big snowstorm".

"We'll shove some i' th' bowster", said Billy. "It needs a blood transfusion or summat".

Downstairs Mrs. Midwinter hammered on the gong.

"Tay must be ready", said Billy. "There'll be a row if it's rabbit-meight an' jam".

"We want no rows in front o' t' other lodgers", said Maggie. "They'll think we clem a'whoam".

"They con think what they'n a mind", said Billy. "Ah'm not payin' fifteen-an-a-tanner a day to scrat about wi' a couple o' sheets o' lettuce".

"Let's unpack th' box afore we go down", said Maggie, "mi frock'll have that monny creases Ah'll ha' to screw it on".

"Leave it till we've seen what th' tay's like", advised Billy. "We're not forced to be stoppin'"".

MORE ROSSENDALE ANECDOTES

A farmer's lad at Bacup was out courting, and to break a long lull in the conversation, his young lady said: "Tha's nowt to say", so he asked: "Will ti' wed me?" "Aye", she replied. They went on in silence for some time longer until she again said: "Tha's nowt to say". His rejoinder on this occasion was: "Aw've said enough already fer one neet".

A tackler who had papered his house was very proud of his work when he had finished it and asked his friend in to look at it. "Tha's med a good job o' thad", sed his friend, "bud wod's them brass knobs for uts dotted up an' deawn o' t' walls?" "Brass knobs?" said the tackler, "them's drawing-pins. Tha knows Aw might be flittin' next year".

"Nine B's" -- Billy Brown, Best Blooming Blower in Bacup Borough Brass Band.

EMILY SARAH HOLT

Whilst Lord Byron was Lord of the Manor of Rochdale, a number of freeholders in Brandwood who had rights on waste or common land agreed to divide the common land amongst themselves. They built a stone wall around 145 acres, giving them title to the surface and to the more valuable coal and other minerals beneath.

By March 1833, the lord of the manor was a Mr. Dearden, who commenced an action at Lancaster Assizes, claiming the land was part of the manor, having descended from Stanlaw monastery to the monastery at Whalley.

His suit was against James Maden of Greens House, Bacup, who was successful, thereby determining without doubt not only his own title but the rights of the other land-owners. His third daughter was Judith -- who in due course married John Holt of Stubbylee (bought by Bacup Corporation in 1914 and subsequently used as their Town Hall).

At the dissolution of the monasteries by King Henry VIII, large tracts of land held by Whalley monastery passed to a Thomas Holt of Gristlehurst in the Rochdale district. He was one of the Holts of Stubley of that locality. Thomas died in 1561, and the branches of the Holt family continued several hundred years.

In due course the land upon which Stubbylee is built passed to James Holt, a woollen manufacturer. It was his son John who married Judith Maden of Greens. They had several children: James Maden Holt, born 18 October 1829, Emily Sarah Holt, born 25 April 1836, Julia Anne Elizabeth Holt (who died 24 October 1843), and Mary Holt whose name only is known.

James Maden Holt married Anna, a daughter of the Rev. John Haworth of Penistone. She died in 1903, and he in 1911, They had no children, and lived in London as well as at Stubbylee. Besides a successful Parliamentary career, James Maden Holt built St. Saviour's Church, and endowed it with his own private fortune in 1865.

The Holt family were well known for their anti-Roman Catholic attitude, and their very Low Church inclinations. Emily Sarah Holt lived mainly in London, and very little is known of her personal life, though she was of a very retiring disposition, and, along with her sister Mary, was well known for her liberality amongst the poor of the district -- according to the Rossendale Free Press in 1900.

She was a prolific writer, and wrote some 50 historical novels. The Spectator called her "a careful student of history; her books are not only highly readable, but historical studies of much value", whilst under the pen-name of "Hermentrude", she was a frequent contributor to the London "Notes and Queries", and to "Christian Armour". Emily Sarah Holt also wrote numerous religious tracts, stories, books on ancient customs, and "How to achieve social success", which last item was published posthumously.

Still remembered by some Bacupians as "an aristocratic, retiring lady", Miss Holt died on Christmas Day, 1893, at Balham House, Surrey, and was subsequently interred in the family vault in St. Saviour's Church, where the Rev. W. Johnson preached a special sermon in her memory -- "She hath wrought a good work upon me". When her will was proved her estate was over £26,000.

Exhaustive research has failed to locate the Maden and Holt family papers, so comparatively little is known. However, an eyewitness has described Miss Holt and her sister as having a demure walk, with figures straight and upright. And to Emily Sarah Holt is attributed this enigmatical local rhyme:

"Abraham, Isaac and Jacob
Lived in a little house a bit aboon Bacup;
Abr'am delved and Isaac span,
And Jacob ran about with a little kitty can."

Historical appendices to many of her works show that Miss Holt was a keen student of history, and spent many hours researching in the library of the British Museum, State Paper Office, and other sources to verify the historicity of her novels. Her first book was published in two volumes in 1861 -- "Memoirs of Royal Ladies". Many of her later books are in a series entitled by the publisher, John F. Shaw of London, "Tales of English life in the Olden Time": many of them in the stock of Bacup Public Library.

* * * * * * * * * * *

THE POPULATION OF BACUP

Population figures for the present Borough of Bacup are notoriously difficult to detail separately before the middle of the nineteenth century. Population statistics were related in the main to Poor Law Townships (Bacup being divided between Newchurch and Spotland), and these did not necessarily fall entirely within the boundaries of the borough.

The entire population of the Forest of Rossendale in the year 1500 totalled about 20. By the time the New Church was built in 1511, the population had increased tenfold, by 1551 was about 1000 and a hundred years later was rather more than 3000. In 1660 the population of Bacup was deduced by Mr. M. B. Ormerod in the course of researches into his family pedigree. He calculated that 102 persons paid tax, and an estimated further 40% did not, making a total population of 143 for Bacup itself. This did not include Stacksteads -- then known as Tunstead -- which similarly admitted 32 taxpayers, with a further 40% making 45 inhabitants in that area. Cowpe, which today is divided between the boroughs of Rawtenstall and Bacup, showed 28 persons paying tax, with a further 40% making an estimated total of 39.

Compounding these three separate estimates, the population of the area covered by the present borough of Bacup in 1660 can be estimated at about 200 persons.

In 1790 the whole population of the Forest of Rossendale did not exceed 10,000, but by 1798 the population of Bacup stood at 1426, and some 24 years later had doubled in number. At this time, Bacup was part of the chapelry of Newchurch, which also included Deadwin Clough and Wolfenden, and was part of the Parish of Whalley in the Hundred of Blackburn. The estimated population of the Forest of Rossendale 150 years ago was about 17,000.

Thomas Newbigging, the immigrant Scotsman who became the historian of the Rossendale Valley, listed the population of the area according to the national censuses:–

	1801	1811	1821	1831	1841	1851
Newchurch, Deadwin Clough, Bacup and Wolfenden	5046	6930	8557	9196	11,668	16,915
Part of the Township of Spotland, viz:- Brandwood Higher and Lower Ends	1527	2078	2591	3059	3403	4507

The precentage increase in the population during the first half of the nineteenth century has been calculated as follows:–

1801 to 1811	--	by 37%
1811 to 1821	--	by 23%
1821 to 1831	--	by 7%
1831 to 1841	--	by 27%
1841 to 1851	--	by 45%

In 1851 to became possible to realise a truer figure for the population of Bacup, though this still excludes the Stacksteads area of the town, which was not formally annexed until the year 1876, and in practice about a third of the present population of the borough live in that area. The 1851 Census recorded a population in Bacup of 10,313.

The remarkable increase in the population of Bacup and Rossendale during the middle years of the nineteenth century was due primarily to the cotton trade, which by the time Bacup was incorporated as a borough could boast 67 cotton mills.

The population figures since 1851 can be briefly summarised according to the official Census figures:

1851 --	10,313	1901 --	22,505
1861 --	10,935	1911 --	22,318
1871 --	17,199	1921 --	21,263
1881 --	25,034	1931 --	20,590
1891 --	23,498		

Because of the Second World War, the national census due in 1941 could not be carried out, and the earliest date at which a reliable population figure can be ascertained is in 1946, from which date the figures are given every five years:

1946 --	17,858	(estimated figure)
1951 --	18,374	(Census return)
1956 --	18,190	(Registrar General's estimate)
1961 --	17 295	(Census return)
1966 --	16,750	(Registrar General's estimate)
1971 --	15,102	(Census return)

This is by no means an exhaustive account of the population changes of Bacup -- a task which does not fall within the purview of Bacup Miscellany.

WAS ROSSENDALE LIKE THIS IN TUDOR TIMES?

Tudor Rossendale was dull,
    When rubbish dumps got heaped and full,
Because of this the town would smell.
    For water all come to the well.

When Rossendale the Queen came through,
    The poorest folk had jobs to do,
They had to fix the Booth highway,
    And when she came, the Queen would say:

"Oh, my people,
    How clean and neat
  Are all your roads,
    And every street".

And Rossendale
    Then had no schools,
So none were clever
    And all were fools.

And travelling through the countryside,
    Travellers always had to hire a guide,
For ruts, and holes, and furrows ploughed
    Would tumble both the poor and proud.

—— I don't think Tudor times would be
The kind of life for you and me.

(This poem won the First Prize in the Junior Section of a Poetry Competition organised by Bacup Public Library in February 1968, and was composed by a pupil of Tunstead C.E. School, Ida Marshall, aged 9.)

WHITHER ROSSENDALE?

From the window of my study at home I look over a Rossendale upon which the evening sun shines after two days of rain, which on Cribden blows in horizontally on the westerly wind. Rossendale is in its smokeless weekend mood, twelve idle chimney stacks, a solitary pylon on the hillside. Cloughfold gasworks as lifeless as the set for "Coronation Street", the stillness of Hall Carr with its battalion of wet roofs and no sign of human life. It is Sunday and no-one stirs; everyone is rendering silent tribute to the telly. In the valley the Skipton bus lopes its way towards Lancashire's most monstrous traffic island, whilst high above on desolate Balladen, streaks of snow hide the scars and to the right are the grey greens of Horncliffe quarries. The wind has veered north westerly, the rain clouds driven beyond the great semi-circle of hills that divide us from Yorkshire. Somewhere in that vast amphitheatre lies Bacup in its Pennine close, as isolated a town as you will find in Northern England. To the south the eye can see as far as Manchester and the hills of Cheshire, but it is Sunday and in the valley no-one stirs.

We came here in the rain from the limpid luminous beauty of Wharfedale. But to visit Rossendale in the rain is to misjudge it. It should be seen for the first time on a fine anti-cyclonic summer day or in February when an easterly air stream gives the outline of the hills a knife edge sharpness and Cowpe Lowe emerges like a sentinel parading its coat of many colours. I first approached Rossendale from the Whitworth road and having previously spent some days in East London, even this, surely the most drab of the valley highways, enabled me to breathe again amongst the hills after flat dreary Dagenham. Having lived for many years on the respectable fringes of large cities, I was pleased to part company with the landscape of brick semis but not so happy to walk on the moors, littered with old bread vans and iron bedsteads, which no-one is public-spirited enough to clear away. The valley itself reminded me of the 1930's in Birmingham, except that there were no war wounded standing all day on street corners or propped against lamp posts.

The isolation of Rossendale has led to the preservation of human characteristics which are, on balance, to its advantage. The people have corporate unity, a sociability, and a pride in their homes which characterise few other industrial areas. Strong non-conformity has produced a conformism which has certain virtues in this age of unrest and spurious values. The youngsters have a solidity often revealed in a stubborn refusal to be pushed but a willingness to be led. And if both parents usually work they do so within at most a few miles of home, and lack of mobility is almost as typical now as it was a hundred years ago.

It is in fear and trepidation that, as a newcomer I look into the future, especially as a Rawtenstall councillor, when speaking of the bus station controversy, criticised those who had not been in the valley for eighteen months for having the impertinence to possess views of their own. Perhaps the spectrum of our experience, coming as we do from beyond Sharneyford, is too wide and our objectives are to be distrusted. How will the valley fare when it is divided between Selnec, Blackburn and Burnley? Or will this change make very much difference to its destiny? In moments of dismay I can visualise an area of decay, the industrial equivalent of the Scottish crofters where the old remain with their memories, the young have gone, the schools are closed and only industrial archaeologists come to muse.

At other times I hope that new industry will be attracted at least to the Western end of the valley opening out on the Irwell Vale with its better communications and its three and a half miles of sinuous motorway, linking one bottleneck with the next. But in the fight for light industry or new industry Rossendale's voice is a small one compared with West Cumberland or Durham. And then on one of those glorious anti-cyclonic days of blue sky when the hills no longer oppress but recede to welcome us, I think of what a superb area this could be for Manchester (sorry, Selnec) commuters to live. There would be disadvantages. We would witness the dynasty of commuterdom, with its idol, the motor car, a symbol of purposeless mobility. The Sunday club of car washers and colour supplement readers would descend upon us. We might become a valley of vertical golf courses. But what an opportunity there would be to create in this valley a linear city, at night a golden ribbon, with buildings of varying heights to take advantage of the landscape, the blight of the nineteenth century removed. Everyone would have access to the moors, partly wild, partly afforested, partly refurbished as green recreation areas. We might even tolerate the odd golf course. As Cheshire prices itself out of the housing market what can it offer that Rossendale could not, given its urban revival and the removal of its blight? Who knows, Rawtenstall might even get its bus station, instead of that medium sized piece of tarmac so narrow that no self-respecting bus can stand sideways.

The evening sun sets in a reddening sky. A lone bird sings. The magpies flash black and white as they balance with precarious confidence on frail branches, suspended hundreds of feet above the valley. There are no magpies in Dagenham. When I travel out of Manchester in the evening rush hour of a lengthening winter day and the bus emerges from the swirling traffic and moves freely along Bury New Road, I catch a glimpse of the Rossendale hills and with affection think: there lies my home and home is where you make it.

MORE ROSSENDALE ANECDOTES

At one time one could stand by the Big Lamp at Haslingden and count 30 public houses. A quarryman with the nickname of "Walloper", a very big man of remarkable strength, used to go the rounds and then stand under the Big Lamp shouting and singing. The police would try to remove him, and he used to shout: "Ah'm noan shiftin' until there's 10 on yo".

A city girl on a visit to a village was asked by one of the local lads to go for a walk. He was very shy, though, and after a while the girl asked him if he knew anything about sex.

"Sacks", he said, "Aw should do. Aw filled moor nor twenty wi coil this mornin' ".

CHURCHES AND CHAPELS IN BACUP

A census of attendance at worship on Sunday, January 22nd, 1887, showed that 17% of the population of Bacup were estimated to have gone to church that day. The figures recorded for attendance are as follows:

	Morning	**Afternoon**	**Evening**	**Total during day**
BAPTISTS:	1769	780	813	3362
* (Waterbarn	355	384		739)
(Ebenezer	392		282	674)
(Zion	268		229	497)
* (Irwell Terrace	235		173	408)
* (Doals	152	224		376)
* (Acre Mill	197		129	326)
(Particular Baptist	98	93		191)
(General Baptist	72	79		151)
WESLEYAN METHODISTS:	1444	281	1317	3042
(Mount Pleasant	532		451	983)
(Wesley Place	278		222	500)
* (Stacksteads	301		194	495)
(Thorn	202		262	464)
* (Heald		206	98	304)
(Britannia	131		90	221)
* (Sharneyford		75		75)

(**Note:** Sharneyford gave up one service for Thorn "Missionary Sermons").

CHURCH OF ENGLAND:	1127		971	2098
* (St. John's	229		387	616)
* (Trinity, Tunstead	296		275	571)
* (Christ Church	242		143	385)
* (St. Saviour's	360		166	526)
SALVATION ARMY:		572	648	1220
* ROMAN CATHOLICS:	569	269		838

(**Note:** St. Mary's had two morning services, at 9 and 11 a.m.).

PRIMITIVE METHODISTS:	155	185	276	616
(Bacup, North St.	155		158	313)
(Stacksteads		133	91	224)
(Change		52	27	79)
UNITED METHODIST FREE CHURCHES:	168	204	240	612
* (Britannia		204	117	321)
* (Waterside	168		123	291)

	Morning	Afternoon	Evening	Total during day
* SPIRITUALISTS:		196	217	413
CONGREGATIONALISTS:	134		120	254
GOSPEL MISSION:	114		96	210
BLUE RIBBON MISSION:			103	103

(Total worshippers: 5480 morning, 2487 afternoon, 4801 evening: 12,768 altogether.)

* These churches are still in use, though Irwell Terrace Baptists after two amalgamations have been known since November 1962 as Trinity Baptists. Britannia U.M.F.C. is now known as Beulah. Waterside U.M.F.C. is now Central Methodist.

Brief notes follow on those churches listed above which have since closed:

BOOTH ROAD PRIMITIVE METHODISTS: Derived from the "Bacup Mission" of the early 1800s, first chapel opened 1850 in premises now "Chapel Cottages"; larger chapel built 1874, closed May 1952, merged with Samuel Chadwick Memorial Chapel, as Stacksteads Methodist Church.

BRITANNIA WESLEYAN METHODISTS: Sunday School established 1870. Met in a hired room, new school-chapel opened 1873. Closed about 1936, was subsequently used by Nestor Manufacturing Co. as a shoe factory.

CHANGE PRIMITIVE METHODISTS: Sunday School began in a mechanics' shop, moved to a room over the blacksmith's shop at Lower Change. Chapel built 1871, closed 1919, later demolished. Now the site of "Chapel Villas".

EBENEZER BAPTISTS: Founded between 1720 and 1736 by Rev. David Crosley. Church built 1746, rebuilt 1777 and 1812, new school 1825, day school 1860, old buildings converted to schools 1866, chapel on new site 1868–70. Merged with Union Baptist Church in November 1962, Ebenezer buildings later demolished.

LOWER ROCKLIFFE: Recorded in the 1887 Census as the Blue Ribbon Mission, was an off-shoot of Ebenezer Baptist Church. Nothing further discovered.

MOUNT OLIVET BAPTISTS: Originally known as the Gospel Mission, Sunday School began January 3rd, 1875, comprised of dissentients from Ebenezer; organised 1880 and church established 1895. Final services January 1st, 1963, building converted into a joiner's workshop June 1963.

MOUNT PLEASANT WESLEYAN METHODISTS: First chapel built 1761, opened in Lanehead Lane by John Wesley; second chapel 1786, third chapel 1840, opened 1841. Schools built 1861, new Sunday schools opened 1876; day school 1844 to 1939. Decision to demolish taken June 1952.

NORTH STREET PRIMITIVE METHODISTS: Cause began in 1820s, schoo established 1825, occupied a room in Lanehead Lane 1831 to 1837, in Unio Street 1837 to 1841, and later one above Duckworth's shop and Greenwood' auction rooms. Church built 1853 on the site of a disused brickworks ("Brick field"), opened Good Friday 1854. Church closed at the end of 1941, late demolished.

PROVIDENCE STRICT BAPTISTS: Sunday School established 1836 a Providence Particular Baptists, church built 1846, enlarged 1851, known a "Tongue Meadow" (Mannex); reconstructed October 1911 (dated stones still visible round the base); closed January 1956. Building subsequently used b Messrs. Bohen as a wholesale fruit warehouse.

SALVATION ARMY: Were in a barracks at the Public Hall, Burnley Road, i 1900, new headquarters opened in South Street January 1934 (room now use by Newgate Mission). Nothing further discovered.

SOUTH STREET CONGREGATIONALISTS: Sunday School opened 1848 church 1851; closed 1957, later used by J. W. Johnson as a warehouse. Roo collapsed June 1959, building later demolished.

SOUTH STREET GENERAL BAPTIST SUNDAY SCHOOL: Formed Octobe 1852, met in Earnshaw Road, Burnley Road, Newchurch Road. School an chapel built in the 1860s; headstones still visible: "General Baptist Chapel 1872". Connected later with Mount Olivet Baptists, subsequently used b Messrs. Tattersall as an undertakers' and joinery works.

THORN WESLEYAN METHODISTS: Sunday School established 1851, carrie on as "Bacup Ragged School" under auspices of Mount Pleasant; official known as Union Street School. Absorbed into Thorn, church built by Apri 1872, opened May 5th. New primary department erected in five months b members, opened October 1953. Church closed at the end of December 1963.

WESLEY PLACE: Off-shoot of Mount Pleasant; Sunday School establishe 1861, chapel 1866. Closed March 1962, demolished June 1966. Now the sit of an electricity sub-station.

ZION BAPTISTS: Originated as a secession from Irwell Terrace on Decembe 24th, 1854; met 1854-57 in the Mechanics' Institute, church built 1857 i Market Street, opened Good Friday 1858. New school 1913, opened 1915 Church declared unsafe May 1947, demolished later. June 1949 – decision t amalgamate with Irwell Terrace Baptists as Union Baptist Church.